Modernist Intimacies

Modernist Intimacies

Edited by
Elsa Högberg

EDINBURGH
University Press

Edinburgh University Press is one of the leading university presses in the UK. We publish academic books and journals in our selected subject areas across the humanities and social sciences, combining cutting-edge scholarship with high editorial and production values to produce academic works of lasting importance. For more information visit our website: edinburghuniversitypress.com

© editorial matter and organisation Elsa Högberg, 2021, 2023
© the chapters their several authors, 2021, 2023

Edinburgh University Press Ltd
The Tun – Holyrood Road, 12(2f) Jackson's Entry, Edinburgh EH8 8PJ

First published in hardback by Edinburgh University Press 2021

Typeset in 10.5/13 Bembo by
IDSUK (DataConnection) Ltd

A CIP record for this book is available from the British Library

ISBN 978 1 4744 4183 4 (hardback)
ISBN 978 1 4744 4184 1 (paperback)
ISBN 978 1 4744 4185 8 (webready PDF)
ISBN 978 1 4744 4186 5 (epub)

The right of Elsa Högberg to be identifie d as the editor of this work has been asserted in accordance with the Copyright, Designs and Patents Act 1988, and the Copyright and Related Rights Regulations 2003 (SI No. 2498).

Contents

Acknowledgements vii
Notes on Contributors viii

Introduction 1
Elsa Högberg

1. Bodies of Water: Fontane, Mann and the Private Performance of Wagnerian Eroticism 16
Axel Englund

2. Stories of O: Modernism and Female Pleasure 31
Laura Frost

3. Burning Feminism: Virginia Woolf's Laboratory of Intimacy 52
Jane Goldman

4. 'Angles and surfaces declared themselves intimately': Intimate Things in Dorothy Richardson's *The Trap* 74
Bryony Randall

5. An Occasion of Intimacy: Duncan Grant, Paul Roche and a Jesus that Bloomsbury Could Live With 92
Todd Avery

6. Cold Intimacy: Compassion, Precarity and Violence in Nathanael West's *Miss Lonelyhearts* 108
Elsa Högberg

7. 'Me you—you—me': Mina Loy and the Art of Ethnographic Intimacy 129
Sanja Bahun

8. The Intimacies of the Modernist Diary 146
   Laura Marcus

9. Leonora Carrington's Poetics of Listening 164
   Anna Watz

10. 'Je me trouve très sympathique': Dada Intimacies 181
    Marius Hentea

11. Overlapping Intimacies: Russian Fever, Domestic Morale and
    the BBC Home Service, 1941–5 197
    Claire Davison

12. The Modernist Nonmodern: Provincialism and the Intimacy
    of Space 215
    Saikat Majumdar

Index 231

Acknowledgements

This book came out of the symposium 'Intimate Modernism', which I organised in Uppsala in October 2015, and which formed part of a collaboration between the Department of English, Uppsala University, and the Department of English Literature, University of Glasgow. I dedicate my warmest thanks to the participants, my colleagues, whose vibrant papers and interactions made this such a stimulating event: Judith Allen, Todd Avery, Sanja Bahun, Jessica Berman, Amy Bromley, Claire Davison, Axel Englund, Laura Frost, Jane Goldman, Marius Hentea, Laura Marcus, Justus Nieland, Bryony Randall, Derek Ryan, Lisa Siraganian, Mia Spiro, Lyndsey Stonebridge, Anna Watz and Jesse Wolfe. I am delighted that so many of these outstanding presentations made their way into this book. Generous funding from Riksbankens Jubileumsfond and LILAe, the literary studies network at Uppsala University, made the symposium possible. Many thanks to the estate of Swedish modernist artist Sigrid Hjertén for granting permission to reproduce Hjertén's *Gosse vid blomsterbordet* on the symposium poster and on the front cover of this volume, and to Bukowskis for the permission to reprint the photograph of Hjertén's painting. Thanks also to graphic designer and illustrator Hannes Högberg for inspirational conversations about the book cover design.

Two major grants financed the different stages of this book project: the Swedish Research Council funded my research as a postdoctoral fellow at Uppsala University and the University of Glasgow (2014–17), while a second postdoctoral grant from Åke Wibergs Stiftelse enabled the completion of the volume. I am most grateful to these foundations for their generous support.

It has been a real pleasure to collaborate with Jackie Jones, Ersev Ersoy and their editorial team at Edinburgh University Press. I am grateful to the Harry Ransom Center for permission to reproduce the D. H. Lawrence illustration 'The Bad Girl in the Pansy Bed'. Every effort has been made to acquire necessary permissions from Paper Lion UK, which controls D. H. Lawrence rights.

Finally, my heartfelt thanks to the contributors of this volume, with whom it has been a privilege and a delight to work.

Notes on Contributors

Todd Avery is Professor in the Department of English at the University of Massachusetts Lowell. His research focuses both on the Bloomsbury Group, especially Lytton Strachey, and on relationships between modernism and radio broadcasting. His publications include *Saxon Sydney-Turner: The Ghost of Bloomsbury* (Cecil Woolf, 2015), the edition *Unpublished Works of Lytton Strachey: Early Papers* (Pickering & Chatto, 2011), *Desmond and Molly MacCarthy: Bloomsberries* (Cecil Woolf, 2010), *Radio Modernism: Literature, Ethics, and the BBC, 1922–1938* (Ashgate, 2006; Routledge, 2016), and numerous essays and reviews. His current book project examines Lytton Strachey as an innovator in the genre of biographical fiction.

Sanja Bahun is Professor of Literature and Film and Dean of Postgraduate Research and Education at the University of Essex. She is the author of *Modernism and Melancholia: Writing as Countermourning* (Oxford University Press, 2014) and the co-editor of *Thinking Home: Interdisciplinary Dialogues* (Bloomsbury Academic, 2018), *Cinema, State Socialism and Society in the Soviet Union and Eastern Europe, 1917–1989: Re-Visions* (Routledge, 2014), *Myth, Literature, and the Unconscious* (Karnac Books, 2013), *Language, Ideology, and the Human: New Interventions* (Ashgate, 2012), *Myth and Violence in the Contemporary Female Text: New Cassandras* (Routledge, 2011), *From Word to Canvas: Appropriations of Myth in Women's Aesthetic Production* (Cambridge Scholars Publishing, 2009), *Violence and Gender in the Globalized World: The Intimate and the Extimate* (Ashgate, 2008; Routledge, 2015) and *The Avant-garde and the Margin: New Territories of Modernism* (Cambridge Scholars Publishing, 2006), and she has published articles and essays on a variety of subjects concerning modernism, world literature and psychoanalytic theory.

Claire Davison is Professor of Modernist Studies at the Université Sorbonne Nouvelle. Her teaching and research focus on intermedial borders and the boundaries of modernism; this includes the translation and reception of

Russian literature in the 1910s–20s, literary and musical modernism, and modernist soundscapes and broadcasting. She is currently exploring European broadcasting archives in preparation for a monograph on modernist arts and cultural diplomacy on air in the 1930s, a project backed by a fellowship with the Uppsala Forum on Democracy, Peace and Justice (2020–1) and the France-Berkeley Fund. Her most recent publications include *Cross-Channel Modernisms*, co-edited with Derek Ryan and Jane Goldman (Edinburgh University Press, 2020), and the first volume of a new four-volume series, *The Edinburgh Edition of the Collected Letters of Katherine Mansfield*, co-edited with Gerri Kimber (Edinburgh University Press, 2020).

Axel Englund is Professor of Literature in the Department of Culture and Aesthetics at Stockholm University. He is the author of *Deviant Opera: Sex, Power, and Perversion on Stage* (University of California Press, 2020) and *Still Songs: Music In and Around the Poetry of Paul Celan* (Ashgate, 2012).

Laura Frost is the author of *The Problem with Pleasure: Modernism and Its Discontents* (Columbia University Press, 2013), *Sex Drives: Fantasies of Fascism in Literary Modernism* (Cornell University Press, 2002), and many articles on modernist and contemporary literature and culture, gender and sexuality.

Jane Goldman is Reader in English Literature at the University of Glasgow and a General Editor of the Cambridge Edition of the Works of Virginia Woolf. She is also a poet. Her critical works include *With you in the Hebrides: Virginia Woolf and Scotland* (Cecil Woolf, 2013), *The Cambridge Introduction to Virginia Woolf* (Cambridge University Press, 2006), *Modernism, 1910–1945: Image to Apocalypse* (Palgrave, 2004) and *The Feminist Aesthetics of Virginia Woolf: Modernism, Post-Impressionism and the Politics of the Visual* (Cambridge University Press, 1998). Building on her published essays on canine aesthetics, she is currently writing a book entitled *Virginia Woolf and the Signifying Dog*. Her poetry collection *SEKXPHRASTICS* is forthcoming with Dostoevsky Wannabe.

Marius Hentea is Professor of English Literature at the University of Gothenburg. He is the author of *TaTa Dada: The Real Life and Celestial Adventures of Tristan Tzara* (MIT Press, 2014) and numerous essays on modernist literature and culture. He is currently completing a monograph on authorship and treason after the Second World War.

Elsa Högberg is a research fellow at the Department of English, Uppsala University. Her published work explores the ethical and political implications of intimacy, affect and lyric in literary modernism and contemporary theory. She is the author of *Virginia Woolf and the Ethics of Intimacy* (Bloomsbury Academic, 2020) and co-editor, with Amy Bromley, of *Sentencing Orlando: Virginia Woolf and the Morphology of the Modernist Sentence* (Edinburgh University Press, 2018).

Saikat Majumdar is Professor of English and Creative Writing at Ashoka University. He is the co-editor, with Aarthi Vadde, of the collection *The Critic as Amateur* (Bloomsbury Academic, 2019), and the author of *Prose of the World: Modernism and the Banality of Empire* (Columbia University Press/Orient Blackswan, 2013/2015), a finalist for the MSA Book Prize 2014, *College: Pathways of Possibility* (Bloomsbury, 2018), a book on the rise of liberal arts education in India, and three novels: *The Scent of God* (Simon & Schuster, 2019), *The Firebird*, published as *Play House* in the US (Hachette/Permanent Press, 2015/2017), and *Silverfish* (HarperCollins, 2007). His work has appeared/is forthcoming in *PMLA, NLH, Cambridge Companion to the Essay, Cambridge History of the British Essay, Cambridge History of the Indian Novel in English, Modern Fiction Studies* and in several popular venues, including a book column in the *Los Angeles Review of Books* and articles on higher education in *Times Higher Education* and *Outlook*.

Laura Marcus is Goldsmiths' Professor of English Literature and Professorial Fellow of New College at the University of Oxford, and a Fellow of the British Academy. She has published widely on nineteenth- and twentieth-century literature and culture. Her book publications include *Autobiography: A Very Short Introduction* (Oxford University Press, 2018), *Dreams of Modernity: Psychoanalysis, Literature, Cinema* (Cambridge University Press, 2014), *The Tenth Muse: Writing about Cinema in the Modernist Period* (Oxford University Press, 2007, awarded the MLA's James Russell Lowell Prize 2008), *Virginia Woolf: Writers and Their Work* (Northcote House, 1997; new edition, Liverpool University Press, 2004) and *Auto/biographical Discourses: Theory, Criticism, Practice* (Manchester University Press, 1994/1998). Current research projects include a study of the concept of 'rhythm' at the turn of the nineteenth and twentieth centuries, in a range of disciplinary contexts, and a monograph on early twentieth-century life-writing.

Bryony Randall is Professor of Modernist Literature at the University of Glasgow. She has research interests in textual editing, women's writing, and literature and the everyday, and has published across these fields. She is a volume editor for the Oxford University Press edition of the work of Dorothy Richardson. With Jane Goldman and Susan Sellers, she is co-General Editor of the Cambridge Edition of the Works of Virginia Woolf, and is co-editing, with Laura Marcus, Woolf's short fiction for that edition. She is co-director of the Textual Editing Lab at the University of Glasgow, and edited a special issue of *Modernist Cultures* on the New Modernist Editing (2020), an output of the AHRC-funded Network of that name for which she was Principal Investigator. She is co-editor, with Jane Goldman, of *Virginia Woolf in Context* (Cambridge University Press, 2013) and author of *Modernism, Daily Time and Everyday Life* (Cambridge University Press, 2007).

Anna Watz is Senior Lecturer in English Literature at Linköping University. She is the author of *Angela Carter and Surrealism: 'A Feminist Libertarian Aesthetic'* (Routledge, 2016) and editor of the volumes *Surrealist Women's Writing: A Critical Exploration* (Manchester University Press, 2021) and the forthcoming *A History of the Surrealist Novel* (Cambridge University Press). She has also published extensively on the writing of Leonora Carrington and on second-wave French feminist theory. Her current research project investigates the intersection between surrealist women's art and writing of the 1960s and 1970s and the emergence of poststructuralist feminism and theories of *écriture féminine*.

Introduction

Elsa Högberg

This book traces modern intimacy back to the first decades of the twentieth century, and shows that modernism played a crucial role in its emergence. Intimacy, in its first two dictionary definitions – '1.a. The state of being personally intimate; intimate friendship or acquaintance; familiar intercourse; close familiarity; an instance of this. b. *euphem.* for sexual intercourse'[1] – can no longer be seen as a wholly private, familiar sphere of life independent of sociopolitical realities. Disruptive and inescapably public, intimacy from the modernist period to the present furthers reactionary and violent as well as progressive and creative forces. The twelve contributors to this volume situate intimacy, conceived as a vital dimension of modernist aesthetic and social practices, in relation to diverse topics from music-making, wartime radio broadcasting and sound poetry to orgasm, queer religiosity and same-sex love. Focusing mainly on literary modernism, they examine its connections with music, painting, avant-garde performance art and radio transmission. In attending to a wide range of print literary texts as well as other media such as church murals and sonic archives, the volume also points to the resonance of modernist intimacies in our own time.

What does it mean to think of intimacy and modernism together? The modernist movement has long been understood as a response to a psychological, social and political crisis of intimacy: an expression of solipsism and alienation in a time when traditional communal bonds organised around religious, class, gender and family hierarchies began to dissolve. In contrast, this volume investigates the emergent, consolidating forms of social and artistic intimacy problematised and created in modernist texts. The events that prompted a transformation of intimacy in the early twentieth century were, amongst others, the world wars with their traumatic legacy and transnational solidarities; the rise of fascism; the emergence of modern psychology, psychoanalysis and sexology; new media such as the radio; the unprecedented number of women in higher education and the professions; the development of birth control and family planning; and the increasing acceptance of homosexual relations. These and other developments, which radically altered the way intimacy was experienced and created in art and life, form the historical context of this book. While *Modernist Intimacies* focuses primarily on Anglo-American, anglophone modernism, it also covers global perspectives on modernist expressions of intimacy ranging from across Europe to South Asian literature.

Over the past two decades, intimacy has become the focus of growing attention in fields including psychology, sociology and economics. Across various disciplines, it has proved to be crucial in accounts of affective, political and ethical relations. The emergence of affect studies in particular has prompted a redefinition of intimacy as commonly understood: relations of familiarity and closeness that, whether between lovers, friends or family, constitute an exclusively private sphere of bodily, sexual and emotional contact. Much recent scholarship has focused on the sociopolitical dimensions of affectively and physically close relations. Intimacy, seen as the very nexus where private and public converge, is a key term in the academic discourse of this century, as the wide range of recent books on the subject attests. This rapidly expanding archive spans multiple fields from sociology, politics and economics to gender and queer studies. Essential titles include *Relating Intimacies: Power and Resistance*, ed. Paul Bagguley and Julie Seymour (1999); *Intimacy*, ed. Lauren Berlant (2000); Eva Illouz's *Cold Intimacies: The Making of Emotional Capitalism* (2007); *Mapping Intimacies: Relations, Exchanges, Affects*, ed. Tam Sanger and Yvette Taylor (2013); and Berlant's *Cruel Optimism* (2011) and *Desire/Love* (2012).[2] Berlant, Illouz and Leo Bersani are among the many theorists to consider intimacy as inextricable from the public realm. However, the literary implications of modern intimacy, and its historical emergence in the modernist period, have only begun to be explored. If intimacy in the twenty-first century is an intriguing crossing of public and private relations, the central argument of *Modernist Intimacies* is that many of these convergences date back to the modernist period, and that modernism played a vital role in the constructions of intimacy specific to the age of modernity.

The aim of this volume, then, is to explore the personal, sociopolitical, ethical, cultural and aesthetic dimensions of intimacy as depicted in key modernist works, and to connect the legacy of literary modernism to contemporary debates around intimate relations. *Modernist Intimacies* brings twenty-first-century accounts of intimacy to bear on modernist innovations in literary form and style, thereby continuing a dialogue initiated in recent works on modernism and affect such as Justus Nieland's *Feeling Modern: The Eccentricities of Public Life* (2008), Julie Taylor's edited volume *Modernism and Affect* (2015) and Jean-Michel Rabaté's *The Pathos of Distance: Affects of the Moderns* (2016).[3] Foregrounding the potential of intimacy as a compelling category for highlighting the sociopolitical implications of interpersonal relations in modernist texts, *Modernist Intimacies* builds on and expands the work undertaken by Jesse Wolfe in his monograph *Bloomsbury, Modernism, and the Reinvention of Intimacy* (2011).[4] Other important studies of modernism and/or aspects of intimacy in early twentieth-century literature include Laura Frost's *Sex Drives: Fantasies of Fascism in Literary Modernism* (2001) and *The Problem with Pleasure: Modernism and Its Discontents* (2013), Sarah Cole's *Modernism, Male Friendship, and the First World War* (2007), Santanu Das's *Touch and Intimacy in First World War Literature* (2005), Jessica Berman's *Modernist Commitments: Ethics, Politics and Transnational Modernism* (2011) and Janine Utell's *Literary Couples and 20th-Century Life Writing: Narrative and Intimacy* (2019).[5] *Modernist Intimacies* takes these critical debates further in historicising intimacy itself as a range of lived experiences shaped and mediated through modernist art. Furthermore, it employs twenty-first-century insights into the complex and often contradictory dimensions of modern intimacies, thereby illuminating historical continuities between modernist and contemporary modes of intimacy, while some chapters also trace their nineteenth-century roots (see Axel Englund's and Bryony Randall's essays).

Apart from intimacy in the senses of close interpersonal familiarity and sexual intercourse, the contributors address alternative definitions of the term, such as 'closeness of observation, knowledge, or the like'.[6] This suggestive definition raises fascinating questions about the role of intimacy in different processes of writing and reading literature, and about the degree of closeness between reading and writing. Addressing the new formalist turn of this century, Marjorie Levinson distinguishes between a nostalgic privileging of aesthetic experience as autotelic, and an 'activist formalism', which restores the close reading of aesthetic form to contextually oriented modes of literary scholarship.[7] Such an activist formalism seems to be a dominant ethos of modernist studies today, and I want to suggest that a contextually alert attention to aesthetic qualities is intimate in the sense of 'entering deeply or closely into a matter'.[8] Intimacy here becomes a question of imagining parallels between artistic and academic creativity. Like literary composition or proficiency in playing a musical instrument, creative critical practices take time and the capacity for pleasurable, focused absorption in the task at hand – a capacity that our digital age of instant communication tends to undermine with its urge for superficial reading, writing and thinking. There is a growing interest in the benefits of slow, deep and immersive reading; the kind of reading where we let ourselves get lost and happily absorbed in a literary text, where we let a single word or sentence take us off-track into imaginary worlds that would have remained hidden on a quick reading.[9] This emergent paradigm inspired *Sentencing* Orlando: *Virginia Woolf and the Morphology of the Modernist Sentence* (2018), a volume I co-edited with Amy Bromley, where each chapter analyses the form and structure of a single sentence from Woolf's *Orlando: A Biography* (1928); together, the contributors reveal obscured historical, political and aesthetic dimensions of a text that is typically read as an enchanting narrative written quickly for light, quick reading.[10] The intense focus on small aesthetic units demands a close intimacy with this text and its alluring range of literary-historical contexts, but it also reveals how modernist art and literature frequently resist intimacy defined as familiarity.

While some chapters in *Modernist Intimacies* explore close connections between intimacy, pleasure and modernist aesthetics, others examine close relations where interpersonal intimacy is uncomfortable and unwilled, or refused altogether. In probing the social, political and ethical capacities and limits of intimacy, the volume engages the vibrant critical discussions around modernism and affect that have materialised in recent years. As Justus Nieland has shown, modernism should not be understood as divided between romantic and classic traditions, where the former cultivates and the latter rejects the intimate in the sense of 'pertaining to the inmost thoughts or feelings; proceeding from, concerning, or affecting one's inmost self; closely personal'.[11] Instead, he suggests that we should think of modernist emotion as ex-centric, that is, emerging in the mass-mediated public life of politics and publicity. In affect studies more generally, affect tends to be seen as undermining the self-contained subject whose emotions can be articulated as personal and conscious. Affect, by this logic, is the impersonal and pre-discursive forces that make intimacy, conceived as private interiority, always open to the other and outside. Teresa Brennan has observed that the transmission of affect as a biological and social reality was taken for granted before the advent of Western modernity, when it was disavowed,[12] and the rich representations of affective transmission in modernist art have yet to be explored. The essays in this collection consider the radical challenge that modernism poses to the still prevalent notion of intimacy as private interiority. They also investigate the sociopolitical implications of this challenge across diverse areas, including sexuality and sexual pleasure, diary-writing, feminism, precarity, and the emergence of new media.

The idea of affect as inevitably public implies that modern, and modernist, intimacy is troubling in several ways. Eva Illouz, for one, traces a historical development in which emotional and intimate relations became central to capitalist expansion. What she calls 'emotional capitalism' emerged in the modernist period: 'a culture in which emotional and economic discourses and practices mutually shape each other' so that 'affect is made an essential aspect of economic behaviour' and 'emotional life [...] follows the logic of economic relations and exchange'.[13] As she demonstrates in *Cold Intimacies*, a communicative model for social relations began to gain ground in the first decades of the twentieth century: a valorisation of freely expressed emotion as a legitimate driving force for social and political action, which continues to shape sociopolitical relations in the present. (It is enough to consider how often contemporary news reporting generates unreflective, emotional responses rather than comprehensive, intimate knowledge, or how we live much of our private lives on Facebook, to confirm Illouz's statement that 'never has the self been so publicly performed'.[14]) The notion of modern intimacy as discursively mediated and performed in the public sphere is a shared conceptual premise in this collection, and the contributors examine the specifically literary and artistic dimensions of such performance.

The modernist writers and artists represented in this volume compel us to expand established definitions of intimacy, exploring relations that probe as well as exceed interiority, familiarity, affective bonds and physical contact. In this sense, their work is strikingly relevant to twenty-first-century debates around power, violence and the limits of intimacy. Freud famously claimed that the construction of communities through intimate (affectionate or erotic) ties can be sustained only at the cost of aggression towards non-members[15] – an issue that resonates strongly with contemporary problems and our increasingly polarised political climate. The contributors to this volume show how modernist intimacy can be a structuring principle of conservatism and socio-economic inequality, but also a progressive force discomposing patriarchal, heteronormative and nationalist perceptual regimes. They thereby address the multiple ways in which modernist writers defamiliarised and reconfigured intimacy in areas including transnational relations, sonic transmission and avant-garde manifestos, same-sex friendship and love, religiosity, and politically and ethically charged modes of reading and writing. In this, the volume both clarifies and widens the scope of 'intimacy' as a critical and theoretical term as well as a phenomenon shaping the private and public worlds of modernity.

In the opening chapter, 'Bodies of Water: Fontane, Mann and the Private Performance of Wagnerian Eroticism', Axel Englund shows how two proto-modernist prose texts, Theodor Fontane's *L'Adultera* (1880/1882) and Thomas Mann's *Buddenbrooks* (1901), transposed the decadent eroticism of Wagnerian opera into the bourgeois home and the private realm of intimate and embodied, domestic musical performance. 'The very sound of Wagner's music was perceived as libidinous', Englund observes,

> and nineteenth-century critics frequently reacted as if the composer were engaging his listeners in reckless acts of aural intercourse. Wagnerian drama not only performed in public the most secret of yearnings – for incest, for adultery, for death; it was aimed at an immersion which made the audience *feel* them.

Focusing on Wagnerian eros as a 'musical torrent', Englund claims that 'the literary transposition of Wagner's music from [large-scale public arenas] to the private sphere allowed these authors to negotiate intimacy and eroticism, and that it did so precisely through an imagery of fluidity'. In Englund's reading, the intimacies made possible by private, physical performances of this oceanic music become a simultaneously erosive and erotically gratifying force propelling modernity itself, one that liquefies the bourgeois subject and its reproductive values.

While Englund explores rich intersections between eroticism and intimacy, Laura Frost decouples them in her chapter, which considers early twentieth-century advocates of female sexual pleasure in light of historical and present-day efforts to illuminate the mechanisms of female sexuality, and specifically orgasm. Examining formulations about female orgasm in the work of Mabel Dodge Luhan and D. H. Lawrence while also touching on writings by Marie Stopes, Virginia Woolf, Anaïs Nin and James Joyce, Frost highlights an aesthetic tendency to depict the female climax as 'an elusive, boundless quality [. . .] that gestures both to and beyond the phenomenon of pleasure or desire', an introspective and intimate mode of figuration which, she argues, made female orgasm susceptible to social and biopolitical 'orgasmic discipline'. She writes:

> For modern fiction and nonfiction writers alike, female orgasm was never only about women's pleasure; it was also an intimate gauge of women's agency and power. At the same time that Luhan and Lawrence depicted sexuality for transgressive or radical purposes – to philosophically and aesthetically expand the limits of representation, and to explore women's interior subjectivity – they deployed that representation toward reactionary, conservative ends [. . .] Their writing, together with that of Freud and birth control advocates who urged specific sexual practices for women, presents an unsettling history of somatic manipulation and control.

Frost thus relates Luhan's and Lawrence's increasingly reactionary conceptions of female pleasure to Luhan's interest in psychoanalysis, to both writers' growing fascination with primitivist spirituality in the Taos art colony, and to the historical backdrop of women's increased emancipation – particularly the late nineteenth- and early twentieth-century 'transformation of intimacy'[16] by which women could eventually exercise reproductive freedom: 'As women made gains as a collective, in both the public and private spheres, they continued to receive spurious and retrogressive advice about their "intimate" sexual lives.'

The contradictory, simultaneously progressive and conservative agendas informing key modern(ist) representations of intimacy remain in focus in Jane Goldman's chapter, 'Burning Feminism: Virginia Woolf's Laboratory of Intimacy'. This chapter presses the notion of textual intimacy between reading and writing as 'closeness of observation', while taking as axiomatic Jessica Berman's insight that intimate relations in Woolf's works hold 'political valences, made salient by [...] the rise of fascism'.[17] Opening with a poem composed of Woolf's conspicuously few mentions of 'feminism' and 'feminist' in her writings, Goldman traces the injunction to burn the word 'feminist' in the anti-fascist 1938 essay *Three Guineas*[18] back to a 'multiplicitously intimate, "inter-textual hot spot"' in Chapter 5 of *A Room of One's Own* (1929): the passage in which 'Chloe liked Olivia. They shared a laboratory together. ....'.[19] Goldman show how this passage, in introducing the fictitious novel *Life's Adventure* by Mary Carmichael – a variant spelling of the scientist and birth control pioneer Marie Stopes's *nom de plume* for her 1928 novel *Love's Creation*, inscribes 'the double feminist shock that is [...] *both* a newly achieved professional intimacy in the collaboration of women in the previously exclusively patriarchal environs of a university scientific laboratory *and* a newly acknowledged possibility of sexual intimacy between women', at the same time as it both echoes and undermines the proto-fascist eugenics that motivated Stopes's work for women's reproductive freedom. Drawing on Spivak and Derrida, Goldman argues that Woolf's intertextual chemist's laboratory manufactures a form of 'teleopoietic', intimate writing and reading, concocting progressive future anteriors out of intertexts turned to anti-fascist, queer feminist advantage:

> We must study [Woolf's prose] closely *in print*: we must become so intimate with this writing about the limits of writing intimacy *in print* that we understand its silences and elisions, what it does not state, but what it nevertheless somehow clearly intimates – the writing in print on intimacies yet to come, 'if we worked for' them.

Bryony Randall continues with the theme of women's intimate sharing of new spaces in early twentieth-century modernity. Her chapter focuses on Dorothy Richardson's *The Trap* (1925), the eighth of the complete chapter-volumes of the modernist *Künstlerroman, Pilgrimage* (1915–67). While the novel's title has been understood to refer to a marriage proposal addressed to the protagonist, Miriam Henderson, here employed as a dental secretary, Randall reads closely the early part of the novel that explores Miriam's vicissitudes of feeling as she moves into shared rented rooms with an acquaintance working as a night-school teacher, Miss Holland, a relationship described as a 'marriage of convenience'. The chapter explorers how Richardson's key technical contributions to modernist aesthetics (her sustained investigation of interiority along with her highly sensual attentiveness to objects and spaces, a style Randall calls 'intimate') create a portrait of a historically unprecedented kind of female intimacy made possible by the social, political and economic changes of the mid- to late nineteenth century, particularly the employment opportunities afforded by the rapid expansion in the education and health care sectors: the sharing of domestic space by two economically independent, single, middle-class working women. Engaging Clive Bell's 'significant form' along with Bill Brown's and Jane Bennett's new materialist theories, Randall focuses on the ways in which inanimate 'things' take centre stage as they mediate and enable Miriam's experiences of intimacy in this shared space, thereby revealing alternative models of intimacy that both exceed and heighten physical and emotional, interpersonal proximity in a 'reconciliation of the material with the affective'.

Such a reconciliation also becomes visible in Todd Avery's chapter, 'An Occasion of Intimacy: Duncan Grant, Paul Roche and a Jesus that Bloomsbury Could Live With'. The celebration and exploration of intimacy as a fundamental human good was central to Bloomsbury's lives and works, and to the group's promotion of sexual freedom as a means of individual, social and political betterment. Avery turns his focus to the world of late Bloomsbury, where an intimate relation developed between one of its original core members and a young writer (who was for a time also a Catholic priest), a relation which sheds new light on Bloomsbury's private, artistic, ethical, political and spiritual commitment to intimacy from the intimate regions of domestic space to non-heteronormative erotic relations. Duncan Grant's friendship with Paul Roche began in the mid-1940s and spanned thirty years. In the course of this relation, Grant took Roche as the model for two portraits: as Narcissus in an unfinished and still unpublished novella, and as the compassionate Jesus in a Lincoln Cathedral mural – 'artistic Bloomsbury's grandest public representation of queer Christian intimacy, which Grant envisions in terms of an ethics of care inspired by the ancient Christian motif of the Good Shepherd' – that together embody an artistically and ethically productive tension between physical desire and spiritual ambition, sensuousness and religiosity, paganism and Christianity. This chapter shows that in the Bloomsbury painters' church murals of the 1940s and '50s, in Grant and Roche's friendship and love, in Grant's pictorial and literary representations of Roche, and in Roche's own writing, 'Bloomsbury's commitment to intimacy achieved a particularly sacred intensity'.

The ethico-political dimensions of (Christian and charitable) compassion also form the focus of my own chapter on Nathanael West's novella *Miss Lonelyhearts*, published in the darkest year of the Great Depression (1933). While West did not explicitly write his radical leftist convictions into his satirical fiction, I argue that *Miss Lonelyhearts* stages a conflict between absent yet massively needed political responses to poverty and precarity (such engagement would only materialise a few years later with the New Deal) and an intratextual world whose 'superrealist' absurdity revolves around the compassionate, male advice columnist Miss Lonelyhearts being held ethically responsible for alleviating the material causes of his correspondents' acute vulnerability. The columnist reacts repeatedly to their suffering with aversion and violence, and this chapter traces an anti-capitalist textual politics in West's unparalleled representation of fraught relations where negative emotions triggering repulsion clash violently with compassion as a positive affect sustaining desire, attraction and love – that is, the realm of intimacy. Enlisting concepts such as Eva Illouz's 'cold intimacy', Lauren Berlant's 'cruel optimism' and Sianne Ngai's 'ugly feelings', I read the text's refusal of compassion and intimacy as a radical rejection of an enduring predicament: an affective-political regime of resilience by which capitalism uses intimate relations and positive emotions to prevent class conflict and socio-economic equality.

Sanja Bahun's chapter, '"Me you—you—me": Mina Loy and the Art of Ethnographic Intimacy', examines the economy of intimacy and affective rapports in Loy's poetry. Focusing on the 'participant observation' characterising Loy's ethnographic writing practice, Bahun probes the affect of discomfort as a mode of intimacy that binds Loy's reader to the subject matter of her early 'Songs to Joannes'/'Love Songs' (1915, 1917, 1923) as well as her mature poems 'Hot Cross Bum' (1949) and 'Photo after Pogrom' (c. 1945), including, in 'Songs to Joannes', sexual intercourse, abortion and bodily functions like sweating and urination, and, in the later poems, homelessness and corpses. The chapter reveals how Loy's multi-sensual and polyphonic poetry uses the poet-ethnographer's simultaneous proximity and reinforced exteriority to foreground the social, ethical and political possibilities, but also limits, of intersubjective, physical intimacy as depicted and mediated by the print text. For Bahun,

> Loy's is a complex economy of intimacy: the reader is made to be intimate with content they might rather avoid [...] through a method that challenges our preconceptions about intimacy and in the print medium that foregrounds it. Her poetry is uncomfortable and it inspects precisely the sources of the writer/ethnographer's and the audience's discomfort [...] It is a world without respite, wherein the sharing of bodily intimacy is the *modus operandi*.

Bahun thus highlights how the participant observation cultivated by Loy's poetry and its social commitments 'challenges the binaries of proximity and distance, attachment and detachment, the inside and the outside, and, for this reason, transforms [...] our understanding of how modernist literature (re-)engaged intimacy'.

Such binaries are also challenged by the introspective writing explored in Laura Marcus's chapter, 'The Intimacies of the Modernist Diary'. This chapter considers the intimate contents and functions of the diaries kept by a group of modern writers in the 1930s, including David Gascoyne, Antonia White and Anaïs Nin, and with reference to Lawrence Durrell's writing as well as the journals of Marie Bashkirtseff, Barbellion and Katherine Mansfield. Gascoyne and Nin not only published fragments from their diaries in the 1930s but also exchanged their diary-writing between themselves, a practice that raises central questions about the diary as a private or public document. For Nin in particular, the diary was something secret and hidden, as well as the repository of secrets, but it also had a public face for her: here the 'intimacy of the diary' (in Nin's phrase) is rendered as an 'extimacy'. Gascoyne was also closely connected to Antonia White in this period: her diary-writing, like Gascoyne's and Nin's, became a way of sustaining writing when the writing of fiction became blocked. Moreover, as with Gascoyne and Nin, her diary-writing became bound up with her psychoanalysis. Situating this archive in relation to the charged historical conditions of the 1930s, with their pressure on the writer's capacity to separate interiority and exteriority, public and private, Marcus looks at the relationships between the dailiness of diary-keeping and of full psychoanalysis, and at the kinds of mirroring and looking represented by, and enacted in, the journal as a mode of writing and as self-analysis.

In the next chapter, Anna Watz traces a poetics of intimate listening in British-born author and painter Leonora Carrington's surrealist novel *The Hearing Trumpet* (written in the 1950s and published in 1974). Carrington was part of the circle of surrealist artists and writers gathered around André Breton in the mid-1930s, and the rupture caused by the arrest of her lover Max Ernst at the outbreak of World War II resulted in Carrington's psychotic breakdown. She subsequently recounted the experiences of her psychosis in the autobiographical *Down Below*, a harrowing text dramatising a search for self-knowledge doomed to fail, in which violence, alienation and isolation in the context of the rise of fascism and Nazism dominate both inner and outer reality. About a decade later, Carrington revisited and rewrote her journey 'down below' in fictional terms, in *The Hearing Trumpet*. Watz shows how the novel, in drawing on 'esoteric narratives, revisionist theology, alternative knowledges, myth and fairy tale', is 'at once a parodic quest narrative, [...] an intimately personal exploration of subjectivity and self-knowledge', and 'a utopian vision of an ethics of being and knowing'. A symbol for the novel's poetics of listening, the protagonist's eponymous hearing trumpet guides Watz's exploration of Carrington's surrealist-feminist text via the philosophy of love and intimacy underpinning Luce Irigaray's twenty-first-century writings. In Watz's reading,

> what is at stake in *The Hearing Trumpet* is a subject configured in close relation to the other (whether human, animal or vegetable), and a philosophy of intersubjectivity in which respect for and an acknowledgement of the other take precedence over coherent self-articulation.

Marius Hentea continues the exploration of avant-garde intimacy in turning his attention to Dada manifestos, sound poetry and intimate interactions with the audience of the cabaret performance. While Dada owed much of its force to the close friendships, physical love and artistic collaborations composing this constellation of 'artists working and sleeping together', Hentea examines another mode of intimacy that inspired the movement's artistic and political ambitions: 'Dada sought to pave the way for the individual to understand the intimate within him- or herself, the spontaneous nature of one's deeply held being, what is "most inner" – an intimacy [...] pertaining to "one's inmost self; closely personal"'.[20] Anticipating the modern form of intimacy described by Anthony Giddens as 'emotional communication, with others and with the self, in a context of interpersonal equality',[21] this utopian quest for self-intimacy, Hentea argues, was a core incentive for Dada's aim to uproot bourgeois intimacies structured around family and nation as metonyms for a 'home' to be defended through war. While even progressive artists turned nationalist during World War I, Hentea shows how the intimacies cultivated by Dada's performances served its internationalist, anti-war politics in severing links between language, culture and nation. To this end, Hentea traces Dada sound poetry's public materialisations of 'the bodily, physical origin of language, the very intimacy of speaking' as manifest in its simultaneous multilingualism, intonations of the word 'Dada', and in Hugo Ball's injunction: 'We must return to the innermost alchemy of the word.'

Claire Davison takes the focus on transnational, sonic intimacy to the BBC Home Service in 1941–5, and its ideologically complex 'Projection of Russia' campaign commissioned to familiarise audiences with a new ally and boost public morale. Her chapter foregrounds the key contributors to this hugely successful cultural project, and the inspiration they drew from some of Russia's twentieth-century artistic landmarks – Soviet film and theatre, modernist music and the Ballets Russes – a process that brought dazzlingly experimental, often trans-medial artworks into the private lives of listeners at home. Contesting the persistent notion of wartime radio as culturally conservative and 'at best, a sober and homely monosphere (seeping from "the cells of [the listener's] most intimate life", as Adorno puts it), at worst an insidiously invasive voice of state-controlled consensus "which no longer appears to come from outside"',[22] Davison's close scrutiny of the *Radio Times*, *The Listener*, *The Gramophone* and the BBC Script and Sound Archives reveals that during the war, 'the Home Service was actually broadcasting its most aesthetically and technologically challenging productions to date', and that in these productions, 'many people's privacies tend to overlap'.[23] Davison's engagement with these archives of sonic modernism and their popularisation through the intimate familiarity of home listening bears out an observation in the unsigned *The Listener* editorial 'Understanding an Ally' (1942): that intimate, transnational and transcultural understanding begins with '"what we have in common": "learning about their background, their views and their traditions, by trying to see things for a few moments as they see them, to think (again temporarily, as an intellectual experience) as they think"'.[24]

In the closing chapter, 'The Modernist Nonmodern: Provincialism and the Intimacy of Space', Saikat Majumdar considers the relevance of literary modernism's attachments to the nonmodern provincial for our present political climate. This essay claims that

> one of the most vital things literature can do today is to disrupt its embeddedness in the modern. That it should seek to find its closest connections with the nonmodern – whatever and wherever such connections may lie [. . .] The betrayal of the individual, the private and the original. Most of all, the celebration of transgressive intimacies that violate both the liberal notion of the individual as well as the traditional conception of community.

In his intimate engagement with South Asian writers Amrita Pritam and Mahasweta Devi alongside a range of modernists as well as his own novels and scholarship, Majumdar charts a restlessness with the cosmopolitan worldview shaping modern literature, and traces how literary modernism's celebration of the provincial as a form of nonmodern spatial intimacy remains overshadowed by the movement's identification with cosmopolitanism. His reflective readings set out to recover 'the organic and visceral power of the provincial [that] has fallen farther and farther out of artistic and intellectual memory', and he argues that exploring the nonmodern spirit of literary aesthetics is an urgent project today in light of the global erosion of liberal modernity and its sociopolitical ambitions. At a time when many of modernity's premises 'seem to be failing miserably before the rise of authoritarian governments backed by jingoistic populism', Majumdar writes, 'the invocation of the nonmodern, as articulated in the celebration of the provincial and the irrational in works of Indian-language modernism [. . .] is at once essential and the best possible gesture of literary activism'. In concluding this volume, Majumdar offers an arresting vista of modernism's lasting intimacies.

Notes

1. 'intimacy, n.', *OED Online*, available at <https://www.oed.com/view/Entry/98503> (accessed 30 September 2020).
2. Paul Bagguley and Julie Seymour (eds), *Relating Intimacies: Power and Resistance* (Basingstoke: Macmillan, 1999); Lauren Berlant (ed.), *Intimacy* (Chicago: University of Chicago Press, 2000); Eva Illouz, *Cold Intimacies: The Making of Emotional Capitalism* (Cambridge: Polity Press, 2007); Tam Sanger and Yvette Taylor (eds), *Mapping Intimacies: Relations, Exchanges, Affects* (New York: Palgrave Macmillan, 2013); Lauren Berlant, *Cruel Optimism* (Durham, NC: Duke University Press, 2011); Berlant, *Desire/Love* (New York: Punctum Books, 2012).
3. Justus Nieland, *Feeling Modern: The Eccentricities of Public Life* (Urbana: University of Illinois Press, 2008); Julie Taylor (ed.), *Modernism and Affect* (Edinburgh: Edinburgh University Press, 2015); Jean-Michel Rabaté, *The Pathos of Distance: Affects of the Moderns* (New York: Bloomsbury Academic, 2016).
4. Jesse Wolfe, *Bloomsbury, Modernism, and the Reinvention of Intimacy* (Cambridge: Cambridge University Press, 2011).
5. Laura Frost, *Sex Drives: Fantasies of Fascism in Literary Modernism* (Ithaca: Cornell University Press, 2001); Frost, *The Problem with Pleasure: Modernism and Its Discontents* (New York: Columbia University Press, 2013); Sarah Cole, *Modernism, Male Friendship, and the First World War* (Cambridge: Cambridge

University Press, 2007); Santanu Das, *Touch and Intimacy in First World War Literature* (Cambridge: Cambridge University Press, 2005); Jessica Berman, *Modernist Commitments: Ethics, Politics and Transnational Modernism* (New York: Columbia University Press, 2011); Janine Utell, *Literary Couples and 20th-Century Life Writing: Narrative and Intimacy* (London: Bloomsbury Academic, 2019).

6. 'intimacy, n.' 1.c., *OED Online*, available at <https://www.oed.com/view/Entry/98503> (accessed 30 September 2020).
7. Marjorie Levinson, 'What is New Formalism?', *PMLA*, 122.2 (March 2007), p. 559.
8. 'intimate, adj. and n.' A. adj. 1.b., *OED Online*, available at <https://www.oed.com/view/Entry/98506> (accessed 30 September 2020).
9. See David Mikics, *Slow Reading in a Hurried Age* (Harvard: Harvard University Press, 2013).
10. Elsa Högberg and Amy Bromley (eds), *Sentencing* Orlando*: Virginia Woolf and the Morphology of the Modernist Sentence* (Edinburgh: Edinburgh University Press, 2018).
11. Nieland, *Feeling Modern*; 'intimate, adj. and n.' A. adj. 2, *OED Online*, available at <https://www.oed.com/view/Entry/98506> (accessed 30 September 2020).
12. Teresa Brennan, *The Transmission of Affect* (Ithaca: Cornell University Press, 2004).
13. Illouz, *Cold Intimacies*, p. 5.
14. Ibid. p. 4.
15. Sigmund Freud, *Group Psychology and the Analysis of the Ego*, in *The Pelican Freud Library. Vol. 12: Civilization, Society and Religion:* Group Psychology, Civilization and Its Discontents *and Other Works*, ed. Albert Dickson, trans. James Strachey (Harmondsworth: Penguin, 1985), pp. 130–1; and Freud, *Civilization and Its Discontents*, in *The Pelican Freud Library. Vol. 12*, p. 305.
16. See Anthony Giddens, *The Transformation of Intimacy: Sexuality, Love and Eroticism in Modern Societies* (Stanford: Stanford University Press, 1992).
17. Jessica Berman, 'Woolf and the Private Sphere', in Bryony Randall and Jane Goldman (eds), *Virginia Woolf in Context* (Cambridge: Cambridge University Press), p. 471.
18. Virginia Woolf, *Three Guineas* (London: Hogarth Press, 1938), p. 184.
19. Virginia Woolf, *A Room of One's Own* (London: Hogarth Press, 1929), p. 125.
20. Hentea's reference is to 'intimate, adj. and n.' A. adj. 2.
21. Giddens, *The Transformation of Intimacy*, p. 130.

22. Davison is citing Theodor Adorno, *Current of Music*, ed. W. H. Kentor (London: Polity Press, 2009), p. 141.
23. Second quote from Louis MacNeice, *Varieties of Parable* (Cambridge: Cambridge University Press, 1965), p. 8.
24. Unsigned editorial, 'Understanding an Ally', *The Listener*, 702 (1942), p. 810.

1

Bodies of Water: Fontane, Mann and the Private Performance of Wagnerian Eroticism

Axel Englund

In a letter from 17 September 1874, Norwegian writer Bjørnstjerne Bjørnson described his experience of a Wagner performance to Edvard Grieg as follows:

> In the autumn, I saw 'Tristan and Isolde'. It is the sickest thing I have ever seen and heard; but in its own deranged way, it is so grand that one is narcotically numbed by it. Even more immoral and weakening than the story is this seasick music itself, which dissolves all contour in its pursuit of colour; in the end, one is nothing but a blob of slime on the seaside, discharged by that opium-masturbating swine.[1]

Bjørnson's remarks, albeit idiosyncratic, succinctly summarise a widely circulated conception of Wagner as a byword of eroticised decadence.[2] Famously advanced by Friedrich Nietzsche and Max Nordau, the idea that Wagner's works threatened moral and physical health was a principal component in the fin-de-siècle image of the composer, from the 1870s onwards.[3] In addition to plots that undermined socially sanctioned sexuality by idealising relations beyond matrimonial mores, Wagner's works combined music, text and drama to achieve unprecedented affective responses. The very sound of Wagner's music was perceived as libidinous, and nineteenth-century critics frequently reacted as if the composer were engaging his listeners in reckless acts of aural intercourse.[4] Wagnerian drama not only performed in public the most secret of yearnings – for incest, for adultery, for death; it was aimed at an immersion which made the audience *feel* them.

Bjørnson's drastic imagery says as much: the listener is swept away and reduced to a shapeless residue of Wagner's musico-sexual fantasy. What I want to emphasise in Bjørnson's account, however, is the liquid form of both the music and the self. The listening subject loses its contours in cascades of diseased music and ends up as a blob of semen spilled on the seashore, waiting to dissolve in the brine. Although humorously deflating it, Bjørnson borrows this idea from the opera he is describing. Isolde's *Liebestod* places the subject on the shoreline of death and desire, deliquescing in the waves of a musical climax: 'In dem wogenden Schwall, / in dem tönenden Schall / in des Welt-Atems wehendem All / ertrinken, versinken, / unbewusst – höchste Lust!' [In the swelling surge, / in the reverberant sound, / in the wafting cosmos of the world breath / to drown, to sink, / unconscious – supreme bliss!]. The poetic analogy between sound and liquid points to the music that accompanies it: its harmonic, melodic and orchestral surge becomes the auditory equivalent of the recurrent water worlds in Wagner's operas.[5] In his theoretical writings, too, Wagner employed a set of interrelated aquatic and sexual metaphors, positing music as the feminine and liquid element, waiting to receive the masculine word and engender music drama.[6] As construed by the discourse of decadence, however, Wagner's fluid eroticism became less procreative than degenerate, as if it had the capacity to liquefy the bourgeois self or indeed the whole bourgeois world by overflowing the familial structures which constituted its moral and ideological foundations. Key tropes of modernity – the dissolution of established values, the melting of all that is solid, the effeminate nervousness that afflicts subject and society – thus found expression in the Wagnerian notion of eros as a musical torrent. This chapter centres on two prose narratives that let this oceanic sexuality leak into the private spaces of bourgeois life: Theodor Fontane's *L'Adultera* (1880/1882) and Thomas Mann's *Buddenbrooks* (1901). My argument, in brief, is that the literary transposition of Wagner's music from the public to the private sphere allowed these authors to negotiate intimacy and eroticism, and that it did so precisely through an imagery of fluidity.

Wagnerian drama was conceived with large-scale public arenas in mind. Yet for nineteenth-century Wagnerians, other channels were necessary to sustain the habit of music-drama consumption. Long before the phonograph, piano reductions of selected pieces brought Wagner into the bourgeois home.[7] This mode of performance is crucial for the spectrum of sexual overtones that Wagner's music brings to literature. In the words of Richard Leppert, the sonorities of the piano 'served as the aesthetic metaphor simultaneously connecting and justifying the connection between public and private life: that is, [...] between bourgeois desire and erotic capacity, on the one hand, and their sublimation [...] on the other'.[8] Through this instrument, Wagner's music gained entry into the private sphere, bringing with it the air of the scandalously erotic and modern. The intimate performance, moreover, not only amplifies the erotic connotations of the music, but also shifts the emphasis from a lofty idealised desire onto the materiality of the performing body. The characters in the texts discussed below are not just perceiving the music of Wagnerian eroticism; they are making it and living its myths.

Nietzsche encouraged his readers to 'translate Wagner into reality, into the modern – let us be even crueler – into the bourgeois! What becomes of Wagner then? Among ourselves, I have tried it. Nothing is more entertaining.'[9] Arguably defining what Fontane and Mann do to Wagner, this notion also points forward to a central aspect of modernism: despite persistent ideas of demythologisation, the confrontation of myth and modern reality was key to works like Eliot's *The Waste Land*, Joyce's *Ulysses*, or Mann's *Doktor Faustus*.[10] If Wagner wanted foundational myths, the grandeur of such a project was inevitably deflated in the clash with modernity. This is how the treatment of Wagner in Fontane and (early) Mann prefigures modernist mythopoeia: throwing myth into relief against bourgeois reality, they simultaneously embrace its fascination and undermine the absoluteness of its claims.

In the stories discussed here, it is the erotic aspects of Wagnerian myth – *Tristan* in particular – that are targeted, as the intimacy that had been made public by Wagner is channelled back into the private world of the German bourgeoisie with consequences variously seductive, humorous and catastrophic. At the same time, of course, these narratives themselves are public discourses, in which music becomes a metaphorical camouflage for the literal intimacy that they are representing. The result is a circuit where erotic intimacy, figured as liquid music, is flowing back and forth between the private and the public, and reflected in the recurrent images of bodies of water and bodily fluids.

In Theodor Fontane's late novella *L'Adultera*, Melanie van der Straaten leaves her well-to-do husband and their daughters to elope with a young lieutenant named Ebenezer Rubehn. In the social circle surrounding this triangle, the issue of Wagnerism is a principal divider. Herr van der Straaten excels in sarcastic remarks about 'Wagner's witchcraft', while his wife is a devout follower of the cult.[11] So is her lieutenant: when Rubehn is introduced into the story, as a visitor at van der Straaten's summer house in the Tiergarten, he is spellbound by a performance of Wotan's farewell from *Die Walküre* at the hands of the piano teacher Anastasia Schmidt (47/41). The lieutenant soon becomes a frequent guest at the house, and van der Straaten has ample opportunity to make fun of the 'pretentious noise' when the Wagnerians gather around the piano (50/43).

Water plays an important figurative part in the adulterous relation that ensues. The first intimate contact between Melanie and Rubehn occurs during an excursion on the Spree, which is erotically charged even before they are on the water. Having coffee on the riverbank, van der Straaten fires off a tirade about the waitress just having stepped out of the river, like a 'Venus Spreavensis and Venus Kallipygos' (63/55) – that is, Venus of the Spree and Venus of the beautiful behind. In this context, his reference to Venus is an allusion to Wagner's *Tannhäuser*, where the love goddess attempts to retain the eponymous singer in her grotto of carnal pleasures, among bathing naiads and sirens. Clueless about his wife's embarrassment, van der Straaten asks for confirmation by the Wagnerians at the table: 'in Greek and in music there's nothing you can't say. Am I right, Anastasia? Am I right, Elimar?' (63/55). Apart from the Venus references designating the river as a source of eroticism, his subsequent observation also pinpoints an important characteristic of musical innuendo: like a foreign language, it divides its listeners into the initiated and the clueless, while its cloak of aesthetic sophistication allows it to escape social censorship. Musical eros is thus precariously poised between the elusiveness that makes it permissible and the precision that makes it suggestive. For van der Straaten, music is a raunchy joke; for his wife, it is a matter of intense passion.

During the boating trip itself, the latter aspect dominates. Melanie and Rubehn end up in the same boat, with no husband to ridicule their tastes. The erotic connotations of the water are right on the surface of the text. As Melanie dips her hand in the water, Rubehn asks, 'Is only the water allowed to touch your hand?', to which she replies, 'It's cooling and I feel so hot' (66/58). The water also retains its connection to music – 'A boating party with no singing is a monstrosity. Even I will concede that', says van der Straaten (52/45) – and songs echo all around on the river. Among them is Eduard Mörike's 'Schön-Rohtraut' – a poem set by Schumann and others – which tells of a servant boy kissing the king's daughter. It is punctuated by the refrain 'Be silent, my heart', which enters Melanie and Rubehn's conversation, sparse but rich in sensual undercurrents: '"Be silent, my heart", Ruben repeated. "Is that what you want?" Melanie did not reply' (68/60). If water is the element of eroticism, Melanie and Rubehn are carried off on its waves: 'the boat rocked gently and drifted [trieb] on the stream, and the question grew louder and louder in Melanie's heart: where are we drifting? [wohin treiben wir?]' (68). This small phrase – notably a *sound*, heard within a heart that ignores the command of silence – heads the chapter, and will recur as a motif of some importance to the love affair. Moreover, it exemplifies the narrative technique of repeating a characteristic phrase which, as we will see below, has often been associated with the idea of the Wagnerian leitmotif in Mann, and which foreshadows many modernist attempts at 'musicalised' fiction.

While the constellation of water, song and erotic innuendo remain in play in this scene, Wagner is not mentioned. He returns, however, to take on a central role in the next chapters, where the adultery is consummated. One day, van der Straaten is away and Melanie and Anastasia spend the afternoon in Rubehn's company. As her husband enquires after her plans, Melanie announces that they will first make music, and then, after a meal, go visit the orchard and the greenhouse, and finally the aquarium. This plan is important to my reading, because it will take them through a sequence of secluded spaces where Melanie and Rubehn's sexual relation is made manifest. About the first, the music room, only a hint is given when Melanie presents her plans to her husband and the following curious little dialogue ensues:

'First we'll sing.'
'Tristan?'
'No. And Anastasia will accompany us. And then we shall have dinner, or anyway, what passes for dinner.' (73–4/65)

Whether purposefully or not, van der Straaten alludes here to his wife's desires: *Tristan* is not only the quintessential story of transfigured adultery, profoundly influenced by Wagner's own extramarital sentiments for Mathilde Wesendonck in the 1850s, but also the apex of Wagner's musical expression of erotic longing.[12] Having denied the implicit allegation, Melanie swiftly changes the topic. In most of the passages dealing with music, the novella excels in specifying what is heard, and it contains allusions not only to Wagner, but also to specific songs by Schumann, Mendelssohn and others. But here, we only learn that it goes on for an hour and a half (75/67). Instead, the chapter centres on the next interior space they visit: 'an old-fashioned greenhouse' (76/68). In the greenhouse, under a cupola, we find the space where their love affair is physically consummated – a secluded bower: 'It was a magical arbor formed by the leafy treetops, and completely enclosed; orchids climbed all over the trees and up the ribbing of the dome [. . .] Melanie felt her nerves giving way under the intoxicating scent' (82/73). The hothouse was a favourite topos of French decadence, furnishing authors from Zola to Huysmans with a symbol of exquisite artificial sensuality.[13] In the love affair between Fontane's two Wagnerians, however, the allusion is more specific. In April of 1858, Wesendonck wrote the poem 'Im Treibhaus' [In the Greenhouse], which Wagner immediately proceeded to set. It belongs to the set of five songs usually referred to as the *Wesendonck-Lieder*, first performed in 1862. But 'Im Treibhaus' is also part of the music Melanie *denies* playing on this day, namely *Tristan*. It is not just that the song makes use of the Tristan chord.[14] Wagner called it a 'Studie für Tristan und Isolde', and its music went straight into the opening of the third act, finished in 1859: its diatonic minor version of the rising desire motif also accompanies the languishing Tristan, and its repeated fading phrases are typically heard as a musical expression of his physical weakness.[15]

To be 'Im Treibhaus', then, is not only to be in a secluded space of olfactory bliss, away from the prying eyes of husbands and friends. It is also to be in the musical world of Wagner's death-bound adultery. Just before yielding to their own desire, Melanie and Rubehn return in their minds to the nexus of water and song. As Melanie remarks that Anastasia will not find them where they are hiding, he says he will not miss her, only 'that song she was singing the day we crossed the river in the boat' (82/73) – that is, 'Schön-Rohtraut', the Schumann song about the illicit kiss. Yet the private space that enfolds their embrace is thoroughly Wagnerian: after having made music at the piano – not *Tristan*, but perhaps so close that Melanie prefers not to let her husband have a second guess – they step right into the fragrant air of the Wesendonck song, acting out the extramarital love story of which that song is the product. The hothouse scene, in other words, is not just a physical place they visit in the realist narrative. It is also an imaginary space of erotic fulfilment, invoked by their Wagnerian fantasy.

Notably, the river and its erotic undercurrents also trickle into the greenhouse, by way of the pun on *trieb* and *Trieb* – that is, the past tense of the verb 'to drift' (*treiben*) and the noun 'drive' (*der Trieb*). The *Treibhaus*, as it were, is also a *Triebhaus*. It answers Melanie's repeated question: 'Where are we drifting?'; the act taking place in the bower is the telos of the sexual drive as well as of the boat drifting on the water, and afterwards she still *hears* this thought (its metaphorical audibility is significant) in her heart. Once they get out of the greenhouse, it is too late to visit the final station that Melanie had planned for: the aquarium. Instead, they go home and make more music. Interestingly, however, the music room has now acquired traces of the greenhouse, the river and the aquarium:

> All the windows and doors stood open, and a balmy air wafted from the freshly mown meadows. Anastasia sat down at the piano and sang, and began a bantering conversation with Rubehn, who made an effort to fall in with her tone. But Melanie stared in front of her and was silent and far away. On the high seas. And in her heart the question rose [Fontane uses 'klang', that is, 'resounded'] again: where are we drifting? (83/74)

Through the open doors and windows, reminders of what has happened enter the room: the balmy air recalls the hothouse and its perfumes, and the waters beneath Melanie's question of drifting have grown from river to high seas. The emotional intensity of her silence — and of the phrase that still *resounds* in her heart — blends with the music heard in the room, which, in turn, is implicitly paralleled by the imaginary inundation.

At the same time, Fontane slyly punctures the pathos he creates. The flooded room with its sea of emotions has a down-to-earth parallel in the aquarium, which was repeatedly emphasised as the afternoon's final goal. One water-filled room, as it were, is substituted for another. The parallel becomes clear in van der Straaten's response to the idea of going there. He warns them of the aquarium by way of a comical anecdote about how water — still the erotic element par excellence — cannot be contained, which suggests that he knows exactly what might happen. On a previous visit, he recalls, one of the glass panels suddenly broke:

> and there, before we could count three, not only was the whole aquarium floor under a foot of water, but all the monsters of the deep were wriggling [zappeln] all around us, and a large pike was investigating Melanie's instep to the deliberate neglect of Aunt Riekchen's. He must have been a connoisseur. And in a fit of mad jealousy I had him killed and personally devoured his liver. (74/66)

This image is a droll alternative to the high seas in the music room, but perhaps with a streak of seriousness, emphasising the husband's potential course of action if struck by sexual jealousy.

Interestingly, Fontane recycled the image of the floundering fish soon after writing this. In a letter to Karl Zöllner from 13 July 1881 — that is, in-between the journal and book publications of *L'Adultera* — he used it in an amusing rant about the lewdness of Wagner:

> There is nothing to do with 'ether', everywhere the lowest drives are twitching [zappeln] [. . .] which appear so objectionable precisely because you see Richard Wagner, personally, twitching along [. . .] And the great aim, the world riddle and the redeeming word, what does it all add up to? To use [an] often-quoted phrase: 'Father, buy me an apple' [. . .] But with Wagner, one never really knows whether, instead of the apple, a sour herring is not intended.[16]

The wish for an apple — a symbol of knowledge, lust and fertility, whether it is the biblical forbidden fruit or Freia's rejuvenating produce — as the answer to the riddle of the universe already cuts Wagner's sexual metaphysics down to size. Add the pungent herring, mirroring here the composer twitching in the net of his sexual impulses – *zappeln* is an eminently corporeal verb, suggesting the inability to curb bodily movement – and Fontane's broadside almost rivals Bjørnson's sperm splotch on the beach. It hardly matters that it is a different fish that twitches in the novella; the constellation of uncontrollable sexuality and Wagnerism knits the passages tightly together.

Fontane develops two images of Wagner's oceanic sexuality flowing into the reality of the bourgeoisie: to Melanie, it is the high seas of passion that inundate the music room, while, to van der Straaten, it is the nuisance of wet feet and fish on the floor. After these scenes, Wagner disappears from the novella. Melanie never perishes in love-death, but leaves her husband to start over. After the emotional, practical and social complications of the divorce, she comes out on the other side with a new child and a new husband, and takes a job as a language teacher. There presumably lay the real scandal of the story for Fontane's contemporaries: not in the adulterous woman, but in the adulterous woman who does not think it fit to be punished by tragic demise. Fontane thus effectively defuses Wagnerian decadence by showing that its spell will break against the real world, and that those involved may just pick up the pieces and get on with their lives.

While Fontane took an interest in Wagner as a cultural phenomenon, he nevertheless remained fundamentally unmoved by his music. By contrast, the young Thomas Mann, who considered Fontane one of his most important role models, nurtured a lifelong (if increasingly fraught and ambiguous) love for the works of his 'Master and Nordic God'.[17] Wagner's work was of immediate importance to Mann from the first to the last – not least as mediated through Nietzsche's mixture of profound admiration and acrimonious criticism, which corresponded closely to Mann's own complicated Wagnerism. My focus here will not be the intertwinement of music with the catastrophe of German history in *Doktor Faustus*, even though this nexus is related to sexuality through Leverkühn's syphilitic bargain, nor the technologically mediated enjoyment in *Zauberberg*, where Wagner has to stand back for French and Italian composers. Instead, I will look at scenes of domestic music-making in *Buddenbrooks*, to show how they foster a Wagnerian association of music with water and eroticism.[18]

In the extensive research on Wagner's impact on Mann, the erotic element has tended to be overshadowed by two other aspects: on the one hand, the idea of Wagner's influence on the structure of Mann's narrative and, on the other hand, Mann's increasing uneasiness with the political aspects of Wagner's work, especially in light of its subsequent misappropriation by the Hitler regime.[19] Hans Rudolf Vaget's authoritative work is a case in point.[20]

Vaget's chief perspective on Mann is that of a *Mentalitätsgeschichte*, where Wagner plays a crucial role in the development of a German culture that gave birth to both Hitler and Mann, which leaves the theme of sexuality in the margins. In relation to *Buddenbrooks*, his focus is on the idea of the Wagnerian leitmotif as structural principle.[21] Based on the repetition and variation of key phrases, this technique is strikingly proto-modernist: Mann structures narrative time by attempting to emulate a musical model, a strategy that would become instrumental in modernism's formal innovations and departure from plot-bound linearity, in Mann's own works as well as those of Joyce, Woolf, Huxley, Gide and others.[22] The problem with this focus is that it directs attention away from the corporeality of music-making: to serve as a model for narrative structure, music must be abstracted from its instantiation in performance. But music's role in *Buddenbrooks*, I will argue, hinges precisely on such instantiation: it is the physical act of *playing* that turns music into a medium of intimacy.

For the devout Wagnerian Hanno, the last frail twig on the family tree, the ocean feels like home. He spends the family vacations in Travemünde adoring the ocean,

> the endless green and blue, from which came a gentle swishing sound bearing a strong, fresh, and aromatic breeze that wrapped itself around your ears [...] a kind of muted numbness that silently, peacefully dissolved every constraint, so that you lost all sense of time and space.[23]

Hanno hears in the ocean sounds the same sensual dissolution and death that pervade *Tristan* (and Mann draws on the same tropes that inform Bjørnson's letter: the seaside is the site of numbness and loss of contour). The ocean is, for Hanno, 'no longer simply the backdrop or symbol for an erotic liberation, but the object of desire itself'.[24] On the wet days when the 'rain fell in sheets, melting heaven, earth, and sea into one another' and 'drops became streams' on the windows, we find Hanno amusing himself with the pianino in the entertainment hall, which has 'a muted, gurgling [glucksender] tone' (699–700/615). The contours of the elements dissolve in the deluge, and the word *glucksen* connotes a soft sound of water, thus letting the music from the old instrument blend with the more massive flow of the sea and the rain outside.

The close relationship between music and the ocean is brought forward by Mann's verbal imagery and insistently connected with illicit sexual impulses or actions. Water vocabulary reoccurs in the novel's key scenes of music-making, as an essential component of Mann's carefully crafted descriptions of music. For instance, when Hanno's mother Gerda Buddenbrook starts making music with

Lieutenant von Throta in the salon, while her worried husband is confined to his study, their harmonies roll and roar ('rollen und brausen'), and embrace in frothing spume ('aufschäumend umschlingen') (712). Moreover, it is the very privacy of the space from which the unmusical Thomas Buddenbrook is excluded that nourishes his suspicion and speculation. The same is true of the house itself, as Thomas imagines it perceived from the outside, fearing that people may see the lieutenant enter his house, where 'upstairs his beautiful wife was making music with her lover – and not just music' (713/626). The house and the salon are like Chinese boxes: their innermost content always remains secret to the surrounding society and to Thomas, yet the liquid music seeps out as a reminder of the intimacy they conceal. The only thing that bothers him more than the music-making is the silence that follows. In this silence, it seems, nothing prevents music from transforming from a symbolic, sublimated version of sexual desire into the foreplay to something more real. When Thomas decides to barge in, the oceanic music itself surges up to prevent him: 'the moment he took hold of the white door's burnt-gold handle, a storm of music surged up again [setzte mit einem stürmischen Aufbrausen die Musik wieder ein] and he shrank back' (715/628). Music-making, after all, always has the unquestionable alibi of respectability.

The novel's most spectacular scenes of Wagnerian musical eroticism are those describing Hanno's piano-playing. The reader is given two lengthy descriptions of pianistic orgasms. In the first, he is only a child. He has heard his mother play *Tristan* with Herr Pfühl, who is a stern Bach admirer and initially appalled when Gerda makes him play Wagner:

> It is the end of all morality in the arts. I will not play it! [...] And think of the child, the child sitting there in his chair. He stole in here quietly to hear music – do you wish to poison his mind for good and all? (548/488)

The child, however, is already seduced by the music in question. For his eighth birthday, he composes a small fantasy, the ending of which is borrowed directly from *Tristan*. Mann uses Pfühl's pedagogical pedantry as an alibi for a technical specification of the allusion: 'but why did you decide suddenly to leave B major for a fourth-sixth chord, for this interval of a fourth with a diminished third – that's what I want to know? Mere tricks. And you add a *tremolo* besides' (555/493–4). The harmonic progression described both here and when Hanno actually performs the piece – the passage from a B major tonic to E minor and back again – is the one that underlies Isolde's final phrase in the *Liebestod*: 'unbewusst – höchste Lust!' [unconscious – supreme bliss!]. Harmonically speaking, this is not just any cadence, but the final resolution of a tension that has been building for hours on end. Hanno's piece, by contrast, is a mere two minutes, and the comedy of the scene derives from the tacking of a disproportionately grandiose climax onto Hanno's childish ditty.

In Mann's protracted description of this final cadence, the figurative veil of the musical performance is only just enough to cover the quasi-pornographic impulse of the prose. Here is a short excerpt:

> He refused to resolve the chord, withheld it from himself and his audience [...] not yet – one moment more of delay, of unbearable tension that would make the release all the more precious [...] Hanno's upper body slowly straightened up, his eyes grew large, his tightly closed lips quivered, he jerked back, drawing air in through his nose – and then that blessedness could be held back no longer. It came, swept over him, and he no longer fought it. His muscles relaxed; overwhelmed, he let his weary head sink back on his shoulders. His eyes closed, and a melancholy, almost pained smile of unutterable ecstasy played about his mouth. (557/495)

The musical orgasm is thus depicted in thoroughly physical terms. When Hanno performs his Wagnerian climax on the piano, the erotic sensuality of the music is not of an idealised or immaterial kind, but an emphatically corporeal activity. The pleasure he experiences is not the detached excitement of the listener, but the exhausting physical effort of the performer.

Just as in the other musical scenes, the fluid imagery is prevalent here. Accompanying him on the violin, his mother releases 'a sparkling, bubbly flood of cadenzas'; the E minor chord is wrapped in her 'sparkling, bubbling runs'; when Hanno adds the sixth as a passing tone, we learn that her Stradivarius 'surged and dashed sonorously around the same C sharp'; and the final arrival at the tonic is a 'submersion [Hineinsinken] into B major' (556–7/494–5). In short, the music insistently acts like water: surging, roaring, sinking, flowing and spuming. Far from a making a purely musical allusion by quoting a harmonic progression, Mann mobilises the entire water-soaked sexuality of *Tristan* and – quite provocatively – places it in the body of a prepubescent child who is finding the keys to his sexuality at the piano.

If the liquid element of music is epitomised in *Buddenbrooks* by the grandeur of the ocean, it is also, when it so explicitly emanates from the performer's flesh, a bodily fluid. As has been pointed out by several critics, Hanno's musical pleasures have strong overtones of masturbation.[25] The climactic passage clearly suggests an ejaculation and, again, Bjørnson's formulation of the *Tristan* experience – a kind of narcotic self-gratification that turns its listener into an emission of the composer – is not far off. The same is true of Hanno's final performance. Despite his guilt-laden resolution to abstain from playing, the now sixteen-year-old boy draws the curtains to guarantee privacy and sits down at the piano. Mann still relies on fluid vocabulary to portray the climax of the improvisation: 'it came, it could not be held back any longer, the convulsions of desire could not be prolonged'; an 'unrestrained orgy' of his musical theme was 'spilling through every octave, weeping, [. . .] sobbing'; and it 'sucked hungrily at its last sweet drops' until 'its excesses trickled off in a long soft arpeggio' (827/721). Again, the pleasure and the exertion are physical as much as mental. Afterwards he throws himself on the bed: 'He was very pale, his knees had gone weak, his eyes burned' (828/721). In accordance with the logic of decadence, this musical auto-eroticism seals the sickly boy's fate: immediately following this chapter, he dies from typhus.

Hanno's music-making is thus aligned with the notion of masturbation as the wasting of an essence. According to this early-sexology perspective, to ejaculate without procreating equals a leakage of vital energy, as if life were leaving the body in fluid form. In *Buddenbrooks*, this idea finds an analogy in tears. Hanno's inability to live is given another expression by his consistent weeping, also associated with his predilection for music: 'Whenever the senator voiced his objections to Hanno's passionate preoccupation with music, he would fix on these very points: the dreamy softness, the weeping, the total lack of vigor and energy' (562/500). Although no one is more teary-eyed than Hanno, the other musical characters in the novel are also typified by a watery gaze: Gerda's eyes are 'radiant and moist from the music' (546/487), and those of her musical companion, Lieutenant von Throta, are also 'shimmering' and seem to glow 'in bottomless depths' (710/626). From the bodies of these aesthetes, as it were, a musical fluid is constantly seeping. When summer vacation is over and Hanno needs to leave Travemünde, the association is presented as a substitution: 'slowly, and hiding his tears [langsam, mit heimlichen Thränen], little Johann learned to miss the sea again [. . .] finding solace in Kai, Herr Pfühl, and his music' (702/617). The tears, Mann's sentence says, are the means by which the music is able to stand in for the vast body of water. Through his music-making body, the great Wagnerian waters enter Hanno's private space, carrying with them the connotations of the Tristanesque desire for an erotic dissolution in death.

In both *L'Adultera* and *Buddenbrooks*, the notion of music as fluid and erotic goes hand in hand with a thematisation of the liminal structures that fail at their task of guaranteeing stability. In relation to the human body, music is associated both with vast bodies of water and with discharged fluids such as tears and semen, which also serve as manifestations of the psychological porosity of the individual subject. In relation to architecture – which is particularly important because the house is a principal image of the solidity of bourgeois life – music is that which may at any moment overflow the boundaries of the private space. Sometimes music leaks or bursts out, sometimes it is insufficiently or temporarily contained. In relation to symbolisation, finally, music represents a floating between the figurative and the literal, between keeping secret and making known – to the readers of the stories as well as the listeners in them. The erotic overtones of music resound clearly enough to be picked up by the already initiated, yet they are vague enough to go unregistered by custodians of bourgeois decorum. While making music remains a sanctioned cultural activity, it may nevertheless serve as an expression of what is perceived as the most reprehensible desires.

The walls that structure privacy never seem quite impermeable, and the domestic Wagnerian performance serves as a conduit through which an oceanic musical eroticism, originally created for the arena of the opera house, flows into the architecture of the bourgeois world via the bodies engaged in intimate performance. Whether lampooning it, admiring it, or both, these stories never limit Wagner's music (and the sexuality it is called upon to represent) to the position of elevated or disembodied greatness. On the contrary, it is continuously returned to the physicality of the performing body, to crude sexuality and to lewd humour, and whether it manifests itself as pregnancy and life or illness and death, its ultimate consequences are emphatically physical. Alongside and beyond a supposed literary use of leitmotifs, this intimate deflation of Wagnerian myth through its injection into the bourgeois world constitutes a significant proto-modernist facet of these texts. When Fontane and Mann have their characters channel Wagner's musical eroticism into their narrative realities – be it as droplets and trickles, be it as a full-scale inundation of its sheltered rooms – it takes the form of a liquid intimacy, which, seeping through boundaries both material and imaginary, insistently dissolves the borders between the internal and the external, between the public and the private, and between the figurative and the literal.

Notes

1. Øyvind Anker, 'Bjørnstjerne Bjørnsons brev til Edvard Grieg', *Edda*, 43 (1943), pp. 170–1. All translations by the author unless otherwise noted.
2. A classic study is Erwin Koppen, *Dekadenter Wagnerismus: Studien zur europäischen Literatur des Fin de siècle* (Berlin and New York: de Gruyter, 1973).
3. See James Kennaway, 'Modern Music and Nervous Modernity: Wagnerism as a Disease of Civilization, 1850–1914', in *Bad Vibrations: The History of the Idea of Music as a Cause of Disease* (Farnham: Ashgate, 2012), pp. 63–98.

4. See Laurence Dreyfus, *Wagner and the Erotic Impulse* (Cambridge, MA: Harvard University Press, 2010).
5. Susan Sontag, 'Wagner's Fluids', *London Review of Books*, 10 December 1987, pp. 8–9.
6. See Thomas S. Grey, *Wagner's Musical Prose: Texts and Contexts* (Cambridge: Cambridge University Press, 1995), pp. 130–79.
7. Nicholas Vazsonyi, *Richard Wagner: Self-Promotion and the Making of a Brand* (Cambridge: Cambridge University Press, 2010), p. 123 et passim.
8. Richard Leppert, 'Sexual Identity, Death and the Family Piano', *19th-Century Music*, 16.2 (1992), pp. 115–16.
9. Friedrich Nietzsche, *The Case of Wagner*, in *The Birth of Tragedy and The Case of Wagner*, trans. Walter Kaufmann (New York: Vintage Books, 1967), p. 175.
10. Michael Bell, *Literature, Modernism and Myth: Belief and Responsibility in the Twentieth Century* (Cambridge: Cambridge University Press, 2009).
11. Theodor Fontane, *The Woman Taken in Adultery and The Poggenpuhl Family*, trans. Gabriele Annan (Chicago and London: University of Chicago Press, 1979), p. 27. For the original, see Fontane, *Werke, Schriften und Briefe: I/2*, ed. Helmuth Nürnberger (Munich: Hanser, 1971), p. 33. Hereafter, references to these editions appear in the text, the page number of the German original followed by the corresponding page of Annan's English translation. The presence of Wagner in Fontane's work, along with motives of the fin-de-siècle decadence, was first noted in Heide Eilert, 'Im Treibhaus: Motive der europäischen Décadence in Theodor Fontanes Roman "L'Adultera"', *Jahrbuch der deutschen Schillergesellschaft*, 22 (1978), pp. 494–517. See also Isabel Nottinger, *Fontanes Fin de Siècle: Motive der Dekadenz in L'Adultera, Cécile und Der Stechlin* (Würzburg: Königshausen & Neumann, 2003).
12. Dreyfus, *Wagner and the Erotic Impulse*, pp. 99–110.
13. Eilert, 'Im Treibhaus', pp. 504–9.
14. Ibid. p. 505.
15. Stephen Downes, *Music and Decadence in European Modernism: The Case of Central and Eastern Europe* (Cambridge: Cambridge University Press, 2010), p. 181.
16. Theodor Fontane, *Schriften und Glossen zur europäischen Literatur, II*, ed. Emil Staiger (Zurich: Artemis, 1967), p. 302.
17. Thomas Mann, *Im Schatten Wagners: Thomas Mann über Richard Wagner*, ed. Hans Rudolf Vaget, 3rd edn (Frankfurt am Main: Fischer, 2005), p. 19.
18. Several other early stories by Mann could have been added, notably *Tristan* (1903), where the physical act of music-making is also described in liquid terms and charged with adulterous eroticism.

19. In the works that form the main exceptions to this tendency, the nexus of physical sexuality, music-making and fluidity, which is my focus here, goes unnoticed: see Koppen, *Dekadenter Wagnerismus*, pp. 184–94, 265–78; Marcel Reich-Ranicki, 'O sink hernieder Nacht der Liebe. Der junge Thomas Mann, der Eros und die Musik', *Thomas-Mann-Jahrbuch*, 7 (1994), pp. 187–98; and Dietmar Krug, *Eros im Dreigestirn: Zur Gestaltung des Erotischen im Frühwerk Thomas Manns* (Frankfurt am Main: Peter Lang, 1997).
20. In addition to two major books – *Seelenzauber: Thomas Mann und die Musik* (Frankfurt am Main: Fischer, 2006) and '*Wehvolles Erbe': Richard Wagner in Deutschland – Hitler, Knappertsbusch, Mann* (Frankfurt am Main: Fischer, 2017) – Vaget has also edited a volume of Mann's writings on Wagner (see note 17 above).
21. Vaget, *Seelenzauber*, pp. 97–121.
22. Cf. Eric Prieto, *Listening In: Music, Mind, and the Modernist Narrative* (Lincoln, NE: University of Nebraska Press, 2002).
23. Thomas Mann, *Buddenbrooks: The Decline of a Family*, trans. John E. Woods (New York: Vintage, 1994), p. 612. For Mann's original, see Mann, *Buddenbrooks: Verfall einer Familie. Große Kommentierte Frankfurter Ausgabe, I* (Frankfurt am Main: Fischer, 2002), p. 696. Hereafter, references to these editions appear in the text, the page number of the German original followed by the corresponding page of Woods's English translation.
24. Krug, *Eros im Dreigestirn*, p. 67.
25. Eckhard Heftrich, *Vom Verfall zur Apokalypse: Über Thomas Mann* (Frankfurt am Main: Vittorio Klostermann, 1982), p. 50. See also Krug, *Eros im Dreigestirn*, p. 69.

2
Stories of O: Modernism and Female Pleasure
Laura Frost

In 1912, Virginia Woolf wrote in a letter from her honeymoon:

> Why do you think people make such a fuss about marriage & copulation? Why do some of our friends change upon losing chastity? Possibly my great age makes it less of a catastrophe; but certainly I find the climax intensely exaggerated.[1]

Despite Woolf's dry humour, both she and Leonard were agitated and they canvassed friends for advice upon their return to England. Woolf's sister Vanessa wrote, 'Apparently [Virginia] still gets no pleasure at all from the act. They were anxious to know when I first had an orgasm.'[2] There were a couple of hypotheses about why orgasm eluded Woolf — namely, her attraction to women, and childhood abuse by her half-brother — but she was hardly alone in her dilemma.

Six years after Woolf's anticlimactic honeymoon, Marie Stopes's *Married Love* (1918) became a British bestseller, with its daring contention that 'woman like man has the same physiological reaction, a reciprocal need for enjoyment and benefit from union in marriage distinct from the exercise of maternal functions'.[3] Stopes reported that '70 or 80 per cent of our married women (in the middle and intellectual classes) are deprived of the full orgasm'.[4] The message was clear: female orgasms were essential to a healthy marriage and most British women were not having them. This news, in Stopes's own words, 'crashed into English society like a bomb-shell'.[5]

Women's orgasmic discontent was not just an English predicament. When André Breton led his fellow surrealists in a series of discussions about sexuality, his first query was: 'A man and a woman make love. To what extent is the man aware of the woman's orgasm?'[6] The painter Yves Tanguy answers, 'Hardly at all.' When Breton persists, 'Do you have any objective ways of telling?' the writer Raymond Queneau insists: 'There are no ways', and poet Benjamin Péret agrees: 'No way.' By contrast, when Breton turns to the male orgasm, things are considerably more transparent. 'It is a matter of a more or less conclusive local examination after the man has finished', he pronounces.[7]

Were women holding out on revealing their orgasmic experience, as Jacques Lacan would suggest in his response to Bernini's sculpture of St Teresa's ecstasy?[8] Hardly. In the first half of the twentieth century, far from a pleasure that dare not speak its name, female orgasm was spoken of as a conundrum, a challenge, a problem to be solved. In this period, female orgasm was considered not just a scientific matter, but also a sociopolitical issue. Medical practitioners, sex reformers and fiction writers alike began to view female orgasm as a fraught reflection of – and a means of regulating or disciplining – women's autonomy and agency. Variously identified as a vital sign of health or as an index of psychological development, female orgasm was widely thought to require management.

Woolf, Stopes and Breton demonstrate how orgasm had, by the early decades of the twentieth century, become a matter of public biopolitics. Annamarie Jagose proposes that

> as a central cipher for modern sex, orgasm is closely bound to its fortunes and consequently shaped by its historical transformations: by altered understandings of love [and] by the rise of intimacy as a social value that takes sex as one of its communicative forms.[9]

Given the uneven historical developments for men and women in the first half of the twentieth century, it follows that a different set of pressures would be brought to bear upon the somatic, and culturally construed as 'intimate', phenomenon of orgasm.

Male orgasm has also been subject to cultural constraints, but it has typically been understood as definitive and vital, self-contained, and strongly delineated.[10] Female orgasm, meanwhile, has been figured as elusive, ambiguous and dependent upon outside influence. Linda Williams has argued, in the context of visual pornography, that the ostensible inscrutability of female pleasure is based on the premise that women's orgasms are not visible or tangible as men's are.[11] This is true for literary as well as visual representation. Men's orgasms tend to be figured as direct, localised, physical and external (as in Breton's description), whereas women's tend to be imagined as a nebulous and largely internal sensation.

So, for example, in *Ulysses* (1922), James Joyce marks the numerous orgasms that transpire on 16 June 1904 differently depending upon the sex of the body in question. In the 'Nausicaa' episode, Joyce describes Leopold Bloom's orgasm mechanically, as a hand working in a pocket and a metaphorical ejaculation of fireworks; meanwhile Gerty MacDowell's climax, 'a little strangled cry, wrung from her, that cry that has rung through the ages',[12] is filtered through a preoccupation with proper appearance and etiquette. Male orgasm, for Joyce, is a release with mostly physical implications, while female orgasm is relational, provisional and ultimately dependent upon male sexuality.

And as for women's descriptions of orgasm? Anaïs Nin, a pioneer in articulating women's sexual experiences from both a psychological and a physical point of view, wrote in her 1937 diary,

> The entire mystery of pleasure in a woman's body lies in the intensity of the pulsation just before the orgasm. Sometimes it is slow, one-two-three, three palpitations which then project a fiery and icy liqueur through the body. If the palpitation is feeble, muted, the pleasure is like a gentler wave. The pocket seed of ecstasy bursts with more or less energy, when it is richest it touches every portion of the body, vibrating through every nerve and cell [...] A rainbow of color strikes the eyelids. A foam of music falls over the ears. It is the gong of orgasm.[13]

Nin deploys a succession of metaphors for a flurry of sensations and motions that envelop the whole body. Strikingly, she describes orgasm without specifying any conventional erotic zones, as a generalised and diffuse sensation. This passage bears a close resemblance to Woolf's description of Clarissa Dalloway's youthful feelings for Sally Seton in *Mrs Dalloway* (1925) as

> a sudden revelation, a tinge like a blush which one tried to check and then, as it spread, one yielded to its expansion, and rushed to the farthest verge and there quivered and felt the world come closer, swollen with some astonishing significance, some pressure of rapture, which split its thin skin and gushed and poured with an extraordinary alleviation over the cracks and sores! Then, for that moment, she had seen an illumination; a match burning in a crocus; an inner meaning almost expressed.[14]

This symphony of blushing, swelling, spreading and quivering evokes female passion – perhaps even female ejaculation – in one of the most emblematic modernist descriptions of female eros. Disappointed with the sexual aspects of marital life, Woolf was quite able to imagine ecstasy outside the bounds of heterosexuality, between women. Lesbian and queer desire remained beneath the radar of the public, medical and social discourses of female orgasm, except for pathologising sexological case studies, censorship trials of texts such as Radclyffe Hall's *The Well of Loneliness* (1928) and scandals such as the 1918 Maud Allan trial, which warned the British public about 'the cult of the clitoris'.[15] Female orgasm was, significantly, mainly a 'problem' for heterosexuality – and this would be underscored in later sexological studies showing that lesbians reported 20 per cent more orgasms than heterosexual women.[16]

The significance that Joyce, Nin and Woolf attribute to erotic ecstasy is commensurate with its suggestive nature: 'an inner meaning almost expressed'; a definite set of sensations without a specific connotation; an elusive, boundless quality; 'some astonishing significance' that gestures both to and beyond the phenomenon of pleasure or desire. This quality of unspecified yet vital importance, combined with epistemological uncertainty, rendered female orgasm susceptible to social cooptation and outside directives.

In this chapter I will consider modern writers who made female orgasm central to their work, and two in particular who imagined conspicuous forms of what I call 'orgasmic discipline': a regulative programme to explicitly alter women's sexual practices for personal or sociopolitical reasons. Mabel Dodge Luhan, whom Christopher Lasch described as 'a pioneer in the cult of the orgasm',[17] left a remarkable account of her attempt to attain orgasmic heteroconformity. Her colleague D. H. Lawrence was equally invested in sexual reform, which he effected in his fiction through his female characters' struggles to conform to particular erotic practices. Luhan and Lawrence make manifest how female orgasm was understood as a vehicle of acculturation by Freud and others who had powerfully affected the modern understanding of female sexuality.

Across a wide range of modern thought, female orgasm – whether posited as a developmental milestone, a reproductive imperative, an expression of gender conformity, a marital duty, or a spasm of liberation – is (1) figured as an enigma, but an enigma of personal and social importance well beyond the production of pleasure; (2) closely correlated with the sociocultural fate of women and the limits of their freedom and autonomy; and (3) framed as requiring management or control – whether restriction or promotion. What is at stake in these modern discourses of female orgasm is nothing less than women's autonomy, agency and sociopolitical power.

*

The ancient Greek prophet Tiresias told Zeus and Hera that women enjoyed sex nine times more than men, and thousands of years later, sex researchers such as Masters and Johnson and Shere Hite substantiated women's capacity for multiple orgasms and lengthier orgasms than men's.[18] In between, knowledge about women's sexual pleasure was full of leaps and recursions. What female orgasm is, what its function is, how it is produced – and in particular, knowledge about the clitoris – is a conversation that has happened in every era, only to be seemingly erased and started anew.[19] To set modern representations of orgasm in an accurate frame, then, it is essential to first briefly look back at these incremental spirals of discovery and apparent amnesia. In the medieval period, female orgasm was widely believed to be necessary for conception, and hence the clitoris was routinely part of midwifery manuals and medical models. This makes all the more conspicuous the fact that an 'anatomical aporia' in medical discourse around women's sexuality set in in the early eighteenth century.[20] Thomas Laqueur argues that

> the erasure of female pleasure from medical accounts of conception took place roughly at the same time as the female body came to be understood not as a lesser version of the male's (a one-sex model) but as its incommensurable opposite (a two-sex model).[21]

Women's bodies and desires were now thought to be entirely different from – and the inverse of – men's. Medical models downplayed the clitoris because it was not thought to be crucial to conception, and this consequently shaped suppositions about the nature of female sexuality.

While female orgasm was fading out of anatomical discourse, it was also being produced by medical treatments aiming to resolve 'female complaints'. From the first century AD through the Victorian period, genital massage was seen as an effective medical treatment for hysteria. Orgasm in this context was a panacea for a host of problems, not least of which was lack of sexual satisfaction. As Rachel Maines explains, 'the demand for treatment had two sources: the proscription on female masturbation as unchaste and possibly unhealthful, and the failure of androcentrically defined sexuality to produce orgasm regularly in most women'.[22] With the advent of electricity, vibrating appliances allowed women to stimulate their own bodies, but women's sexuality was understood more as a matter of hygiene and health than of pleasure.

Freud's theories about female sexuality moved the conversation about orgasm in another direction entirely. In *The Question of Lay Analysis* (1926), Freud famously described female sexuality as 'a "dark continent" for psychology', as a void or enigma.[23] In *Three Essays on the Theory of Sexuality* (1905), he cast female pleasure as analogous to male sexuality, with the clitoris a sort of stunted penis, and argued that a normal female's erogenous zone shifts, in the course of maturity, to the superior organ, the vagina, where erotic sensation would coincide with intercourse.[24] In Freud's account, sexual practices such as oral sex and masturbation are conspicuously absent, banished along with lesbian desire. The effects of Freud's ideas were pernicious and long-lasting; Marie Bonaparte was one of their most famous casualties. An aristocratic patient of Freud and an analyst herself, Bonaparte devoted herself to the quest for the Holy Grail of vaginal orgasm, writing that women's 'frigidity caused by clitoral fixation can only be cured by a mixture of surgery and psychoanalysis'.[25] Bonaparte underwent three operations between 1927 and 1931 to have her clitoris surgically moved closer to her vaginal opening, so that it might be more easily stimulated during sex. The operations were not successful, and Bonaparte continued to think of herself as frigid. This notion that vaginal orgasms were superior to clitoral ones would persist well into the second half of the twentieth century.

To be sure, there were stirrings of clitoral consciousness at this time. In *Married Love*, Stopes clearly identified body parts and pleasures – for example, 'the woman has at the surface a small vestigial organ called the clitoris, which corresponds morphologically to the man's penis, and which, like it, is extremely sensitive to touch-sensations'.[26] Despite describing the clitoris as essentially a small penis (as per the one-sex model) and as 'vestigial', as having outlived its original function (pleasure), Stopes tried to explain women's arousal in enough detail for her readers to replicate, describing sexual positions conducive to women's orgasm and emphasising the importance of foreplay, which 'takes time. More time indeed than the average husband dreams of spending upon it.'[27] However, in asserting that if women did not have a 'full' orgasm during sex they would be 'nervous' and 'anxious', Stopes iterated the old paradigm of female sexuality as both a disease and cure.[28] While introducing women to their own bodies and making pleasure a priority, Stopes also presented female orgasm in heterosexual intercourse as a compulsory pleasure.

*

The notion that female sexuality is an enigma requiring management sat uneasily alongside women's emancipatory movements, and their achievement of new fields of employment for women in conjunction with the legal right to own property, divorce, vote and exercise reproductive freedom. As women made gains as a collective, in both the public and private spheres, they continued to receive spurious and retrogressive advice about their 'intimate' sexual lives. Mabel Dodge Luhan left a vivid record about living at this crossroads of conflict. Raised in a wealthy family, with emotionally distant parents who gave her a lifelong desire to create alternative communities, Luhan made her mark on modernism primarily in founding a series of international salons and hosting leading writers, painters, musicians, philosophers and political activists to discuss modern art, politics, psychoanalysis, socialism, feminism, birth control and other issues of the day. Luhan also helped organise and promote the landmark 1913 International Exhibition of Modern Art at the New York Armory, and wrote an essay to accompany Gertrude Stein's 'Portrait of Mabel Dodge at the Villa Curonia'. Luhan later mused that 'if Gertrude Stein was born at the Armory Show, so was "Mabel Dodge"'.[29] Luhan's life represented the exhilarating innovations of modernity, but also the struggles for women to define their sexuality.

Less well known than Luhan's organisational activities is her four-volume autobiography *Intimate Memories* (1933–7), in which she writes about her friendships, her salons, her psychoanalysis and her sex life. For Luhan, sex was 'perhaps the cornerstone of any life, and its chief reality'; she was inspired by the American birth control activist Margaret Sanger, 'an ardent propagandist for the joys of the flesh'.[30] Sanger, Luhan wrote, 'taught us the way to a heightening of pleasure and of prolonging it, and the delimiting of it to the sexual zones, the spreading out and sexualizing of the whole body'.[31]

This remark coincides with Woolf's and Nin's descriptions of expansive female erotic pleasure; it also brings to mind Anthony Giddens's idea of 'plastic sexuality'.[32] One of the key shifts in the 'transformation of intimacy' occurring around the end of the nineteenth century and into the early twentieth, Giddens contends, was contraception and the freedom to enjoy sex without reproductive consequences. But that pliability also made women's sexuality vulnerable to more disciplinary measures. Luhan's conception of women's sexuality was shaped not just by champions of erotic freedom, but also by voices insisting that traditional gender roles were essential to social harmony and individual happiness.

In the course of her memoirs and correspondence, Luhan narrates the story of her first orgasm not once but four times. Her successive tellings show how her initial association of orgasm with freedom and agency changes once she is under the influence of psychoanalysis. In the second volume of *Intimate Memories*, Luhan reports that she experienced orgasm for the first time with her husband Karl Evans, whom she married in 1900 when she was twenty-one. She describes their sex as a 'blind, passive, unsurprised and unmoving experience to which I submitted myself without either pleasure or pain'.[33] But one night, that changed as they made love on the rug at her parents' house. She was surprised by an

> amazing explosion of the internal fireworks. I had never heard of that gentle transformation that is, in sensation, as though the nerves expressed themselves in the manner of silent, fiery fountains falling on black velvet [...] No one had ever told me about this definite, so definite and surprising thing. And I had never read of it.[34]

Like Nin and Woolf, Luhan narrates erotic sensation through a series of metaphors and as an expansive, radiating, all-enveloping pleasure as well as a 'new illumination', a 'central marvel to life', a 'new adventure of my *vie intérieure*'.[35]

In contrast to Stopes's conviction that orgasm binds couples and cements their spiritual union, Luhan admits that

> I did not remember [Karl] as a vivid part of my new experience, nor take him with me on the long, internal exploration I was making of life by the light of the new lantern I held within me. No, he was the accident in all this.[36]

Far from fostering closeness or intimacy, orgasm delivers Luhan into sexual autonomy as well as interior exploration.

Luhan recounts the same event differently in her unpublished autobiography. Although the setting is the same, now she claims that what brought about her first climax was fantasising about her gynaecologist: 'I invented a new method for myself. I closed my eyes and pretended it was the doctor I was with. And for the first time since we had been married the strange, unknown miracle occurred in my body.'[37] As with her first account, Luhan underscores the novel nature of her orgasm; here, she also accentuates her own will and creativity. And the orgasm is accompanied by another 'miracle': Luhan becomes pregnant. In this second iteration, orgasm is an act of erotic agency that resolves Luhan's conflict between marital fidelity/motherhood and carnal desire.

Luhan's images of a 'lantern' and a 'new illumination' of her '*vie intérieure*' resonate strongly with non-heteronormative formulations of female pleasure such as Woolf's, whose 'match burning in a crocus' suggests the 'Chloe liked Olivia' passage in *A Room of One's Own*, and its 'torch' lit 'in that vast chamber where nobody has yet been'.[38] These modernist tropes of female radiance and exploration might be read as a critical appropriation of Freud's 'dark continent' metaphor about female sexuality. And yet, Luhan's conception of female erotic autonomy would go in a very different direction under the guidance of psychoanalysis.

Luhan tells her orgasm tale a third time in a letter to her analyst Dr Smith Ely Jelliffe, whom she began seeing in 1916 in New York. Jelliffe believed, as Lois Palken Rudnick writes, 'that woman's biology was her destiny, and that her highest fulfillment came through bearing and raising children; and that to have sex properly, a woman must lie passively under the phallus and make sure she experienced orgasm in her vagina'.[39] Luhan took on Jelliffe's orders in the most literal terms imaginable. She writes in a letter to him: 'You have told me repeatedly that no relation between a man & a woman was justified save in that it was productive & I have repeatedly told you that I wanted it to be so.'[40] She insists that she has never had a sexual relationship without desiring a child, '*but* as you said – I was *unconsciously* using my femaleness *malely* – & I never conceived for that reason'.[41] Applying Jelliffe's stereotypes of male aggression and female passivity, Luhan superimposes social roles on biological function. There was scant room for a woman to pursue professional or sexual fulfilment when any ambitions were interpreted as penis envy. Within the psychoanalytic narrative, passivity is key to successful womanliness, but it has to be an effortless passivity, rather than a wilful passivity. 'When I was first married I tried to keep myself blank to my husband', Luhan writes. 'I didn't strain to him & try to seize him as I had. I just tried to preserve myself [...] by a nullified passiveness.'[42] And then 'one night to my real horror something *took* me – took place in me – in spite of my *not* straining to bring it about & in spite of my willful non-participation'.[43] The result of this performance of pure passivity, she tells Jelliffe triumphantly, is pregnancy.

She goes on to note that 'for fifteen years it never happened again', but then, 'last week [...] the same thing happened'; 'It was not only that the orgasm took place in the vagina because that has occurred more or less since the analysis directed it there.'[44] This aside is astonishing evidence of the disciplinary power of psychoanalysis. From Luhan's first account of her explosive and diffuse orgasm, the sensation is now emphatically 'in the vagina' as 'directed' by Jelliffe. She continues,

> while my own will on that night seemed to me torpid – slow – indifferent some other will in me seemed to act – seemed to open up the walls of the uterus to receive the flow [...] I was even at the moment certain it meant a baby. My body and an unconscious will in me had operated together – while – *I* – my own strong self had lain there – hardly doing more than observe.[45]

By suspending her agency in an almost out of body experience, 'an unconscious will' takes over. 'If ever there was a psychoanalytic baby', Luhan remarks, 'this is one'.⁴⁶ Days later, she sent a follow-up letter to Jelliffe admitting that she was panicking and considering terminating the pregnancy, but also boasting of how she has 'brought about the submission of the female organs' through her tactics of sexual passivity.⁴⁷

At the same time that Luhan was aiming to achieve a psychoanalytic standard of womanliness, she was also investigating different forms of spirituality. This search led her to found an art colony in Taos in 1917, a 'Red Atlantis' of primitivist fascination that seemed to promise a flight from modern gender roles. In the final volume of *Intimate Memories*, called *Edge of Taos Desert: An Escape to Reality* (1937), Luhan recalls how, in New York, she had been 'grabbing things for years, to try and satisfy an unnameable hunger' and 'learned to use the name of sex for that strong autonomous serpent in the blood that once unleashed took full possession of all my other activities, and rode me unmercifully'.⁴⁸ She revisits the narrative of her first orgasm in the Taos context, recalling

> the first surprising involuntary orgasm that Karl caused to break in me on the hardwood floor of my mother's house [. . .] Since that, nothing real had happened to me or in me. I had been merely repeating that experience or repressing it, and I was as immature as I had been at eighteen.⁴⁹

Attributing the action to Karl, Luhan reduces her past erotic life to a juvenile repetition compulsion. By contrast, 'in Taos I was awake to a new experience of sex and love, more mature and more civilized that any I had known before'.⁵⁰ The epitome of these new experiences was her marriage to Tony Luhan, a Pueblo Native American. If Luhan was 'born' into the exhilarating modernity of the Armory show, she was born again, by her own account, by gender stereotype in Taos.

One of the most important influences on Luhan at this time was D. H. Lawrence. In the interwar period, having seen a generation of young men killed in the war while women attained new sociopolitical powers, both Luhan and Lawrence were drawn to pre-industrial cultures to overcome what they saw as a spiritual vacuum and a crisis of sexuality. Lawrence's work took a decidedly conservative turn at the end of World War I, moving from sympathetic representations of new women to the hostile and threatened stance of 'Tickets, Please' (1918), for example, with its nightmarish scenario of women's castrating attempts to appropriate men's power. This tendency developed over the interwar period, in works such as 'The Woman Who Rode Away' (1924), his leadership novels of the 1920s (*Aaron's Rod* [1922], *Kangaroo* [1923], *The Plumed Serpent* [1926]) and *Lady Chatterley's Lover* (1928). Considering Luhan's acceptance of conservative gender stereotypes in the context of her therapy, it is not surprising that she would be open to Lawrence's views, even, as Rudnick puts it, 'revering him as the prophet of female submissiveness'.[51]

While Lawrence fantasised about founding an idealised community that he called Rananim, Mabel coaxed him into joining her in Taos in 1922, along with his wife Frieda. Luhan claimed to intuit a sexual power struggle between Lawrence and Frieda, whom she described as 'the mother of orgasm and the vast, lively mystery of the flesh'.[52] Both Luhan and Lawrence viewed erotic dominance as more appropriately male than female, and Luhan perceived that Lawrence was 'tied' to Frieda and also 'limited' by her, noting rather comically that Lawrence was physically dwarfed by his wife: 'Lawrence hid behind her big body. I scarcely saw him, but we all knew he was there, all right!'[53] Lawrence, in turn, recognised Luhan's intensity, capability and commitment to her vision, but he was a poor mentor, responding to her poems by remarking that 'the essential you, for me, doesn't know and could never write: the Eve who is Voiceless like the serpent, yet communicates'.[54] Later, Lawrence would discourage Luhan from publishing her *Intimate Memories* ('I don't think it's wise, while your mother lives'[55]).

The fraught relationship between Luhan and Lawrence and her ambivalence about female autonomy are embodied by a poem Luhan wrote in Taos, 'The Ballad of a Bad Girl' (1924). The poem begins with a female speaker being pushed from her cradle by her mother. She rebounds by 'snatch[ing] up in the hall Father's silver-headed walking-stick, / And, a-straddle it', she 'hastened after God'. Trading maternal love for a paternal phallus, she flies 'higher, past the Higherarchy'; learning 'things no other woman knows', she soars through the cosmos, 'pushing past all barriers and beyond locked gates'. At last she meets God himself and is 'ready to plunge [her] eager hand within His burning Breast' when she is confronted by a 'very, very angry man, / With blue, blue eyes and a red, red crest' who harangues her: 'Get out of here! [...] Back, back to earth to where you belong. / This is no place for *women* here!'[56] The furious man proceeds to give the bad girl a kick and she tumbles to earth – '*all of a sudden* I forgot my lovely secrets'. It is seemingly a defeat, but in the penultimate stanza the speaker unexpectedly announces: 'On the way [down to earth] I learned a secret [...] That a *woman* can be saved by a fall, fall, fall!' Remorsefully, the girl replaces her father's silver cane and 'lay down in the pansy-bed', whispering 'Mother! Mother me, / And teach me how to mother and that's all, all, all!'[57]

In a jarringly abrupt shift, the brazen girl punished for her defiance and audacity considers herself 'saved' by this *felix culpa*. As in Luhan's accounts of submissive sex and dutifully directed orgasm, the 'bad girl' acquiesces to her postlapsarian maternal role. Is the poem comic? Parodic? Luhan wrote in a letter to Carl Van Vechten that 'The Ballad of a Bad Girl' 'is an indictment against all Feminism' and an 'earnest appeal to women to leave off trying to steal the world away from men [...] Let them leave off stealing the masculine secrets of the will-to-power' – a language that is strongly reminiscent of Lawrence's from the period.[58] Rudnick reads the 'angry man' in the ballad as Lawrence, in keeping with his antagonistic response to Luhan's attempts to write.[59] The bad girl's dizzying shift from joyful adventurer to chastened daughter/prospective mother enacts a narrative of New Woman comeuppance that Lawrence inscribed in his own interwar fiction.

Underscoring the influence, 'The Ballad of a Bad Girl' was printed in the Taos journal *Laughing Horse* accompanied by an illustration by Lawrence. The drawing, captioned 'The Bad Girl in the Pansy Bed by DHL', shows a nude woman falling onto a flowerbed teeming with a giant snake, a snail and a beetle-like insect, along with three pansy-faced men, none of which are indicated in Luhan's poem. Lawrence brought his own set of images and his own interpretation to the ballad. *Pansies* would become the title of his 1929 collection of poems, which he explained as a pun on Pascal's 'pensées': ephemeral thoughts that were as 'fleeting as pansies, which wilt so soon, and are so fascinating with their varied faces, while they last'.[60] Hovering in the background of Lawrence's illustration, above the falling girl, is Lawrence's personal totem of renewal, the phoenix. In Luhan's poem, the girl falls back into traditional maternity. In Lawrence's interpretation, she seems like a New Eve figure, returned to nature, that is reminiscent of a cancelled passage in Lawrence's novel *The Plumed Serpent* imagining how gender roles might be restored: 'the snake coils in peace round the ankle of Eve, and she no longer tries to bruise his head'.[61] It is almost as if Lawrence attempts to achieve in his illustration of Luhan's work something he struggled to effect in life: bringing the New Woman into submission.

Their collaboration on 'Bad Girl' reflects Luhan's and Lawrence's shared fixation on gendered battles of power expressed through sexuality. Both Luhan and Lawrence viewed women's orgasm as a vehicle to correct the gender imbalances of modernity. During the 1920s, Lawrence wrote several narratives in which a white woman falls in thrall to excitingly primitive 'Indian' men who demand sexual passivity and impose orgasmic discipline. In Lawrence's short story 'The Woman Who Rode Away' (1924) and *The Plumed Serpent*, an aloof modern heroine (American in one case, British in the other) goes to Mexico and becomes entranced with swarthy men whose ideology is founded on Aztec cosmology and male dominance.[62] In *The Plumed Serpent*, the New Woman protagonist, Kate Leslie, travels to Mexico City, where she meets the leaders of the Quetzalcoatl movement who call for the return of

Figure 2.1 'The Bad Girl in the Pansy Bed', D. H. Lawrence, reproduced by permission of Harry Ransom Center.

ancient Aztec gods, authoritarian politics, and racial and gender hierarchy. Kate is aroused by the charismatic general Cipriano and his colleague Don Ramón, sensing in them the 'intensity and the crudity of the semi-savage'.[63] The men display a 'barbarian consciousness'[64] and virile, animalistic masculinity that Kate finds irresistible. She pronounces herself 'cursed' with an 'itching, prurient, knowing, imagining eye', 'the curse of Eve' that lusts for knowledge and 'spasmodic desire'.[65] When Cipriano asks Kate to become the 'First Woman of Itzpapalotl', she initially resists, wondering, 'how could she [...] give her body to this death?'[66] Nevertheless, 'she felt herself submitting, succumbing. He was once more the old dominant male [and] she swooned prone beneath, perfect in her proneness.'[67]

> It was the ancient phallic mystery [...] Ah! and what a mystery of prone submission, on her part, this huge erection would imply! [...] Ah! what a marriage! How terrible! and how complete! [...] She could conceive now her marriage with Cipriano; the supreme passivity, like the earth below the twilight, consummate in living lifelessness, the sheer solid mystery of passivity.[68]

Like Luhan's 'bad girl' realising that 'a *woman* can be saved by a fall', Kate comes to the conclusion that 'I ought to *want* to be limited. I ought to be *glad* if a man will limit me with a strong will and a warm touch.'[69]

One of the limitations Cipriano imposes upon her is orgasmic discipline. 'He made her aware of her own desire for frictional, irritant sensation [...] and the spasms of frictional voluptuousness.'[70] Cipriano actively curbs these tendencies:

> When, in their love, it came back on her, the seething electric female ecstasy, which knows such spasms of delirium, he recoiled from her [...] And succeeding the first moment of disappointment, when this sort of 'satisfaction' was denied her, came the knowledge that she did not really want it, that it was really nauseous to her.[71]

Critics have generally understood this passage as Cipriano demanding that Kate renounce her clitoral 'spasms of frictional voluptuousness' for more 'potent' vaginal orgasms. Kate will gain the 'mystery of passivity' in a marriage to 'the old dominant male' only by relinquishing her 'seething electric female ecstasy', her Eve-like modern desire for transgressive knowledge, and her exploration of clitoral pleasure.

After several novels in which he searched for spiritual rejuvenation abroad, Lawrence turned back to England in *Lady Chatterley's Lover* where, even more explicitly than in *The Plumed Serpent*, he challenges his female seeker to adopt the correct kind of orgasm as a means of transcending the malaise of modernity. Constance Chatterley's first sexual experience is an 'anti-climax', and subsequent ones are just as dispiriting.[72] Pondering how 'she could use this sex thing to have power over' a man, she discovers that

> she only had to hold herself back in sexual intercourse, and let him finish and expend himself without herself coming to the crisis; and then she could prolong the connexion and achieve her orgasm and her crisis while he was merely her tool.[73]

By describing everything through the lens of power, Lawrence ascribes a mercenary attitude to what is essentially an accommodation of mutual orgasm. When Constance repeats the technique later in her affair with a writer, Michaelis, he bristles:

> You couldn't go off at the same time as a man, could you? You'd have to bring yourself off! You'd have to run the show! [...] You keep on for hours

after I've gone off [...] and I have to hang on with my teeth till you bring yourself off by your own exertions.[74]

The gamekeeper Mellors, who sexually liberates Constance, has even more damning things to say about women's sexuality. He tells the tale of his diabolical ex-wife Bertha Coutts and her castrating orgasmic etiquette: 'She'd try to lie still and let *me* work the business. She'd try. But it was no good. She got no feeling off it, from my working. She had to work the thing herself, grind her own coffee.'[75] The men in Lady Chatterley are openly hostile about the women's attempts to achieve orgasm, as if pleasure is a zero sum game.

The sex scenes in Lady Chatterley's Lover present Constance with a sequence of orgasmic instruction. At first when she and Mellors have sex, it is unremarkable. He enters her and 'she lay still, in a kind of sleep, always in a kind of sleep. The activity, the orgasm was his, all his.'[76] Afterward, 'her tormented modern woman's brain still had no rest. Was it real? – And she knew, if she gave herself to the man, it was real. But if she kept herself for herself, it was nothing.'[77] She is able to achieve proper passivity the next time they have sex – 'Her will had left her [...] She was giving way. She was giving up'[78] – and Lawrence's most extended description of female orgasm follows. 'There awoke in her new strange thrills rippling inside her, rippling, rippling, like a flapping overlapping of soft flames.' The sensation induces her 'womb' to 'open' and to 'clamou[r] like a sea-anemone under the tides', and her 'tormented modern woman's brain' is finally swayed by 'the unspeakable motion that was not really motion, but pure deepening whirlpools of sensation, swirling deeper and deeper through all her tissue and consciousness'.[79]

Although Lawrence's approach to sexuality is innovative in many respects, his representation of pleasure in Lady Chatterley's Lover is also oppressively pedagogical. So, for example, female orgasm in the previous scene is enigmatic and non-local, but the ideological direction in which Lawrence takes that description demonstrates how a modern/ist metaphoric poetics of intimate sensation renders female orgasm susceptible to different forms of discipline than men's. Constance's sensation of orgasm shifts to dogmatic instruction in the couple's postcoital pillow talk as Mellors tells Constance, 'We came-off together that time [...] It's good when it's like that. Most folks live their lives through and they never know it.'[80] Her sexual experience moves increasingly toward limitation. The next time the couple is together, Mellors approaches her from the rear, introducing 'wonder that was also awe, terror', which brings about her metaphorical dissolution and rebirth through sexual passivity: 'She was gone, she was not, and she was born: a woman.'[81] In the following scene of anal penetration, Lawrence only very briefly mentions Constance's orgasm as 'piercing thrills of sensuality'[82] occurring at the beginning of the scene, shifting the centre of gravity to Mellors's orgasm. After that, a pregnant Constance and Mellors are together one more time in a London hotel and the sex is unremarkable. Lawrence thus plots the progress of his female protagonist in *Lady Chatterley's Lover* in terms of a disciplinary programme that ultimately restricts her agency and pleasure. This path runs parallel to Luhan's trajectory, and her 'bad' girl's fall into motherhood.

For modern fiction and nonfiction writers alike, female orgasm was never only about women's pleasure; it was also an intimate gauge of women's agency and power. At the same time that Luhan and Lawrence depicted sexuality for transgressive or radical purposes – to philosophically and aesthetically expand the limits of representation, and to explore women's interior subjectivity – they deployed that representation toward reactionary, conservative ends: Luhan's 'escape to reality' and Lawrence's phallic 'bridge to the future'.[83] Their writing, together with that of Freud and birth control advocates who urged specific sexual practices for women, presents an unsettling history of somatic manipulation and control.

Certainly, there were efforts in the first half of the twentieth century to imagine expanded erotic experience for women. For example, Anaïs Nin wrote in her 1943 diary,

> Let me celebrate my *freedom*. I am as free as man has been – I am free to enjoy – today I experienced for the first time an orgasm within adventure. For the first time I did not feel the orgasm linked to emotional fidelity, as an emotional surrender, as necessarily and fatally bound to love.[84]

For Nin 'orgasm within adventure' is a traditionally male prerogative, and distinct from the intimacy, monogamy and relationality that she associates with female sexuality. While seeming to strive for a new kind of female sexual autonomy (anticipating Erica Jong's 'zipless fuck' in *Fear of Flying* [1973]), Nin's vision conforms to the one-sex model in which sexual freedom is male, rather than imagining something new. By contrast, Woolf's orgasmic passage in *Mrs Dalloway*, and her emphasis on exploration and illumination in *A Room of One's Own*, as well as Luhan's original account of her first orgasm, promise an alternative mode of female sexual experience: a mode based on open-endedness and multiplicity as a counterpoint to discipline and restrictive heteronormativity.

After Kinsey and Masters and Johnson debunked Freud's myths of female sexuality, second-wave feminists made the late 1960s and 1970s the golden age of female orgasm. A proliferation of writings by feminist sex researchers and educators, including Shere Hite's *Hite Report on Female Sexuality* (1976),

Kate Millett's *Sexual Politics* (1970), Betty Dodson's *Liberating Masturbation* (1974), Anne Koedt's 'The Myth of the Vaginal Orgasm' (1968) and Susan Lydon's 'The Politics of Orgasm' (1970), argued for women's sexual pleasure as a political and civil right.[85] With an increasing awareness of how women's sexuality had been repressively yoked to their sociopolitical destiny, they identified how techniques of orgasmic discipline like Freud's were a symptom of patriarchy that tried to 'cure' a problem which was essentially cultural. They countered this with education about women's sexuality together with a critique of patriarchy.

And yet, forty years after second-wave feminism, the 'problem' of women's orgasm apparently persists. Indiana University's 2009 National Survey of Sexual Health and Behavior found that 91 per cent of men reported that they had an orgasm during their last sexual encounter, but only 64 per cent of women could say the same. There is a new name for this old problem: the 'orgasm gap'. Discourses on female orgasm have changed with the times, and with the logic of late capitalism and neoliberal self-care. The orgasm gap – perpetuating the premise that female pleasure is a nebulous but crucial aspiration requiring improvement – has become big business as media tells women to upgrade their orgasm. Big Pharma, lifestyle companies and 'sextech' have eagerly capitalised on the idea that women are in need of expensive products of dubious value to attain so-called 'orgasm equality'.[86] Orgasmic discipline has been monetised.

In framing female orgasm as a malleable intimate experience linked to sociopolitical being, modernism set the stage for second-wave feminism to connect the dots between patriarchy and women's sexuality, and to argue for systemic change. But the perception of female orgasm as elusive and enigmatic endures. Modernism's key formulation about female orgasm – that it reflects ambivalence about women's changing cultural status – remains trenchant. Women's autonomy, power and pleasure – among modernity's most galvanising legacies – are a still-unfolding story of twenty-first-century culture. If female orgasm remains a marker of the unfinished feminist revolution, it also gives us hope for more pleasure to come.

Notes

1. Virginia Woolf, *The Letters of Virginia Woolf*, vol. 2, ed. Nigel Nicolson and Joanne Trautmann (New York: Harcourt Brace Jovanovich, 1976), p. 6.
2. Vanessa Bell, *Selected Letters of Vanessa Bell*, ed. Regina Marler (New York: Pantheon, 1993), p. 132.

3. Marie Stopes, *Married Love: A New Contribution to the Solution of Sex Difficulties*, 9th edn (London: Putnam, 1921), p. 135.
4. Ibid. p. 93.
5. Marie Stopes, *Marriage in My Time* (London: Rich & Cowan, 1935), p. 44.
6. José Pierre (ed.) and Malcolm Imrie (trans.), *Investigating Sex: Surrealist Research 1928–1932* (New York: Verso, 2011), p. 3.
7. Ibid. p. 4.
8. Jacques Lacan, *Feminine Sexuality*, ed. Juliet Mitchell, trans. Jacqueline Rose (New York: W. W. Norton, 1985), pp. 146–7.
9. Annamarie Jagose, *Orgasmology* (Durham, NC and London: Duke University Press, 2013), p. 83.
10. See Thomas W. Laqueur, *Solitary Sex: A Cultural History of Masturbation* (Cambridge: Zone Books, 2003).
11. Linda Williams, *Hard Core: Power, Pleasure, and the 'Frenzy of the Visible'* (Berkeley: University of California Press, 1989).
12. James Joyce, *Ulysses*, ed. Hans Walter Gabler (New York: Random House, 1986), p. 300.
13. Anaïs Nin, *The Diary of Anaïs Nin*, vol. 2, ed. Gunther Stuhlmann (New York: Harvest, 1967), pp. 263–4.
14. Virginia Woolf, *Mrs Dalloway*, ed. Mark Hussey (New York: Harvest, 2005), p. 31.
15. Lucy Bland, 'Trial By Sexology? Maud Allan, Salome, and the Cult of the Clitoris Case', in Bland and Laura Doan (eds), *Sexology in Culture: Labelling Bodies and Desires* (Chicago: University of Chicago Press, 1998), pp. 183–97.
16. See Jennifer Finney Boylan, 'What a Greek Prophet Can Tell Us About Sex', *New York Times*, 16 May 2018, available at <https://www.nytimes.com/2018/05/16/opinion/greek-prophet-sex-tiresias.html> (accessed 15 September 2019).
17. Christopher Lasch, *The New Radicalism in America, 1889–1963: The Intellectual as a Social Type* (New York: Knopf, 1965).
18. See William H. Masters and Virginia Johnson, *Human Sexual Response* (New York: Bantam Books, 1966); and Shere Hite, *The Hite Report: A National Study of Female Sexuality* (New York: Macmillan, 1976).
19. See Thomas Walter Laqueur, *Making Sex: Body and Gender from the Greeks to Freud* (Cambridge, MA: Harvard University Press, 1990); Emily Nagoski, *Come as You Are: The Surprising New Science That Will Transform Your Sex Life* (New York: Simon & Schuster, 2015); Rebecca Chalker, *The Clitoral Truth* (New York: Seven Stories Press, 2002); and Laurie Mintz, *Becoming Cliterate: Why Orgasm Equality Matters and How to Get It* (New York: Harper, 2017).
20. Laqueur, *Making Sex*, p. 175.

21. Ibid. p. viii.
22. Rachel Maines, *The Technology of Orgasm: 'Hysteria', the Vibrator, and Women's Sexual Satisfaction* (Baltimore: Johns Hopkins University Press, 2001), p. 3.
23. Sigmund Freud, *The Question of Lay Analysis: The Standard Edition*, ed. James Strachey (New York: W. W. Norton, 1990), p. 38.
24. Sigmund Freud, *Three Essays on the Theory of Sexuality*, ed. James Strachey (New York: Basic Books, 2000).
25. Anna Clark, *Desire: A History of European Sexuality* (London: Routledge, 2008), p. 175. See also Alison Moore, 'Relocating Marie Bonaparte's Clitoris', *Australian Feminist Studies*, 24.60 (2009), pp. 149–65.
26. Marie Stopes, *Married Love or Love in Marriage* (New York: Critic and Guide, 1918), available at <http://digital.library.upenn.edu/women/stopes/married/1918.html> (accessed 5 September 2019).
27. Ibid.
28. Ibid.
29. Cited in Lois Palken Rudnick, *Mabel Dodge Luhan: New Woman, New Worlds* (Albuquerque: University of New Mexico Press, 1984), p. 68.
30. Mabel Dodge Luhan, *Intimate Memories: Volume Three. Movers and Shakers* (New York: Harcourt, 1936), pp. 263, 69.
31. Ibid. p. 71.
32. Anthony Giddens, *The Transformation of Intimacy: Sexuality, Love, and Eroticism in Modern Societies* (Stanford: Stanford University Press, 1992).
33. Mabel Dodge Luhan, *Intimate Memories: Volume Two. European Experiences* (New York: Harcourt, 1935), p. 36.
34. Ibid. p. 36.
35. Ibid. p. 36.
36. Ibid. p. 38.
37. Patricia R. Everett, *Corresponding Lives: Mabel Dodge Luhan, A. A. Brill, and the Psychoanalytic Adventure in America* (New York: Routledge, 2018), p. 15.
38. Virginia Woolf, *A Room of One's Own* (London: Penguin, 2004), p. 98.
39. Lois Palken Rudnick (ed.), *The Suppressed Memoirs of Mabel Dodge Luhan: Sex, Syphilis, and Psychoanalysis in the Making of Modern American Culture* (Albuquerque: University of New Mexico Press, 2012), p. 29.
40. Ibid. p. 35.
41. Ibid. p. 35.
42. Ibid. p. 35.
43. Ibid. p. 35.
44. Ibid. p. 35.
45. Ibid. p. 35.
46. Ibid. p. 37.

47. Ibid. p. 37.
48. Mabel Dodge Luhan, *Intimate Memories: Volume Four. Edge of Taos Desert: An Escape to Reality* (New York: Harcourt, 1937), p. 215.
49. Ibid. p. 216.
50. Ibid. p. 273.
51. Rudnick, *New Woman, New Worlds*, p. 213.
52. Mabel Dodge Luhan, *Lorenzo in Taos: D. H. Lawrence and Mabel Dodge Luhan* (Santa Fe, NM: Sunstone Press, 2007), p. 45.
53. Ibid. p. 45.
54. Ibid. p. 136.
55. Ibid. p. 309.
56. Mabel Dodge Luhan, 'The Ballad of a Bad Girl', *Laughing Horse* (May 1924). Reprinted in Luhan, *Lorenzo in Taos*, pp. 95–7.
57. Ibid. p. 97.
58. Edward Burns, *The Letters of Gertrude Stein and Carl Van Vechten, 1913–1946* (New York: Columbia University Press, 2013), p. 100.
59. Rudnick, *New Woman, New Worlds*, p. 214.
60. D. H. Lawrence, *The Complete Poems of D. H. Lawrence*, ed. Vivian de Sola Pinto and F. Warren Roberts (New York: Penguin, 1977), p. 423.
61. Keith Sagar, *D. H. Lawrence: Poet* (Humanities-Ebooks, 2007), p. 95.
62. For fuller readings of the erotic politics of 'The Woman Who Rode Away' and *The Plumed Serpent*, see Laura Frost, 'Orgasmic Discipline: D. H. Lawrence, E. M. Hull, and Interwar Erotic Fiction', in *The Problem with Pleasure: Modernism and Its Discontents* (New York: Columbia University Press, 2013), pp. 89–129; and Frost, 'The Libidinal Politics of D. H. Lawrence's "Leadership Novels"', in *Sex Drives: Fantasies of Fascism in Literary Modernism* (Ithaca: Cornell University Press, 2002), pp. 38–58.
63. D. H. Lawrence, *The Plumed Serpent*, ed. L. D. Clark (New York: Cambridge University Press, 1987), p. 67.
64. Ibid. p. 82.
65. Ibid. p. 184.
66. Ibid. p. 248.
67. Ibid. p. 311.
68. Ibid. p. 311.
69. Ibid. p. 439.
70. Ibid. p. 421.
71. Ibid. p. 421.
72. D. H. Lawrence, *Lady Chatterley's Lover*, ed. Michael Squires (London: Penguin, 2006), p. 7.
73. Ibid. p. 7.

74. Ibid. p. 54.
75. Ibid. p. 202.
76. Ibid. p. 116.
77. Ibid. p. 117.
78. Ibid. p. 133.
79. Ibid. pp. 133–4.
80. Ibid. p. 134.
81. Ibid. pp. 174–5.
82. Ibid. p. 246.
83. D. H. Lawrence, 'A Propos of *Lady Chatterley's Lover*', in *Lady Chatterley's Lover*, p. 327.
84. Anaïs Nin, *Mirages: The Unexpurgated Diary of Anaïs Nin, 1939–1947*, ed. Paul Herron (Athens, OH: Ohio University Press, 2013), 28 June 1943.
85. See Kate Millett, *Sexual Politics* (Garden City, NY: Doubleday, 1970); Betty Dodson, *Liberating Masturbation* (New York: Bodysex Designs, 1974); Anne Koedt, 'The Myth of the Vaginal Orgasm' (first published in pamphlet form by New England Free Press in 1968); and Susan Lydon, 'The Politics of Orgasm', in Robin Morgan (ed.), *Sisterhood is Powerful: An Anthology of Writings from the Women's Liberation Movement* (New York: Vintage Books, 1970), pp. 197–205.
86. See Laura Frost, 'The Cult of the Clitoris', *Los Angeles Review of Books*, 16 June 2017; and Frost, 'Cracking the Clit', *Logic*, 2 (2017), available at <https://logicmag.io/02-cracking-the-clit/> (accessed 4 December 2018).

3

Burning Feminism: Virginia Woolf's Laboratory of Intimacy

Jane Goldman

FEMINIST WOOLF: A POEM

1. (1916-1935)
    I become steadily more feminist
        & Lady R is a feminist, & Molly is not.
    But the Lady R.s ought to be feminist
        & its the feminists who will drain off this black blood
            of bitterness which is poisoning us all
        If I were still a feminist
  also I shall be attacked for a feminist & hinted at for a sapphist
        if I were a feminist
        —no thats too patently feminist
            "even feminists cd. wish to segregate & label the sexes"
        —history, politics, feminism, art, literature

2. (1919-1938)
  "Cassandra is what they call a Feminist," Katharine went on.
      "Or rather, she was a Feminist six months ago"
    Miss Julia Hedge, the feminist, waited for her books. They did not come.
      "The arrant feminist! She says that men are snobs!"
  why was Miss West an arrant feminist for making a possibly true if
            uncomplimentary statement about the other sex?
  carefully eschewing "the arrant feminism" of Miss Rebecca West
      "The editor forbids feminism," I interposed severely.
        "What is feminism?" they screamed with one accord
      The word "feminist" is the word indicated.
      The word "feminist" is destroyed; the air is cleared;
        "feminists" were in fact the advance guard
      "Feminism", we have had to destroy.

Burning Feminism

I made this poem by systematically gleaning from a digital word search of Virginia Woolf's writings every instance of her usage of the words 'feminism' and 'feminist'.[1] The first stanza records in chronological order her more personal and private deployment of the terms in her letters and diaries from the first in 1916 to the last in 1935.[2] The second stanza likewise records her every usage in print from the first in 1919 to the last in 1938.[3] The poem allows us to see at a glance the arc of usage. It is astonishingly infrequent in the writings of an author so intimately associated with feminism in popular culture and academic criticism.

We can see that 'feminist' occurs in only two novels: in *Night and Day* (1919) where Katherine comments on the taciturnity of Cassandra's feminism, a taciturnity that extends to Woolf herself whose feminism too runs hot and cold; and in *Jacob's Room* (1922) where the feminist Julia Hedge is noticed in the British Library vainly awaiting her books. On 23 January 1916, Woolf connects her self-avowed feminism to her pacifism when she writes to Margaret Llewelyn Davies (1861–1944), her friend and General Secretary of the Women's Cooperative Guild:

> I become steadily more feminist owing to the Times, which I read at breakfast and wonder how this preposterous masculine fiction [the war] keeps going a day longer – without some vigorous young woman pulling us together and marching through it – Do you see any sense in it? I feel as if I were reading about some curious tribe in Central Africa – And now they'll give us votes.[4]

On Friday, 17 February 1922, she writes in her diary of a conversation with Molly McCarthy about Lady Rhondda,[5] a prominent suffragette (notorious for her attempted bombing of a Royal Mail post-box in 1913):

> Lady R. is a feminist, & Molly is not. But the Lady R.s ought to be feminists, I said; & you must encourage them, for if the rich women will do it, we neednt; & it is the rich women who will drain off this black blood of bitterness which is poisoning us all.[6]

And by 1924 Woolf is writing, 'If I were still a feminist.'[7] Just before publishing her manifesto, *A Room of One's Own*, she was worrying it would cause her to 'be attacked for a feminist & hinted at for a sapphist',[8] just as the text itself reports on how patriarchy denounces Rebecca West as 'an arrant feminist'.[9] In April 1931, still wavering she writes, 'if I were a feminist'.[10] In February 1932 she worries over a new project: 'whats it to be called? – "Men are like that?"

– no thats too patently feminist'.[11] By 1933 her plan includes 'history, politics, feminism, art, literature'.[12]

In the essay 'Why' (1934) for *Lysistrata*, the short-lived magazine for women students at Oxford, the speaker finds 'wealth' to be 'the great obstacle to asking questions openly in public'.[13] This is at odds with Woolf's earlier private remarks on leaving organised feminism to the rich. Yet when the questions that probe the speaker find *Lysistrata*'s 'women's colleges poor and young' and therefore conducive to asking such questions, including of the colleges themselves – 'Are they not inventive, adventurous? Are they not out to create a new –?' – she cuts them off with 'The editor forbids feminism', only to be bombarded with the unanswerable 'What is feminism?'[14] Is it possible that she has censored or redacted the creating of a new feminism, if that is indeed the new creation? Is it so radically new it requires a new word? Or has 'feminism' now become too dangerous a word to be uttered in public even here?

In January 1935, Woolf's 'sparring' correspondence with Princess Elizabeth Bibesco shows her probing how anti-fascism sits with feminism. Bibesco writes:

> 'it had not occurred to me that in matters of ultimate importance even feminists cd. wish to segregate & label the sexes. It wd. seem to be a pity that sex alone should be able to bring them together' – to which I replied, What about Hitler? This is because, when she asked me to join the Cttee of the anti-Fascist [Exhibition], I asked why the woman question was ignored.[15]

Woolf pasted Bibesco's letter, which also concedes 'there will of course be a section dealing with the Nazi regime', into her notebook of materials which fed into *Three Guineas* (1938).[16]

Woolf used the word 'feminism' in print, as far as I can establish, for the very last time in *Three Guineas*, three years after her last recorded private diary usage. *Three Guineas* examines the intimate relations between feminism, pacifism, anti-Nazism and anti-fascism. Here Woolf famously urges us to burn the 'dead' and 'corrupt' word 'feminist' – perhaps in satirical parody of earlier suffragette militant incendiary acts on buildings and works of art, perhaps in satirical parody of more recent patriarchal Nazi book-burning:

> Let us write that word in large black letters on a sheet of foolscap; then solemnly apply a match to the paper. Look, how it burns! What a light dances over the world! [...] The smoke has died down; the word is destroyed. [...] The word 'feminist' is destroyed; the air is cleared; and in that clearer air what do we see? Men and women working together for the same cause.[17]

Citing Josephine Butler, she claims that the progressive socialism and antifascism of her time form a common cause, rooted in nineteenth-century feminism: 'The daughters of educated men who were called, to their resentment, "feminists" were in fact the advance guard of your own movement.'[18] Woolf's final recorded usage, '"Feminism", we have had to destroy', is followed by her dismissing the 'tags and labels' applied to feminists of premature 'anti-Fascism' or intellectual and cultural libertarianism, to emphasise the diverse *emotional* forces inspiring

> the daughters' opposition to the infantile fixation of the fathers, because, as biography shows, that force had behind it many different emotions, and many that were contradictory. Tears were behind it, of course – tears, bitter tears: the tears of those whose desire for knowledge was frustrated. One daughter longed to learn chemistry; the books at home only taught her alchemy. She 'cried bitterly at not being taught things'. Also the desire for an open and rational love was behind it. Again there were tears – angry tears.[19]

Perhaps the point of such a declaration of the word's destruction, followed by this acknowledgement of the historical, lived, embodied 'angry tears' shed by feminists is to point up how this visceral, emotional force has ebbed out of the term in current usage. This tear-drenched disavowal may be an attempt to make strange a term that is of course impossible to destroy, but one that is in danger of becoming meaningless if we do not pay it close attention as a word with its own histories and usages, not least its lived emotional hinterland. Feminism is not like death and taxes. It has not always been with us. And the printed evidence suggests that 'feminism' and 'feminist', not terms that frequently flow from Woolf's pen in any case as my poem demonstrates, do in fact disappear from her own discourse after 1938. Outside of Woolf's late writings, of course, both terms do indeed seem to have thrived, having arisen phoenix style from her metaphorical torching, and are certainly not in danger of extinction. The pointed reference to chemistry and alchemy suggests this torching is an experiment somewhere between Enlightenment science and arcane ritual magic.

Yet by aping earlier incendiary suffragette protests as well as Nazi book-burning in order to destroy the word 'feminism' in the cause of 'all men and women', is Woolf getting at some problematic elements in 'feminism' whereby it may be equated with or has become tainted by nationalism or even national socialism? The precedent is there in the spectrum of political positions embraced by the suffragettes, who were by no means all left-wing, including in their ranks, for example, the Conservative and Unionist Women's Franchise Association.[20] The suffragettes frequently engaged in imperialist, colonial and nationalist discourses and symbolism, not least in their 'Pageant of Empire' for the Women's Coronation Procession, 17 June 1911.[21] At the outbreak of the Great War, Emmeline and Christabel Pankhurst, contra the pacifist feminism of Sylvia Pankhurst,

> seized the opportunity to become in effect political leaders for the government they had opposed, committing the WSPU to mobilise the women of Britain in national service, supporting internment, making recruitment speeches, calling for conscription, organising what Annie Kenney called an 'anti-Bolshevist' campaign in the trade unions and handing white feathers to men not in uniform.[22]

The notorious suffragette arsonist and hunger-striker, Mary Richardson, who had made headlines in 1914 when she took an axe to Velázquez's painting, *The Rokeby Venus*, in the National Gallery, London,[23] joined Oswald Mosley's British Union of Fascists in 1932, becoming in 1934 its Chief Organiser for the Women's Section. She opened the National Club for Fascist Women in April 1934.[24] She was not the only suffragette to turn fascist.[25] Nor were the German Nazis without some 'feminist' support in the same era.[26]

What interests me here is the way *Three Guineas* is invoking the scene of pedagogy, the chemist's laboratory, in *A Room of One's Own* (1929), a text that similarly points up the rise of fascism in the 1920s and where both 'love' and 'chemistry' light up their flames in intimate proximity. Does the demonstrative burning of the word 'feminism' in *Three Guineas* fall within the domestic 'alchemy' reviled by daughters of educated men, or does it belong in the science laboratories to which women were still fighting to gain access? To answer these difficult questions we need to enter Woolf's own laboratory of intimacy, itself located in a fictitious novel illuminated in *A Room of One's Own*, where famously 'Chloe liked Olivia', and where also lurks a pioneering woman scientist and intimate of laboratories who did much to advance the cause of women and yet who was also a eugenicist and an admirer of fascism and Nazism – Marie Charlotte Carmichael Stopes (1880–1958).

Woolf's Laboratory of Intimacy

> 'What are they, I wonder, the very intimate things, one says in print?'
> – Virginia Woolf, Letter to Vita Sackville-West
> (15 September 1926)[27]

'Intimacy' means the 'quality or condition of being intimate' and is '*euphemistic* for sexual intercourse' but also means 'closeness of observation, knowledge, or the like'.[28] And I would like to press the notion of textual intimacy between writing and reading available in the sense of 'closeness of observation', while taking as axiomatic Jessica Berman's observation on Woolf's inscriptions of the private sphere where 'Gender, sexuality, and intimate relations all come to contain not just ethical but specifically political valences, made salient by the disruption of war and the rise of fascism.'[29]

By Woolf's laboratory of intimacy I refer to the multiplicitously intimate, 'inter-textual hot spot',[30] a site of all such intimacies, in chapter 5 of *A Room of One's Own*, the laboratory shared by Chloe and Olivia. Here we are introduced by one narrator, the fictitious Mary Beton (a descendant or variant character from a Scottish ballad, 'The Four Maries'/'Mary Hamilton'), to the fictitious novel, *Life's Adventure*, written by the fictitious Mary Carmichael (another descendant or variant character from the same Scottish ballad):

> 'Chloe liked Olivia. They shared a laboratory together. . . .' I read on and discovered that these two young women were engaged in mincing liver, which is, it seems, a cure for pernicious anaemia; although one of them was married and had – I think I am right in stating – two small children. Now all that, of course, has had to be left out, and thus the splendid portrait of the fictitious woman is much too simple and much too monotonous.[31]

If the narrator's parenthetical injunction in chapter 1 to '(call me Mary Beton, Mary Seton, Mary Carmichael or by any name you please – it is not a matter of any importance)'[32] encourages us to think of the Scottish ballad about infanticide at the court of Mary, Queen of Scots as a source for Mary Carmichael's name, then chapter 5 prompts recognition of its variant spelling of Marie Carmichael, the publicly acknowledged *nom de plume* of the controversial pioneer of birth control, Marie Stopes, adopted for her 1928 novel *Love's Creation*.[33] The marital and maternal status of Chloe or Olivia further fuels the powerful subtext of *A Room of One's Own* concerning marriage and motherhood as obstacles to women's creativity, education and entry into the professions. The doubling intertext in Mary Carmichael that points to the ballad and to Stopes prompts us to consider if progress has been made now that efficient birth control and family planning are available, albeit within the bounds of marriage. It also prompts alertness to other possible allusions to Stopes in Woolf's manifesto. Mary Beton ponders after the laboratory scene how

> literature is impoverished beyond our counting by the doors that have been shut upon women. Married against their will, kept in one room, and to one occupation, how could a dramatist give a full or interesting or truthful account of them?[34]

And the narrator of chapter 6 repeatedly refers to women's historical lack of 'intellectual freedom' which has meant women 'have not had a dog's chance of writing poetry'.[35] Both passages might well be in dialogue with Stopes's *Married Love* (1918), where 'modern marriage' is seen to give 'more and more freedom to each of the partners', yet 'far too often, marriage puts an end to woman's intellectual life. Marriage can never reach its full stature until women possess as much intellectual freedom and freedom of opportunity within it as do their partners.'[36]

By the close of chapter 5, *Life's Adventure* along with Mary Carmichael's formal technique, her circumstances and education, her literary antecedents and possible descendants have all been intimately examined: 'She will be a poet, I said, putting *Life's Adventure*, by Mary Carmichael, at the end of the shelf, in another hundred years' time.'[37] Stopes, famous for her best-selling work on birth control, was also a published poet, so this becomes a somewhat cruel aside on her already published volume of (rhyming) poetry, *Man, Other Poems and a Preface* (1914),[38] if she is read off as the literal to Beton's (or Woolf's) fictitious novelist. The narrator does not favour 'the less interesting branch of the species' as she calls Mary Carmichael '– the naturalist-novelist, and not the contemplative',[39] perhaps a barbed reference to Stopes's fictional style in *Love's Creation*, which itself opens in a university laboratory, a familiar setting to Stopes who was a botanist and palaeontologist, and in 1904 the first woman scientist employed by the University of Manchester.

But regardless, for the moment, of possible intertexts, what interests me here in this famous 'Chloe liked Olivia' passage is how Woolf manages to inscribe in the same continuum of words the double feminist shock that is the simultaneous acknowledgement of private and public experiences of women in modernity: *both* a newly achieved professional intimacy in the collaboration of women in the previously exclusively patriarchal environs of a university scientific laboratory *and* a newly acknowledged possibility of sexual intimacy between women. If the sauciness of the eliding ellipsis in the text cited from *Life's Adventure*, whether Mary Carmichael's or Mary Beton's (and we would need to think through the provenance of both the ellipsis and the sauciness), is in a sense *undone* by the information supplied in the next sentence where it is reported (not directly cited) from the novel 'that these two young women were engaged in mincing liver' (fear not for they are scientists cutting up into very small pieces a large glandular organ of the digestive system in a medical laboratory and gaining intimate scientific knowledge of that object), it is also simultaneously *compounded* by those very same words. The clause begins with an utterance that might belong in a conventional romantic novel ('these two young women were engaged', presumably not to each other, although that socially startling idea for 1929 is present), but 'engaged in' suggests something more active than passive betrothal; it suggests something conspiratorial and shocking, possibly worthy of a police report. And this is before we have reached the innuendo-laden constructions, 'it seems' and 'although'.

And as for the slang-worthy 'mincing liver', aside from this imagery's numerous lewd connotations of applying friction to meat, it is worth noting that the liver is historically the 'bodily organ regarded as the seat of love or other passionate emotion, as anger, bitterness, etc.'[40] Here we see the 'angry tears' of *Three Guineas* cited above already stoking in *A Room of One's Own*. The liver is also associated with the ancient arts of divination and prophecy (and the laboratory shared by Chloe and Olivia is loaded with futurity). It is also worth noting that 'mincing' is also the 'action of extenuating, minimizing, palliating, or glossing over a matter; the suppression of part of a fact or statement. In later use chiefly: the moderation of one's language.'[41] So Chloe and Olivia may be understood to be engaged in suppressing their passions, just like the preceding ellipsis may do, and these women are possibly therefore not even in a scientific laboratory at all. The teasing, slippery, evasive rhetoric of *A Room of One's Own* manages to hide in plain sight the most lubricious of utterances. 'Mincing', therefore, in this sense is precisely what Woolf's prose itself is doing, given that Woolf must watch her words if her work is to avoid the fate of Radclyffe Hall's *The Well of Loneliness* (the lesbian love novel banned for obscenity in 1928), the spectre of whose chief prosecutor, Conservative Home Secretary Sir William Joynson-Hicks, is raised a few pages later.[42]

And because her prose is mincing in that suppressive sense, it is 'mincing', even further, in its arch sense of the 'habit of speaking or acting in an affectedly refined or elegant [or effete] manner'.[43] And because Woolf's prose is so affectedly mincing in all these senses, it becomes apparent that merely hearing it read out as a lecture viva voce, which may give thrilling licence to dangerous innuendo, cannot do justice to its considerable complexities and subtleties. We must study it closely *in print*: we must become so intimate with this writing about the limits of writing intimacy *in print* that we understand its silences and elisions, what it does not state, but what it nevertheless somehow clearly intimates – the writing in print on intimacies yet to come, 'if we worked for' them (to borrow from the messianic-feminist closing line of *A Room of One's Own*).[44] For *A Room of One's Own* is ripe with a multiplicity of feminist future anteriors, for which we must collectively labour if we are to bring them to term. In this manifesto, Woolf 'expects attentive reading',[45] Gayatri Chakravorty Spivak observes, demonstrating in her own attentive reading how this text constructs the notion, delicate and destabilising, of 'the future anterior, where one promises no future present but attends upon what will have happened as a result of one's work'.[46] This is Derrida's messianic concept of 'teleopoiesis': 'We are not yet among the philosophers of the future, we who are calling them and calling them the philosophers of the future, but we are in advance their friends.'[47] This form of literary criticism, Claire Colebrook explains, creates 'a discipline that reverberates, plumbs desires, sends out relays, and conductively makes something happen in the world'.[48] In the doubly fictive Chloe and Olivia's laboratory, then, there is access, as Spivak points up, to 'the unimaginable future "to come"', in 'an unpredictable filiation [...] between Woolf' and contemporary 'subaltern cultural formations' that 'intuit an originary queerness, within which the heterosexual bond is loosely contained as a social focus of loyalty and parenting'.[49] Thus Woolf's 'intuitions of a general queerness within which reproductive sexuality can find its limited socialization (Chloe likes Olivia but goes home to her children) is an open-ended structure that can be reconstellated, levered off from its textual location, copied from Bloomsbury and pasted'[50] onto new narratives. This moment in the laboratory, then,

> serves as a model for reconstellating, copying and pasting for editing, teleopoiesis. It seems to inhabit the same structure – heteronormativity contained within the 'queer' – that I intuit in the precapitalist formation for which I have been working. For Woolf the structure heralds a new gendered collectivity – a gendered notion of friendship.[51]

Whereas we are always indeed free to practise teleopoiesis, to 'cut and paste from even the most restrictive text'[52] (and *Love's Creation* may be such a text, I would add), what Woolf's mincing laboratory of intimacy does is to manufacture teleopoiesis itself, to demand teleopoiesis of its readers, to make them teleopoietic writers in turn. Two recent, brilliant such responses, in my view, which both superbly reconstellate key tropes from *A Room of One's Own*, not least the 'fine negress', are Kabe Wilson's multimedia work, '*Of One Woman or So* by Olivia N'Gowfri' (2014), and Shola von Reinhold's novel, *Lote* (2020).[53]

'The whole book is full of nooks and corners which I enjoy exploring', Woolf writes, in September 1926, to her lover, Vita Sackville-West, on reading the proofs of her novel, *Passenger to Teheran* (1926): 'Sometimes one wants a candle in one's hand though – That's my only criticism – you've left (I daresay in haste) one or two dangling dim places. It's a delicious method.'[54] And while we can see the candle in Vita's dim places here to prefigure the 'candle' with which, in chapter 5 of *A Room of One's Own*, one goes 'peering' in 'serpentine caves', as well as the 'torch' that Mary Carmichael lights 'in that vast chamber where nobody has yet been',[55] it is Woolf's observations in this letter on print and intimacy that I would like to connect with her manifesto published three years later:

Indeed, it is odd that now, having read this, I have picked up a good many things I had missed in private life. What are they, I wonder, the very intimate things, one says in print? There's a whole family of them. Its the proof, to me, of being a writer, that one expresses them in print only.[56]

'Intimate' and 'intimacy' frequently recur in Woolf's private and public writings, and are deployed in a gamut of contexts, suggesting her intimacy with a very broad range of its possible meanings. Yet neither word appears in the printed version of *A Room of One's Own*. And in the light of Woolf's letter to Sackville-West, it is interesting to shine a torch into the 'nooks and corners' of its minced and mincing manuscript for the following singular instance, which occurs (deleted) in a draft of the imagined life of Judith Shakespeare, as she is driven by 'the force of her own gift' and her 'cursed love of poetry' to London:

> Perhaps a rough man laughed at
> her: ~~Certainly, at the age of 16~~ a pretty girl <of 16> could no more
> ~~walk to London without~~ walking along a country road,
> standing in the street, alone, a London street ~~would~~ <without> soon have
> met with ~~an~~ a violence & a bewilderment which if not
> rational – **sex, they say** <[I say?] it> ~~the idea of~~ **chastity**
> ~~may be a~~ <is> fetish, something we invent, in civilised countries
> for obscure reasons, ~~that are probably~~ foolish – ~~but~~ still
> ~~certainly as things are~~ <were> ~~even~~ are, nobody can deny its
> profound ~~& **intimate** connection with every one~~
> importance in the ~~mind~~ <life> of woman; or ~~its the~~ dirt
> immense nervous stress & dilemma which a
> girl would be thrown into who came up to London
> ~~alone as Judith did to mix~~ & stood alone at a stage
> door.   Thus, if women had written then,
> their what they wrote would ~~her~~ have been twisted, &
> deformed ~~with all those~~ <with> morbid imaginations;[57]

'Chastity' replaces 'sex' as the 'fetish' foolishly invented for obscure reasons by civilised countries. This silly fetish, chastity, then, according to the speaker rather than others, no one can deny is of profound importance in the life (previously the mind) of woman, a statement that takes precedence over the earlier assertion that nobody can deny the 'profound & intimate connection with every one' (regardless of gender) of chastity (previously sex). Here, just as 'fetish' applies more logically to 'chastity' than to sex itself, so 'intimate' will not do to describe the import of the foolish fetish of chastity for the life of 'woman'. This draft, shedding its incomplete utterances on 'sex' and a sense of universal 'intimate connection', transmutes, or chastens itself, into print in chapter 3 as follows:

> No girl could have walked to London and stood at a stage door and forced her way into the presence of actor-managers without doing herself a violence and suffering an anguish which may have been irrational – for chastity may be a fetish invented by certain societies for unknown reasons – but were none the less inevitable. Chastity had then, it has even now, a religious importance in a woman's life, and has so wrapped itself round with nerves and instincts that to cut it free and bring it to the light of day demands courage to the rarest. To have lived a free life in the sixteenth century would have meant for a woman who was poet and playwright a nervous stress and dilemma which might well have killed her. Had she survived, whatever she had written would have been twisted and deformed, issuing from a strained and morbid imagination.[58]

The 'issuing', as in birthing, of writing is in keeping with the dominant disruptive and contradictory tropes, in *A Room of One's Own*, of fertility, nuptials, fathering, mothering, aborting and infanticide. Compare too Woolf's concern over the 'nervous stress' of chastity with Stopes's warning in *Married Love* of the

> imposing list of diseases more or less directly caused by abstinence both in men and in women. These diseases range from neuralgia and 'nerves' to actual fibroid growths. And it is well worthy of remark that these diseases may be present when the patient (as have many unmarried women) has no idea that the sex impulse exists unmastered. [...] There is, however, no disease I know of which is caused by the normal and mutually happy marriage relation – a relation which, certainly to most has positive healing and vitalizing power.[59]

Had the pregnant Shakespeare's sister lived (rather than killing herself as we soon learn), furthermore, she may well have expelled into the patriarchy something that resembles the 'Fascist poem' contemplated in a dreaded fascist future anterior in chapter 6, which

> one may fear, will be a horrid little abortion such as one sees in a glass jar in the museum of some county town. Such monsters never live long, it is said; one has never seen a prodigy of that sort cropping grass in a field. Two heads on one body do not make for length of life.[60]

Woolf here reinscribes the then absolutely pervasive discourse of eugenics as received information ('it is said') against itself: fascism – or a poem conceived as fascist – is by its own eugenicist ideology a monstrous unviable herbivorous animal foetus. This dangerous, contradictory rhetorical strategy gives pause to any reader of Woolf's shocking private diary entry for 9 January 1915 describing her passing in Kingston 'a long line of imbeciles' and 'realis[ing] that every one in that long line was a miserable ineffective shuffling creature, with no forehead, or no chin, & an imbecile grin, or a wild suspicious stare. It was perfectly horrible. They should certainly be killed.'[61] Fourteen years later does the author of *A Room of One's Own* still subscribe to such shocking eugenicist views? The ironic turning of the discourse against itself in *A Room of One's Own* seems to undercut the eugenicism on display; and in *Three Guineas* this trope of fascism as monstrous birth continues as 'the egg of the very same worm [. . .] in embryo the creature, Dictator'.[62]

Were the suicidal Judith Shakespeare able to access the methods of birth control pioneered and advocated by Stopes, on the other hand, how different her story might be. This speculation seems implicit in *A Room of One's Own*, whose readers would be well aware of the feminist ramifications of progressive developments in family planning. Yet anyone visiting one of Stopes's clinics or making use of her patented contraceptive rubber cap could hardly disambiguate these from the zealous eugenicism that drove her campaign for 'wise scientific prevention' of pregnancy. However, Stopes was no supporter of 'criminal abortion'.[63] Her Mothers' Clinics, the first of which opened in 1921, were 'the practical instrument of her Society for Constructive Birth Control and Race Progress'.[64] Between 1934 and 1945 she opened five regional clinics and operated two travelling caravan clinics.[65] Every rubber cap was stamped with its patented name 'Pro-Race' and issued with spermicidal birth control suppositories called 'Racial Solubles'.[66] Later the cap's trade name was the 'Racial Occlusive'.[67] The rubber in these contraceptives promoting white racial supremacy was extracted by slave labour in the horrific plantations of the Congo Free State and Ceylon, Singapore and Malaya.[68]

But, family planning matters aside, the collective feminist work urged in *A Room of One's Own* to hasten the coming of a feminist counter-prodigy, Shakespeare's sister, we would do well to note, is here pitched against the Fascist imperatives of the 'unmitigated masculinity' (a twice repeated epithet) of Mussolini's dictatorship to hatch an implicitly patriarchal poet as Mary Beton reports on how 'I began to envisage an age to come of pure, self-assertive virility, such as the letters of professors (take Sir Walter Raleigh's letters, for instance) seem to forebode, and the rulers of Italy have already brought into being.'[69] Note how the professor's name bridges Shakespeare's era and present-day England as parallels with contemporary Fascist Italy:

> At any rate, according to the newspapers, there is a certain anxiety about fiction in Italy. There has been a meeting of academicians whose object it is 'to develop the Italian novel'. 'Men famous by birth, or in finance, industry or the Fascist corporations' came together the other day and discussed the matter, and a telegram was sent to the Duce expressing the hope 'that the Fascist era would soon give birth to a poet worthy of it'. We may all join in that pious hope, but it is doubtful whether poetry can come of an incubator. Poetry ought to have a mother as well as a father.[70]

The literary eugenics of fascism questioned here are reflected back on the nationalism implicit in the fatal project of a woman poet who sets out to rival Shakespeare as the embodiment or 'Absolute Subject'[71] of a national (English) literature. Judith Shakespeare, in William Shakespeare's era, prefers suicide over the prospect of continuing with an illegitimate pregnancy – such was the stigma of motherhood outside wedlock. This is one way to read her suicide (and many do); but perhaps what is intimated here is that Judith Shakespeare, if embodied in 1928, would still prefer suicide over the role of patriarchal incubator and the prospect of birthing the forced 'twisted and deformed' poetic progeny of a fascist patriarchy. The endless deferral of the arrival of such a Judith Shakespeare (that is, one serving a national, racial imaginary), among the multiplicitous future anteriors, as yet unwritten, to which collectivities (of women) might work suddenly seems well judged. And it is the sense of collectivity rather than a neo-fascist paradigmatic individualism that the closing feminist messianic passage of *A Room of One's Own* intimates: 'I am talking of the common life which is the real life and not of all the little separate lives which we live as individuals.'[72] The text allows the reader to ponder the limits of this 'common life'. Is it exclusive to women? Does it include or exclude the much debated 'fine negress' (apparently not 'a woman' nor 'an Englishwoman'),[73] or the figure of a 'lamb with a dogs head' birthed by a sheep, then aborted from the text for publication,[74] or the fascist eggs 'we can still shake out from newspapers' in *Three Guineas*,[75] or the line of disabled people Woolf terms in her diary 'imbeciles'?

As well as turning, as Bradshaw and Clarke do in their Explanatory Note, to *The Times* of 26 May 1928, page 14, to verify Woolf's text with reference to 'the report on the first meeting of the Italian Fascist "Academy of Ten"', the attentive reader might also follow up at length on their brief sampling of the matter excised at this point from the manuscript. For Woolf has aborted from her matter prepared for the printed text the following passage, perhaps preferring it to be still-born than to live on in print:

> And the trouble is likely to increase, I thought, putting Forsyte Saga back on the book case, for self conscious virility is probably in the ascendant. One has only to travel in Italy at least to see that it is perfectly possible for one sex to suppress the other completely. And I remembered the network of regulations in Italy, the dining cars and the railway carriages, and how one must not put one's foot here and one must not take off one's coat there. On every little grocer's shop there was stamped the head of a swarthy man whom one was invited to live for ever. And wherever there was a blank wall large enough to display a poster, vast black letters celebrated the flight of some aviator, or the triumph of some General. Flags and banners urged all the little boys to march under them and wherever there was a court yard large enough to receive them grown men in black shirts wheeled and turned in response to the shouts of officers. It was all very military and masculine and dry (I mean to a woman), I thought, remembering Rome but the military side of it is beyond my purview; what effect has all this drumming and trampling on poetry, I wondered? Well, apparently, there is a certain anxiety about fiction in Italy.[76]

Woolf's motives are not accessible for suppressing this account of the black printed letters already on Italian walls. However, the effects of this aborted but surviving passage (which is now in print for the first time in an appendix to the published avant-texte *Women & Fiction*) – its effect on readings of the printed version of *A Room of One's Own*, and its relation to it – need careful consideration. For one thing a clearer line from the more latent anti-fascism of *A Room of One's Own* to the more overt anti-fascism and anti-Nazism of *Three Guineas* less than a decade later is discernible, the latter a regrettable embodiment of a feminist resistance necessitated by a dreaded future anterior pointed up in the former – a feminist resistance, furthermore, that requires the destruction of the word 'feminism' itself. A possible reading here is that if the eugenicist Stopes is a feminist, and already linked in subtext to fascism in *A Room of One's Own*, the more overtly anti-fascist *Three Guineas* is obliged not only to confront socialists and anti-fascists with their forgotten common cause and roots in feminism, but also to confront feminists and socialists with past and current overlapping interests in the very eugenics promulgated by fascists.

Back in the intertextual hotspot of the laboratory where 'Chloe liked Olivia', such 'political valences' haunt their 'intimate relations'.[77] Woolf's laboratory of intimacy appears to be concocting something new out a number of sources, including Hélène du Coudray's *Another Country* (1928), a debut novel written by an Oxford woman student; Radclyffe Hall's lesbian love story, *The Well of Loneliness* (1928), banned for obscenity; and her own queer text *Orlando: A Biography* (1928), which evaded prosecution.[78] But here I want to look at the quite overt intertext with Stopes's *Love's Creation* (1928), *pace* David Bradshaw and Stuart Clarke who protest, 'But Woolf does not have Stopes in mind at this point in the book, and the discussion that follows is of an imaginary novel, not Stopes's,'[79] They rightly point out that *Life's Adventure* is imaginary, but in so far as it exists at all in the interstices of Woolf's chapter, it is in many ways, in both its cited passages and its paraphrased episodes, a teleopoietic exercise in mincing the very liver of Stopes's *Love's Creation*.

Perhaps Woolf's chapter 5, and *A Room of One's Own* itself, is an inception of a possible future anterior to Stopes's novel, a many-mothered hybrid or a mutant descendant? The last thing I think Woolf is doing here is offering a faithful account of anyone's novel, not even Mary Carmichael's fictitious one, never mind Marie Stopes's all too real and published one. Indeed, having read it most attentively (in a wonderfully informative new edition prepared by Deryn Rees-Jones) I almost find myself concurring with Muriel Spark's exasperated remarks on the older post-war Stopes who crossed her when she was editor of *Poetry Review*: 'I used to think it a pity that her mother rather than she had not thought of birth control.'[80] And 'What about Hitler?' we may well ask with Woolf. On 12 August 1939, Stopes sent her *Love Songs for Young Lovers* (1939) to Adolf Hitler to share with 'the young people of your nation',[81] a gesture that confirms the alarming intimacy of Stopes's brand of feminism with extreme racism and nationalism prior to Hitler's Nazi ascendancy.

But, in Woolf's intimate engagement with *Love's Creation* in *A Room of One's Own*, and not merely in chapter 5, I have come to see how such works may be continually open to being turned to anti-fascist feminist (to salvage the latter from the flames) advantage – in the spaces in which attentive readers identify their possible future anteriors. Woolf's playful, contradictory and densely allusive text (much more so than Stopes's didactic text) positively encourages such readerly engagement. To cite a text is not to repeat it. And Woolf's manifesto does seem to riff on Stopes's novel. Rees-Jones, building on the work of Elizabeth Abel and Donald Childs in connecting Stopes and Woolf, demonstrates their common 'evolutionary' discourse, and common engagement in the ramifications of social Darwinism.[82] But it is precisely this common discourse, I suggest, where the two radically diverge. Rees-Jones points up many of 'the complex, elusive and telling' 'displacements that are going on in Woolf's reconfiguration of Stopes's novel', not least 'the subtle shift in author' (Woolf's shifting of Stopes's pseudonym drawn from the latter's own mother's name) and shift in 'titles of the novels' (from 'creation' to 'adventure') that point 'to a narrative for Woolf which on the one hand favours a maternal line while on the other eschews the biologically maternal'.[83] In doing so Woolf eschews and satirises quite specifically 'the biologically maternal' at work in Stopes's novel, which as we will see below, is in many respects a paean to fascist eugenics.

I would also emphasise that both *Love's Creation* and *A Room of One's Own* may be read teleopoietically as queer campus novels, Stopes's against itself, while Woolf's queers Stopes's more 'restrictive', less self-consciously teleopoietic proto-queer episodes further. Certainly, Woolf's detailed discussions of the funding and fabric of universities, and of denied and limited access to education on grounds of gender and race and class are prefigured in *Love's Creation*, which even has a chapter entitled 'The Endowed Chair' and includes plenty of bitching about academics' pay! As for 'Sapphic' intimacy, Jane Marcus was incorrect in stating that *Love's Creation* opens with a chapter in which two *women* share a scientific laboratory.[84] In fact it is two men and a boy (Dr Kenneth Harvey and Dr Nicholson, 'his co-lecturer', and Tom, 'the attendant's boy').[85] But very soon in the novel a man and a woman (Dr Kenneth Harvey and Miss Lilian Rullford) share a laboratory, and they soon marry each other. But a marriage between laboratory collaborators, however heteronormative, cannot fare well in Stopes's universe. It is cut short by the wife's death. And the plot is certainly driven by the narrative conventions of compulsory heterosexuality. But it is as 'compelling and provocative' as D. H. Lawrence's *Lady Chatterley's Lover* (banned for obscenity in 1928).[86] In Stopes's novel – peppered by the way with the term 'intimate'[87] – there is a penchant for a kind of double entendre that perhaps allows (where Lawrence fails) its risqué enterprise into print, and which Woolf is surely matching, countering and turning Sapphic in her own laboratory of intimacy.

I will end with a brief taste and feel of *Love's Creation*, with which both *Life's Adventure* and *A Room of One's Own* I am now convinced are on pretty intimate terms. The plot revolves around Kenneth Harvey's eugenic research and his marriages, first to Lilian and then, after Lilian's death, to her sister, Rose Amber, herself a widow whose first marriage, she confides to Kenneth's mother, gives her no sexual pleasure:

'He even kisses my feet, and when he is beside me my body seems to stir him so that he quivers and pants and almost groans with the thrill of it, and I – I am frightened: I can't imagine really what he is feeling. It is terrible to stir anyone so much and not feel like that too, and not to understand'.

'My darling – ' Mrs. Harvey did not know what to say. Rose Amber was a wife; how could she tell her that she was a wife bodily unawakened, unstirred? Mrs Harvey knew well how many women wait for years, or for ever, before they experience and understand the thrilling joys of the body.

[...] Mrs Harvey's lips were tremulous at the thought of how much Rose Amber, in her tender humility, revealed, unaware of her lack of mated fusion.

'There are things for you to learn yet, dear'. Mrs. Harvey's fingers softly touched the curls on her neck.[88]

If Mrs Harvey's rehearsal of Stopes's tenets in *Married Love* also suggests a frisson of lesbian desire, a glimpse of Spivak's 'originary queerness' perhaps, it is merely to triangulate Rose Amber with Mrs Harvey's son, Kenneth. Such is the didacticism of Stopes's plot that Rose Amber's sexually unarousing first marriage is surpassed (following her sudden widowhood) by the perfect match with Kenneth. The latter's own apparently blissful but untenable marriage of intellects and bodies to his former laboratory partner Lily, Rose Amber's sister, is terminated shortly after the wedding by Lily's death in a bicycling accident. Dr Kenneth Harvey, between sisters, takes leave of his safe university career for the middle chapters of the novel, involving scrapes with 'beastly niggers', 'idiot' 'coolies' and 'myriads of Chinamen',[89] to pursue his post-Darwinian research into his quasi-fascist theory of the Greater Unit, which he expounds in the chapter so titled: '"Don't you see that the war, instead of being as so many think, the crash and break-up of our civilization and good old order, is really the rearrangement of the units of life at the beginning of a higher phase – a new and better order."'[90] In Dr Harvey's arms, the newly wed Rose Amber in an 'interval of rapture' becomes 'woman-like, eager to provide a material body for the dreams her lover shared with her'.[91] Unlike her now deceased professionally ambitious, laboratory-dwelling sister, she gets the chance to bear his children and steers clear of his laboratory. Is this the kind of marriage experienced by whichever one of Woolf's Chloe or Olivia is married? The novel closes with the Harveys confidently looking forward down the generations to the like-minded higher units to come:

> Rose Amber was eager. 'Don't you see how your work is the key of all I was striving after for humanity [...] the singing of a paean of joy to God in two lives may mean something sublime in the life of the Greater Unit'.
>
> [...] 'But I fear, I fear I'm only the epoch-maker's *grandfather*! How long can you love a man whose only claim to greatness is that he will be a grandfather?' He tossed back his head, the sunlight caught the firm pillar of his throat. Rose Amber kissed it.
>
> 'So long as he is also the father of my child – *always*'.[92]

Little wonder, then, that a year after these words appeared in print, we find in *Life's Adventure*, as rendered by *A Room of One's Own*, Chloe and Olivia have taken over the laboratory, fascist poems are aborted, and heteronormative motherhood itself is under queer erasure, while Shakespeare's sister is still yet to 'put on the body which she has so often laid down'.[93] And if there is a scintilla or spark of the 'feminist' in the pioneering scientist Marie Stopes, little wonder that Woolf returns to the laboratory nine years later in *Three Guineas*, rhetorically at least to burn the word 'feminism'.

Notes

1. Mark Hussey (ed.), *Major Authors on CD-ROM: Virginia Woolf* (Reading: Primary Source Media, 1997).
2. Line 1: Virginia Woolf, 23 January 1916, Letter to Margaret Llewelyn Davies, in *The Letters of Virginia Woolf*, 6 vols, ed. Nigel Nicolson and Joanne Trautmann (London: Hogarth Press, 1975–80), vol. 2, p. 76; lines 2–5: Woolf, 17 February 1922, in *The Diary of Virginia Woolf*, 5 vols, ed. Anne Olivier Bell and Andrew McNeillie (London: Hogarth Press, 1979–85), vol. 2, p. 167; line 6: Woolf, 17 October 1924, in *The Diary of Virginia Woolf*, vol. 2, p. 318; line 7: Woolf, 23 October 1929, in *The Diary of Virginia Woolf*, vol. 3, p. 262; line 8: Woolf, 15 April 1931, Letter to Ethel Smyth, in *The Letters of Virginia Woolf*, vol. 4, p. 312; line 9: Woolf, 16 February 1932, in *The Diary of Virginia Woolf*, vol. 4, p. 77; line 10: Woolf, 6 January 1935, citing Princess Elizabeth Bibesco, in *The Diary of Virginia Woolf*, vol. 4, p. 273; line 11: Woolf, 25 April 1933, in *The Diary of Virginia Woolf*, vol. 4, p. 152.
3. Lines 1–2: Virginia Woolf, *Night and Day* (London: Duckworth, 1919), p. 371; line 3: Woolf, *Jacob's Room* (London: Hogarth Press, 1922), p. 173; lines 4–6: Woolf, *A Room of One's Own* (London: Hogarth Press, 1929), p. 53; lines 7–8: Woolf, 'Why?' (*Lysistrata*, May 1934), in *The Essays of Virginia Woolf*, 6 vols, ed. Andrew McNeillie (vols 1–4) and Stuart N. Clarke (vols 5–6) (London: Hogarth Press, 1986–2011), vol. 6, p. 31; lines 9–12: Woolf, *Three Guineas* (London: Hogarth Press, 1938), pp. 184, 185.
4. Woolf, *The Letters of Virginia Woolf*, vol. 2, p. 76.
5. Margaret Haig Mackworth (née Thomas), 2nd Viscountess Rhondda (1883–1958).
6. Woolf, *The Diary of Virginia Woolf*, vol. 2, p. 167.
7. Ibid. p. 318.
8. Woolf, *The Diary of Virginia Woolf*, vol. 3, p. 262.
9. Woolf, *A Room of One's Own*, p. 53.
10. Woolf, *The Letters of Virginia Woolf*, vol. 4, p. 312.

11. Woolf, *The Diary of Virginia Woolf*, vol. 4, p. 77.
12. Ibid. p. 152.
13. Woolf, 'Why?', p. 31.
14. Ibid. p. 31.
15. Woolf, 6 January 1935, citing Princess Elizabeth Bibesco, in *The Diary of Virginia Woolf*, vol. 4, p. 273.
16. See ibid. p. 273n6 on the Cambridge anti-War Council's anti-Fascist exhibition.
17. Woolf, *Three Guineas*, p. 184.
18. Ibid. p. 185.
19. Ibid. p. 185.
20. Lisa Tickner, *The Spectacle of Women: Imagery of the Suffrage Campaign 1907–14* (London: Chatto & Windus, 1987), p. 128.
21. Tickner, *The Spectacle of Women*, pp. 126–8.
22. Ibid. p. 230, citing (without reference) Annie Kenney, *Memoirs of a Militant* (London: Edward Arnold, 1924), p. 282. WSPU stands for the Women's Social and Political Union.
23. Mary R. Richardson, *Laugh a Defiance* (London: Weidenfeld & Nicolson, 1952), pp. 165–73. See also Jane Goldman, 'Virginia Woolf and Modernist Aesthetics', in Maggie Humm (ed.), *The Edinburgh Companion to Virginia Woolf and the Arts* (Edinburgh: Edinburgh University Press, 2010), p. 41.
24. Julie V. Gottlieb, *Feminine Fascism: Women in Britain's Fascist Movement* (London: I.B. Tauris, 2003), p. 52.
25. See Julie V. Gottlieb's chapter on Richardson, Norah Elam and Mary Allen, 'The Legacy of the Suffragettes to British Fascism', in ibid. pp. 147–76.
26. See Richard L. Johnson, 'Nazi Feminists: A Contradiction in Terms', *Frontiers: A Journal of Women Studies*, 1.3 (Winter 1976), pp. 55–62.
27. Woolf, 15 September 1926, Letter to Vita Sackville-West, in *The Letters of Virginia Woolf*, vol. 3, p. 291.
28. 'intimacy, n.', *OED Online*, available at <https://www.oed.com/view/Entry/98503> (accessed 31 August 2020).
29. Jessica Berman, 'Woolf and the Private Sphere', in Bryony Randall and Jane Goldman (eds), *Virginia Woolf in Context* (Cambridge: Cambridge University Press), p. 471.
30. David Bradshaw, '"Vanished Like Leaves": The Military, Elegy and Italy in *Mrs. Dalloway*', *Woolf Studies Annual*, 8 (2002), p. 113.
31. Woolf, *A Room of One's Own*, p. 125.
32. Ibid. p. 8.
33. Marie Carmichael [Marie Stopes], *Love's Creation – A Novel* (London: John Bale, 1928). All further references in the notes below are to Marie Stopes,

Love's Creation: A Novel, ed. Deryn Rees-Jones (Brighton: Sussex Academic Press, 2012).
34. Woolf, *A Room of One's Own*, pp. 125–6.
35. Ibid. pp. 162–3, 163.
36. Marie Carmichael Stopes, *Married Love: A New Contribution to the Solution of Sex Difficulties*, 6th enlarged edn (London: A. C. Fifield, 1919), p. 99.
37. Woolf, *A Room of One's Own*, p. 142.
38. Marie Stopes, *Man, Other Poems and a Preface* (London: Heinemann, 1914).
39. Woolf, *A Room of One's Own*, pp. 132–3.
40. 'liver, n1', *OED Online*, available at <https://www.oed.com/view/Entry/109323> (accessed 31 August 2020).
41. 'mincing, n.', *OED Online*, available at <https://www.oed.com/view/Entry/118728> (accessed 31 August 2020).
42. Woolf, *A Room of One's Own*, pp. 129–30.
43. 'mincing, n.'
44. Woolf, *A Room of One's Own*, p. 172.
45. Gayatri Chakravorty Spivak, *Death of a Discipline* (New York: Columbia University Press, 2003), p. 33.
46. Spivak, *Death of a Discipline*, p. 26.
47. Jacques Derrida, *Politics of Friendship*, trans. George Collins (New York: Verso, 1997), p. 37, cited in ibid. p. 27.
48. Claire Colebrook, 'Woolf and Theory', in Randall and Goldman (eds), *Virginia Woolf in Context*, p. 88.
49. Spivak, *Death of a Discipline*, p. 28.
50. Ibid. p. 28.
51. Ibid. p. 29.
52. Ibid. pp. 28–9.
53. See Kabe Wilson, 'The Dreadlock Hoax', *Studies in the Maternal*, 6.1 (2014), p. 1; and Shola von Reinhold, *Lote* (London: Jacaranda, 2020).
54. Woolf, *The Letters of Virginia Woolf*, vol. 3, p. 291.
55. Woolf, *A Room of One's Own*, p. 126.
56. Woolf, 15 September 1926, Letter to Sackville-West, in *The Letters of Virginia Woolf*, vol. 3, p. 291.
57. Virginia Woolf, *Women & Fiction: The Manuscript Versions of A Room of One's Own*, ed. S. P. Rosenbaum (Oxford: Shakespeare Head Press for Blackwell, 1992), p. 83; bold style mine.
58. Woolf, *A Room of One's Own*, p. 75.
59. Stopes, *Married Love*, p. 75.
60. Woolf, *A Room of One's Own*, p. 155.
61. Woolf, *The Diary of Virginia Woolf*, vol. 1, p. 13.

62. Woolf, *Three Guineas*, p. 96; see also pp. 98, 186.
63. Stopes, *Married Love*, p. 135.
64. Richard A. Soloway, 'The "Perfect Contraceptive": Eugenics and Birth Control Research in Britain and America in the Interwar Years', *Journal of Contemporary History*, 30.4 (October 1995), p. 642.
65. Peter Neushul, 'Marie C. Stopes and the Popularization of Birth Control Technology', *Technology and Culture*, 39.2 (April 1998), p. 247.
66. Soloway, 'The "Perfect Contraceptive"', p. 655; Neushul, 'Marie C. Stopes', p. 256. See also '"Prorace" Cervical Cap', Science Museum Group, available at <https://collection.sciencemuseumgroup.org.uk/objects/co96336/prorace-cervical-cap-cervical-cap> (accessed 31 August 2020).
67. Neushul, 'Marie C. Stopes', p. 256.
68. David Bradshaw, '"Perished Alive": *Dubliners* and the Reek of Rubber', *Essays in Criticism*, 67.1 (January 2017), pp. 20–36. See Roger Casement's *Congo Report* (February 1904) and Edmund Morel's numerous publications including 'the hugely influential *Red Rubber* (1906)' cited in Bradshaw, 'Perished Alive', p. 25.
69. Woolf, *A Room of One's Own*, p. 154.
70. Ibid. p. 155.
71. See Louis Althusser, 'Ideology and Ideological State Apparatuses (Notes towards an Investigation)', in *Lenin and Philosophy and Other Essays*, trans. Ben Brewster (New York: Monthly Review Press, 2001), pp. 85–126.
72. Woolf, *A Room of One's Own*, p. 171.
73. Ibid. p. 76.
74. Woolf, *Women & Fiction*, p. 50.
75. Woolf, *Three Guineas*, p. 186.
76. Woolf, *Women & Fiction*, p. 190.
77. Berman, 'Woolf and the Private Sphere', p. 471.
78. For example, Woolf cites Peter Quennell's anonymous review of du Coudray's *Another Country* (1928) without naming it (*A Room of One's Own*, p. 112); she references the prosecutor of the Radclyffe Hall trial (*A Room of One's Own*, pp. 129–30); and she imports the character Nick Greene from *Orlando* (*A Room of One's Own*, p. 73; *Orlando: A Biography* (London: Hogarth Press, 1928), p. 79). See Jane Goldman, 'Desmond MacCarthy, *Life and Letters* (1928–35), and Bloomsbury Modernism', in Peter Brooker and Andrew Thacker (eds), *The Oxford Critical and Cultural History of Modernist Magazines*, vol. 1: *Britain and Ireland 1880–1955* (Oxford: Oxford University Press, 2009), pp. 428–51.
79. David Bradshaw and Stuart N. Clarke, Note, in Virginia Woolf, *A Room of One's Own*, ed. Bradshaw and Clarke (Oxford: Shakespeare Head Press for Blackwell, 2015), p. 117.

80. Muriel Spark, *Curriculum Vitae: Autobiography* (London: Constable, 1992), p. 178.
81. June Rose, *Marie Stopes and the Sexual Revolution* (London: Faber, 2007), p. 275; Marie Stopes, *Love Songs for Young Lovers* (London: Heinemann, 1939).
82. Elizabeth Abel, *Virginia Woolf and the Fictions of Psychoanalysis* (Chicago: University of Chicago Press, 2001); Donald Childs, *Modernism and Eugenics: Woolf, Eliot, Yeats and the Culture of Degeneration* (Cambridge: Cambridge University Press, 1992).
83. Deryn Rees-Jones, 'Introduction', in Stopes, *Love's Creation*, p. xxi.
84. Jane Marcus, 'Sapphistry: Narration as Lesbian Seduction in *A Room of One's Own*', in *Virginia Woolf and the Languages of Patriarchy* (Bloomington: Indiana University Press, 1987), p. 175.
85. Stopes, *Love's Creation*, pp. 3–4.
86. Rees-Jones, 'Introduction', pp. xxvi, xiv.
87. Stopes, *Love's Creation*, pp. 15, 32, 52, 84, 125, 135, 156.
88. Ibid. pp. 122, 123.
89. Ibid. pp. 96, 97, 101.
90. Ibid. p. 152.
91. Ibid. p. 183.
92. Ibid. p. 183.
93. Woolf, *A Room of One's Own*, p. 172.

4

'Angles and surfaces declared themselves intimately': Intimate Things in Dorothy Richardson's *The Trap*

Bryony Randall

'Intimacy only rarely makes sense of things.'

– Lauren Berlant[1]

The Trap, first published in 1925, is the eighth, and shortest, of the complete chapter-volumes of Dorothy Richardson's thirteen-volume modernist *Künstlerroman, Pilgrimage* (1915–67). This chapter-volume (as Richardson herself called them)[2] covers a period of around a year in the life of the protagonist Miriam Henderson, who comes from an upper-middle-class family thrown into crisis when her father goes bankrupt. Aged seventeen she is sent to earn her keep teaching English in Germany, and continues working as a teacher and governess on her return to England, then moving to central London to take up a post as a dental secretary. After Miriam has spent some years living in a boarding house near Euston Road, *The Trap* (set in 1904–5) sees her take up lodgings in a narrow thoroughfare called Flaxman's Court with an acquaintance, Miss Selina Holland, who is employed as a night-school teacher.

Where there has been anything written on this relatively neglected chapter-volume, the 'trap' of the text's title has generally been read as meaning 'marriage', as Miriam muses on the possibility of accepting a proposal from the eligible Dr Densley. Indeed, the eminent Richardson critic George Thomson regards it as 'the most explicitly thematic of all the books of *Pilgrimage*', the theme being, ostensibly, marriage.[3] But the text opens with Miriam entering into what she will explicitly describe as another kind of marriage, one of 'convenience': the experiment in shared living with Miss Holland (Miriam can never quite bring herself to use Selina's first name).[4] This kind of living arrangement was the product of significant social and economic changes through the mid- to late nineteenth century, in particular the employment opportunities offered by the rapid expansion in the education and health care sectors; as a result, 'for the first time in history a small group of middle-class women could afford to live, however poorly, on their own earnings outside heterosexual domesticity or church governance'.[5] Living arrangements for these women was a key issue: indeed, Emily Gee has argued that 'the big question for the single working woman was "Where shall she live?"'[6] *The Trap* offers an intimate portrait of the attempt of two just such single (educated, middle-class) working women to construct a mutually acceptable alternative living space – an example of these 'new living conditions'[7] – which did not centre on the heterosexual (married) couple.

Since leaving her family home, Miriam has lived in digs provided to her as a teacher or governess, and subsequently in a boarding house.[8] *The Trap* describes the first time she has to navigate the combination of control and compromise required in the sharing equally of an entire habitation with one other person. It seems that this particular arrangement was still an unusual one at the turn of the twentieth century, as (for example) summarised in a 1900 article entitled 'Women Workers: How They Live, How They Wish To Live'. The inadequacy of accommodation options is summarised thus:

> the boarding-house [where meals were also provided] is condemned as 'fussy and frumpish'; the lodging as in most cases uncomfortable and desperately lonely; the supply of women's chambers [...] quite inadequate to the demand, or else found wanting in good food and good arrangement.[9]

Instead, the vast majority of the women surveyed for this article expressed the desire for 'a "combined dwelling" – a combination, that is, of individual privacy with co-operative advantages'.[10] Miriam and Miss Holland's arrangement would, then, appear be propitious for the exploration of what Jesse Wolfe has described as the proliferation of different kinds of modernist intimacy in this period, promising as it does an ideal of mitigating loneliness while providing privacy.[11] But the experiment is not, ultimately, a success, and there are hints of its fragility from the very beginning: at an early stage, Miriam finds herself 'indefinitely committed to live at close quarters with a scorn she was not sure of being able to share'.[12] A further example: the fact that Miriam describes this new kind of intimacy as nonetheless a kind of 'marriage' – indeed, this is how it 'first appeared' to her – naturally invites a comparison between what Densley will then go on to offer, and Miriam to reject; and what life with Miss Holland, or someone like her, might offer.[13] Thus while such a comparison might encourage the reader to reflect on the differences between these kinds of intimacy (for example, while Gloria Fromm convincingly argues that

'Miriam is unwillingly and uneasily attracted to Miss Holland',[14] at least at first, there seems little evidence to interpret the nature of this attraction as sexual or romantic), it also raises the possibility that even a modern living arrangement such as this might pose similar risks to a conventional marriage, as perhaps another kind of emotional trap.

Nevertheless, and before the experiment falls apart, this text does see Miriam inhabiting and imagining various kinds of intimacy in an alternative space from the conventional marital home. This chapter will analyse the ways in which the early part of *The Trap*, which describes Miriam moving into her shared rooms, represents a particular mode of intimacy made possible only by the social, political and economic changes of modernity. My chapter, however, differs from investigations of intimacy which focus on interpersonal relationships. Instead, I explore Miriam's relationship with 'things' in this shared space through attention both to how the word 'things' is itself used, and to how certain individual objects are depicted in the text. As one of my students put it: in this particular chapter-volume it appears that Miriam likes things considerably more than she does people.[15] Yet while Miriam's most intimate experiences in this space occur in interaction with the inanimate, offering alternative models of intimacy in their own right, all these experiences are necessarily inflected – whether positively or negatively – through the fact that this space is shared with Miss Holland. As part of this discussion, I will also propose that 'intimate' is a highly apt term to describe Richardson's intensely focused narrative, and that the paradoxes of her narrative style are in many ways cognate with the paradoxes of intimacy itself.

First impressions: 'the thing she loved'

A key passage from the description of Miriam's first visit to the lodgings she will share with Miss Holland reads thus:

> Very gently she went down her stairs. In this clear upper light, angles and surfaces declared themselves intimately. The thing she loved was there. Light falling upon the shapes of things, reflected back, moving through the day, a steadfast friend, silent and understanding. She had loved it wherever she was, even in the midst of miseries; and always it had belonged to others. This time it was her own. The breath she held facing it was a cool stream, bringing strength; joy. Nothing could be better than this. None of the events, none of the passions of life, better than this sense of light quietly falling.[16]

Here, the interaction between light and physical space – 'the shapes of things' – enthrals Miriam and offers her emotional sustenance. The passage begins with a focus on line and plane that evokes abstract art: it is the 'angles and surfaces' making up the space of (presumably) the staircase which present themselves to Miriam – indeed, 'declar[ing] themselves intimately' as a lover might do in proposing marriage, no less. This perception leads to the revelation or realisation that 'the thing she loved was there. Light falling upon the shapes of things'.

Richardson's articulation of Miriam's visual and emotional experience here resonates strongly with one of the most influential aesthetic theories of the early twentieth century, popularised by Clive Bell as 'significant form' – a response to, description of, and in some ways a manifesto for, a Post-Impressionist visual aesthetic.[17] Firstly, there is Bell's emphasis on form: 'For a discussion of aesthetics it need only be agreed that forms arranged and combined according to certain mysterious laws do move us profoundly.'[18] Secondly, the aesthetic experience is, for Bell, emphatically an emotional one: significant form raises 'a peculiar emotion, called aesthetic'.[19] Miriam's perception and emotional response on the stairs, with their focus on form, appear to be an instance of precisely such an experience. Further, Bell's definition of that which might convey 'significant form' is inclusive, embracing 'pictures, sculpture, buildings, pots, carvings, textiles'.[20] But Richardson's articulation goes further, implicitly asserting that this experience of what we might call 'significant form' could emerge not necessarily from a particular object, as Bell's list seems to imply, nor indeed need it be intrinsic to such an object, but rather might arise from a momentary coming together of a particular set of 'angles and surfaces' appearing as light falls on them in a certain way, and as this visual perception resonates with previous similar instances in Miriam's life.

This 'thing she loved', then, while relying here on particular, material objects (presumably stairs, walls, a ceiling, bannisters, and so forth), resembles one of the 'confederations' of vibrant matter which Jane Bennett proposes in her 'political ecology of things' – a confederation of surfaces, light and 'the seeing self'.[21] Indeed, Bennett makes an argument for the value of just the kind of anthropomorphism in which Miriam indulges in her construction of light as her steadfast, silent friend. For Bennett, as it seems for Richardson, 'a touch of anthropomorphism [...] can catalyze a sensibility that finds a world filled not only with ontologically distinct categories of beings (subjects and objects) but with variously composed materialities that form confederations'.[22] It should be noted, however, that 'things' in *The Trap* do not always map onto the notion of 'thing' as it is understood either by Bennett, or within the influential theory of Bill Brown, whose work I also draw on here.[23] Bennett argues that 'things' are 'vivid entities not entirely reducible to the contexts in which (human) subjects set them, never entirely exhausted by their semiotics' – as, implicitly, 'objects' are;[24] similarly, Brown argues that 'thingness' arises 'when the object is experienced in whatever time it takes (in whatever time it is) for an object to become another'.[25] While there are of course subtle differences between each theorist's definitions, their respective invocations of 'objects' and 'things' broadly align the 'object' with the stable, atemporal, reducible and cognitive, while the 'thing' is vivid, narratable, temporal, most likely transitory and (epistemologically) excessive. In this chapter I will trace Richardson's own use of the term, which sometimes corresponds with Brown and Bennett and sometimes does not. That is to say, sometimes it is used in a way which is broadly synonymous with the term 'object' as defined by Bennett and Brown: clearly identifiable as something singular, bounded and definable. Sometimes, however, it seems instead to invoke the irreducibility, and temporal quality, which Bennett and Brown identify as a characteristic of the thing or 'thingness', as opposed to the object. And there are instances which seem to hover between these categories, on the continuum between them. My focus here is on how the text's own fluctuating use of the terms 'thing' and 'things' helps evoke Miriam's most intense experiences of intimacy.

Returning to the key passage quoted at the start of this section, I want to draw attention to two important characteristics of the 'thing [Miriam] loved' here: the feeling of possession, and the intensity of the positive feelings this 'thing' evokes. This 'thing' is distinguished from previous appearances of this phenomenon in Miriam's life, in that here for the first time Miriam possesses it – it is 'her own', just as the stairs are now 'her[s]'. The feeling of possession is a key quality of the intimacy between Miriam and things which recurs in *The Trap*; indeed, often the sole characteristic given of the things referred to is that they are Miriam's. This emphasis on possession is perhaps unsurprising given the historical development of the legal relationship between women, possession and intimate relations. Until 1870, one key difference between married and single women in the United Kingdom was that 'on marrying, [a woman] relinquished her personal [i.e. moveable] property'.[26] While Miriam does not actually own the dwelling she inhabits, she explicitly views the space as hers, and throughout revels in her possession of 'moveable property'. We recall that this particular chapter-volume is the part of *Pilgrimage* which most explicitly raises the possibility of Miriam's marriage. While her marriage would not, by this point in history, require her to relinquish her rights in such property, the fact that until relatively recently it would have adds a further layer of significance to the emphasis Miriam places upon things, abstract or concrete, being her own.

Further, the presence of 'this sense of light quietly falling' represents nothing less than the greatest ecstasy Miriam can imagine – 'Nothing could be better than this' – and thus relates to the optimism she feels upon entering this phase of her life.[27] When Miss Holland appears and the two women begin to negotiate the practicalities of sharing a living space, Miriam describes herself as 'deep, quite deep, in delight at the prospect of settling down here in intimacy'.[28] Even Miriam's – and likely the reader's – disappointment by the end of the novel that her relationship with Miss Holland has largely broken down cannot negate the intensity and significance of her positive feelings in these early stages. Indeed, her assertion that 'nothing could be better than this. None of the events, none of the passions of life' all but explicitly states that even marriage could not offer the same ecstasy. Thus the quasi-marriage proposal contained in the phrase 'angles and surfaces declared themselves intimately' replaces the intimacy of exclusive heterosexual desire with an intimacy between this interaction of light and surfaces, anthropomorphised as a 'steadfast friend'. But it also anticipates that the intimacy Miriam will achieve with Miss Holland will never offer anything like the satisfaction of this moment of aesthetic, affective response to the significant form of the angles and surfaces of this interior domestic space. In this key passage as elsewhere, it is Richardson's language – in particular, its open-ended, multivalent syntax – which permits the 'thing' to evoke both the material, even political, with the emphasis on possession; and the aesthetic and its associated intensity of affect. As we shall see, this reconciliation of the material with the affective – or perhaps better, an insistence on their inextricability – underpins Richardson's evocation of Miriam's relationship with things.

Ineffable Things

The word 'things' is everywhere in the first chapter of *The Trap*. In this section, I will focus on instances of the term where the referent is more or less unspecified. The word is, as Bill Brown notes, profoundly ambivalent: '*things* is a word that tends, especially at its most banal, to index a certain limit or liminality, to hover over the threshold between the nameable and unnameable, the figurable and unfigurable, the identifiable and unidentifiable'.[29] In this sense, then, certain instances of 'thing' or 'things' can always generate a sense of intimacy where the term is used to refer to items so well known to the narrator that they do not need to be named. If we follow Brown, the word as it is used when Miriam describes the removal of 'the last of her things'[30] from her previous residence in principle refers to the identifiable in that it appears to denote 'material items belonging to Miriam'. But *precisely* what these things are remains, per Brown, unidentifiable by the reader. The effect of this imprecision is to create a focus on the word 'her', indicating possession. There is an intimacy generated by the phrase 'her things', distinct from that generated by the phrase 'her possessions' or 'her objects', which relies on the fact that 'things' are not necessarily material objects. 'Her things' may primarily denote 'her objects, my possessions' but the term's informality, together with its gesture towards the intangible, contributes to the sense that these 'things' have an affective quality, bound up with their possessor's emotional as well as material life.

Later in this first day of moving in, the term 'things', while retaining its alluring combination of imprecision and solidity, comes to operate more specifically as the focus for an expression of Miriam's feelings in relation to the new space of the shared rooms, as she looks back on her first experience of them:

> Her eyes roamed as she moved about putting on her things. Seeking up and down the strip of bedroom for a centre [...] There seemed to be none, though the light was fading and the aspect of the room as it had been when her things were first set down was already in the past. Each glance produced the same picture; a picture seen and judged long ago and with which her eyes could do nothing. She took refuge with single objects, finding each satisfactory, but nowhere reaching home.[31]

Note that the word 'things' is used in this paragraph to mean 'that which belongs to Miriam' in general ('her things were first set down'), and also a specific subcategory thereof – her clothes ('putting on her things'). But this passage then draws attention to the way that the change of light on these things registers time passing and, with it, a change in her affective relationship with this space; the vision of the room as it had been earlier is now making way for something more familiar, less ecstatic. By way of contrast with her earlier elation, here 'single objects' from among her 'things' are not adequately grounding; they do not enable her to reach 'home'. Agnes Heller's definition of 'home' helpfully articulates the way in which this term is commonly understood as the ultimate signifier of intimate space:

> Integral to the average everyday life is awareness of a fixed point in space, a firm position from which we 'proceed' (whether every day or over longer periods of time) and to which we return in due course. This firm position is what we call 'home'. [...] 'Going home' should mean: returning to that firm position which we know, to which we are accustomed, where we feel safe, and where our emotional relationships are at their most intense.[32]

While Heller acknowledges that '"home" is not simply house, roof, family',[33] it is clear that home is emphatically a spatial category – a 'fixed point in space', a 'firm position'. However, as we recall, the first and most intense relationship that Miriam had in her new lodgings was not just *in* this space, but *with* this space – with the 'light falling upon the shapes of things'. With the fading of this light, however, comes a diminution of this emotional intensity. Here, we might legitimately invoke the thing/object distinction as articulated by Brown, who insists on the thing's status as 'outside the subject/object trajectory', and yet only occurring 'in the subject/object nexus [...] where they can be *narrated* as the *effect* (not the ground) of an interaction at once physical and psychological, at once intimate and alienating'.[34] In these terms, the significant form conveyed by a particular, momentary confederation of angles and surfaces, of which 'thingness' was the effect, has dissolved. Miriam attempts here to have recourse to specific, knowable objects that, despite their emphatic materiality, fail to reproduce the sense of intimacy with this space that she initially experienced.

A further, yet more abstract example of the term 'thing' appears earlier in the chapter where 'the thing' (here in the singular) does not apparently mean a tangible object of any kind, and where the level of abstraction provides a particularly striking example of what I suggest we might call Richardson's intimate style. The passage describes a brief moment in which Miriam is alone in one of the rooms she is to inhabit. Her landlord, showing her around, moves momentarily out of sight; instead of following him, Miriam 'turn[s] into the large room' and reflects:

> Long she had stood, with life gathered richly about her, in the empty window-lit space where she now asked whether really she had seen up there while she welcomed this superfluous second room, the thing that lay reflected in her mind, growing dim, changing to a feeling, a part of the warm sense of life all about her.[35]

The thing is, almost literally, at the centre of this syntactically evasive sentence, but it is not clear precisely what it is. Unlike in the 'angles and surfaces' passage, here there is no elaboration of what this 'thing that lay reflected in her mind' might be, other than that it becomes a 'feeling' that is 'a part of the warm sense of life all about her'. It is extremely difficult for the reader to orientate herself in this sentence: when 'had [she] seen [...] the thing'? Where is 'up there'? Is Miriam now experiencing this 'thing', or recalling having experienced it in the past?

None of these questions is answered, precisely because of the intimacy of Richardson's style. The full extent of this intimacy is nicely articulated by one of Richardson's earliest and most sensitively appreciative critics, her fellow novelist May Sinclair, who observed that '[Richardson] must not know or divine anything that Miriam does not know or divine; she must not see anything that Miriam does not see. She has taken Miriam's nature upon her.'[36] And in taking Miriam's nature upon her, she imposes it on us too; Richardson's aim is to make us to all intents and purposes, while reading *Pilgrimage*, identical with Miriam. The implications of this narrative perspective are clear in the passage quoted above, which refuses to provide deictic orientation for 'the thing' – a thought of a kind, 'reflected in her mind', then a 'feeling' – whose location in time and space is either obvious to Miriam and therefore does not need to be stated, or is ineffable to her and therefore cannot be. It may, therefore, be argued that in its excessive abstraction and syntactic ambiguity, Richardson's style resists rather than creates or invites intimacy, making her protagonist inaccessible to the reader. On the other hand, one could argue that Richardson's narrative style is in fact intrinsic to generating the reader's close intimacy with Miriam, as they experience, with her, the ineffability of this experience/thought/feeling.

Exploring slightly different definitions of the term 'intimate' can assist in distinguishing which kinds of intimacy are at play at different levels of Richardson's text. Broadly, the adjective 'intimate' can evoke penetration of or access to an interior (including as a euphemism for sexual intercourse): 'A.1.a. Inmost; most inward; deep-seated; hence pertaining to or connected with the inmost nature of a thing; essential; intrinsic [. . .] A.2. Pertaining to the inmost thoughts or feelings; proceeding from, concerning or affecting one's inmost self; closely personal.'[37] But it can also evoke a slightly different relationship, of proximity or closeness: 'A.3.a. Close in acquaintance or association; closely connected by friendship or personal knowledge [. . .] A.4. Of knowledge or acquaintance: Involving or resulting from close familiarity; close. A.5. Of a relation between things: involving very close connection or union; very close.'[38] While the latter set of definitions may ultimately enable the former – indeed, closeness may be a necessary precursor to accessing interiority – there is, ultimately, a subtle difference between the two.

In *Pilgrimage*, the narrative perspective is arguably as close as it is possible for a reader to be to a narrator, in so far as we only 'know or divine' what Miriam does, and only from her perspective. To this extent, then, the reader's relationship with Miriam is intimate. But here the potential tensions between definitions of 'intimate' emerge. Although there is much in *Pilgrimage* which enables us to know and understand Miriam's thoughts, words and actions, there are moments when the intimate (as in, very close) narrative style – the intimate description of her thoughts, words and actions – seems to mitigate against an intimate understanding of Miriam's interiority, of her most inward, deep-seated essence. Indeed, to provide commentary would disrupt the strict adherence to Miriam's point of view, particularly in instances where she herself does not fully understand what she is perceiving or experiencing. There is an interesting connection here between these different definitions of 'intimate' and Brown's discussion of what is required for the acknowledgement of 'things': namely, 'thinking sensation in its *distinction from cognition*'.[39] Richardson's style, it might be argued, at times sacrifices cognition – the reader's understanding of what precisely is happening, what is being referred to or seen – in favour of sensation, of conveying Miriam's experience of the ineffable.

If this is an extreme example of Richardson's intimate style, then it confirms Berlant's claim that 'intimacy only rarely makes sense of things'.[40] Berlant is not using 'things' here in a technical, theoretical sense, as distinct from objects, but rather in a more general way, so that the term might be replaced by 'the world' or 'life in general'. Her interest is, like mine at this point, in the relationship between intimacy and sense. That is to say, this ineffable 'thing' that Miriam, and thus Richardson, appears to struggle to convey, is offered to the reader as intimately as is possible in narrative (again according to definitions emphasising proximity rather than penetration), but in a way that does not 'make sense'. Cognition is not the point here, nor is coherence; the point is, instead, to convey the sense of a shifting experience of perception, thought and feeling which has particular qualities, certainly, but does not add up to some*thing* of which one can ultimately 'make sense'.

Tangible Things

But what of the attention the narrative does pay, at times, to specific, material objects? When Miriam scrutinises Miss Holland's possessions for the first time, light is once again crucial to her experience:

> Coming back in the afternoon, she found Miss Holland installed, her half of the larger room fully furnished.
>
> From a low camp-bed with a limply frilled Madras muslin cover, her eyes passed to a wicker wash-stand-table, decked with a strip of the same muslin and set with chilly, pimpled white crockery. At its side was a dulled old Windsor chair, and underneath it a battered zinc footbath propped against the wall. Above a small shabby chest of drawers a tiny square of mirror hung by a nail to the strip of wall next the window. No colour anywhere but in the limp muslin, washed almost colourless.
>
> But over the whole of the floor, gleaming, without blemish, was the new linoleum.[41]

Miriam has not yet encountered Miss Holland herself in these rooms, but perceives that she is 'installed' in so far as her belongings are now in situ, indicating the power of belongings to metonymically represent their possessor. While the scene is not explicitly described as lacking light, there is certainly a lacklustre aspect conveyed through the language: 'limply', 'chilly', 'dulled', 'battered' and 'no colour anywhere'. This is emphasised by the contrast between the items enumerated and the 'gleaming [...] new linoleum', introduced in its own paragraph and heralded with an emphatic 'But'. Even the 'tiny square of mirror' describes the absolute attenuation of the possibility of reflection in Miss Holland's side of the room. The contrast with Miriam's description of her own things later in the chapter could not be clearer:

> The new furniture peopled the room with clear reflections. The daylight was dimmed by the street, but it came in generously through the wide high window. And upon the polished surfaces of the little bureau, set down with its back to the curtain, and upon its image, filling the lower part of the full-length strip of mirror hung opposite against the wall, were bright plaques of open sky.
>
> The bureau was experience; seen from any angle it was joy complete. Added to life and independent of it. A little thing that would keep its power through all accidents of mood and circumstance. The inlaid design enclosing the lock of the sloping lid formed a triangle with the small brass candlesticks at either end of the level top, and the brass handles of the three drawers hung below on either side, garlands, completing the decoration.[42]

Here there is a 'full-length strip of mirror' reflecting back the 'bright plaques of open sky' also reflected on the 'polished surfaces' of the bureau as if in a hall of mirrors; the proliferation of light is throughout crucial ('clear reflections', 'daylight [...] came in generously', and later 'pathway of morning light').[43] In being 'added to life and independent of it', the bureau also represents a key feature of Richardson's aesthetic and philosophy: in Richardson's phrase, the 'strange sum of her central being',[44] which I have elsewhere characterised as an addition that 'does not alter that to which it is added'.[45] In being thus associated with the 'strange sum', we understand that this object is vital to Miriam's very sense of self, her 'central being': her most intimate self. Crucially, it is both an object with use-value – perhaps the most important object that Miriam will ever own in terms of her development as a writer – and a thing to be valued for its abstract aesthetic qualities. Miriam's attention dwells on the minute details of the bureau as she focuses on the visual and spatial relationships between the elements forming this object, using a quasi-geometrical vocabulary describing angles, planes and lines. Or, put another way, Miriam appreciates this material thing not just because of what it represents for her as an aspiring writer (its 'semiotics', as Bennett puts it in her definition of the object[46]), but in terms of its significant form, the emotion that its abstract physical qualities evoke. It is the combination of these object-ly and thing-ly qualities which makes the bureau's presence here – indeed, its precise location, generating precisely these reflections, shapes and lines, these 'angles and surfaces' – evoke all the qualities that one would hope to experience in an intimate space (thinking back to Heller's definitions of home): completeness, power and a sense of permanence.

There is one object, however, that defines absolutely Miriam's experience of this space: the curtain that will be erected between the two women's sides of the bedroom. While the curtain is not aestheticised as is the bureau – not admired for its significant form – it too is crucial to Miriam's experience of the intimacy within this space, through its literal demarcation of Miriam's physical relationship with Miss Holland. Indeed, the first thing we hear Miss Holland say mentions this item: '"Yes," she said disdainfully, "that is the curtain".'[47] In hindsight, the 'disdain' in Miss Holland's voice at this early point in *The Trap* reads as a warning of the fundamental incompatibility of the two women. As we have seen, Miriam feels initially optimistic about this experiment in shared living, but with the caveat that it cannot succeed 'until the curtain was up and the strips of privacy were secure'.[48] Certainly, we get the clear impression that the intimacy between Miriam and Miss Holland is sustainable only with the provision of this privacy:

> For herself, the coming of the curtain would be the moment of dropping the mask of attention, the moment of soaring freely within this new life. Things were going ahead too fast. Strong impressions succeeding and obliterating each other too swiftly to be absorbed.[49]

If a key aspiration of working women sharing a living space at this period was 'a combination [...] of individual privacy with co-operative advantages', then the 'individual privacy' in this space is assured by nothing more substantial than a curtain – not even a 'matchboard partition – on the other side of which you can hear your neighbour sneezing or fidgeting' of the kind separating the (unpopular) cubicles from each other in purpose-built hostels.[50]

Nevertheless, the curtain is absolutely necessary, both practically in order to delimit a private space for Miriam, and psychically to arrest the flood of sensations and feelings that arise as Miriam negotiates the sharing of intimate space. As Terri Mulholland notes, 'Miriam's privacy is not only about the demarcation of interior space; it is bound up with protecting her inner life.'[51]

Yet it is notable that a key moment when Miriam experiences contentment in this space happens in the next chapter of *The Trap* where she feels 'in happy communion with Miss Holland, moving busily *the other side of the curtain*'.[52] This moment of 'communion' which arises precisely when Miriam's companion is physically separated from her again evokes the ambiguity of intimacy: for Richardson, genuine intimacy – in apparent tension with the dictionary definitions of the term – depends upon separation.

One further item singles itself out for attention in the first conversation between Miriam and Miss Holland in their shared rooms – a conversation which unsurprisingly focuses on particular objects and their arrangement. This is the tantalisingly named 'indispensable' that Miriam suddenly realises she has forgotten – a 'tragedy', it would seem.[53] While the *Oxford English Dictionary* gives only two definitions for this word as a noun (a kind of ladies' satchel, and as a euphemism for trousers), both are somewhat archaic by the turn of the century, and in any case neither fits particularly well with the context here.[54] Richardson makes a tantalising reference to the term in a letter to her friend and patron Bryher dating from late 1925:

> I thought Alan [Richardson's husband] would expire in shrieks over your 'in des pensible' waste paper basket. He has a complex about indispensables ever since, when he was a small boy, an uncle went mad & came in to dinner with one on his head.[55]

We are unable positively to identify Miriam's 'unmentionable', but precisely the euphemistic quality of the word, and the hysterics into which the young Alan was sent by such an object, make it reasonable to propose that it might serve an intimate purpose, perhaps specifically associated with bodily functions. My interpretation here is doubtless influenced by the presence in *The Trap* of Henry James's 1903 novel *The Ambassadors*. Miriam is reading this book in the early part of the chapter-volume, describing it as no less than 'the centre of her life'.[56] While – or perhaps because – James's novel famously refuses to name the 'vulgar' object, 'wanting in [...] dignity'[57] on the manufacture of which a family fortune has been built, a rumour has arisen in literary critical circles that the item in question is a chamber pot.[58] Nevertheless, this interpretation is not implausible – a chamber pot would, after all, certainly be indispensable – particularly since this omission leads Miriam to remember another tragedy, exclaiming, 'And, oh Lord, a pail! I forgot a pail' to which Miss Holland reassuringly responds, 'There is no need to invoke the Deity. I have several pails.'[59]

The ease with which Miss Holland assures Miriam that she can provide such intimate items is an early indicator of her alacrity to cement this relationship, on a continuum with her willingness to take care of the intimate work of housekeeping. Indeed, it is directly relevant that Miss Holland uses the word 'things' to mean 'housework': she offers to take care of 'things' in return for Miriam dealing with the paying of the rent and associated '*palavering*'.[60] The intimacy implicit here in the term 'things' resides partly in its quasi-euphemistic function, just as with the forgotten 'indispensable', since housekeeping is, ultimately, a process of managing the relationship between bodies – including the detritus shed or residues left by bodies – and the spaces they use or inhabit. Miriam goes on to reflect that while 'housework might [...] hold some strange charm', nevertheless 'always, in relation to household women, she felt herself a man'.[61] Here the relationship comes briefly into sharper focus as what Miriam will call a 'marriage of convenience': Miriam's claim that 'household women [...] included her [...] in the world of men' casts her in the role of husband, and Miss Holland as wife.[62] In a novel that ultimately rejects actual marriage, this can only act as a warning that the relationship between Miriam and Miss Holland is likewise ill-fated. Certainly, the women exist in considerable physical proximity; and there are hints of some emotional intimacy, as Miriam expresses some feelings of sympathy between the two – for example, 'the exchanged glance of delighted understanding' about the need to seek tea as refreshment, bringing them 'immediately together again'; or later, the 'long and eventful [first Sunday], full of talk and laughter', that they spend together.[63] But the negative rapidly outweighs the positive, and it is soon clear that there will never be a true intellectual, emotional or spiritual intimacy between them. Thus the casting of this odd couple as man and wife inevitably raises the question as to the necessary relationship between cohabitation – the most socially valued version of which is of course marriage – and the kinds of intimacy that go deeper than simply sharing a domestic space.

From a feminist point of view, then, the novel's end might be read as a disappointing failure to take up the opportunity to positively represent the new kinds of intimacy between women offered by the evolving economic and cultural context of the turn of the century. Miriam does not 'reach home' in this space, or this text. Nevertheless, *The Trap*, despite its discouraging title, offers a frequently uplifting representation of intimacy in various forms, whether (occasionally) generated in relation to a cohabitee, or (more often) between a subject and the 'things' that surround her: material things, or sensations generated by material things, or even more ineffable affective responses generated by, returning to Bennett, confederations of vibrant matter, including that subject herself. Whether the term 'thing' is used to describe specific objects worthy of particular attention and generating an aesthetically affective response, euphemistically to allude to the physically intimate, or simply to generate a sense of the ineffable, its circulation in this text is a key part of its evocation of an intimate shared space, and the way in which this space might be navigated. These various intimacies form the crucial context for any glimpses the text provides, however limited or ambivalent these might be, of the 'happy communion' or 'companionship' that alternative forms of living might afford the independent woman of the new century.

Notes

I would like to thank Dr Vicky Margree for her invaluable help in revising this chapter.

1. Lauren Berlant, 'Intimacy: A Special Issue', *Critical Inquiry*, 24.2 (Winter 1998), p. 286.
2. Dorothy Richardson, 'To Sylvia Beach, 10 November 1934', in Gloria G. Fromm (ed.), *Windows on Modernism: Selected Letters of Dorothy Richardson* (Athens, GA and London: University of Georgia Press, 1995), p. 276.
3. George Thomson, *A Reader's Guide to Dorothy Richardson's Pilgrimage* (Greensboro, NC: ELT Press, 1996), p. 40.
4. Dorothy Richardson, *Pilgrimage*, vol. 3 (London: Virago, 1992), p. 428; see p. 507.
5. See Martha Vicinus, *Independent Women: Work and Community for Single Women 1850–1920* (Chicago and London: University of Chicago Press, 1985), p. 5.
6. Emily Gee, 'Where Shall She Live?', *Journal of Architectural Conservation*, 15.2 (2009), p. 29.
7. Vicinus, *Independent Women*, p. 6.
8. For an important discussion of Miriam's experience in boarding and lodging houses (and the difference between the two), see Terri Mulholland, 'No Place Like Home: Boarding and Lodging in Dorothy Richardson's *Pilgrimage*', in *British Boarding Houses in Interwar Women's Literature: Alternative Domestic Spaces* (London and New York: Routledge, 2017), pp. 22–47. Mulholland briefly mentions *The Trap*, but focuses on Miriam's relationship with single rooms elsewhere in *Pilgrimage*.
9. Emily Hobhouse, 'Women Workers: How They Live, How They Wish to Live', *The Nineteenth Century* (March 1900), p. 477.
10. Ibid. p. 479.
11. Jesse Wolfe, *Bloomsbury, Modernism, and the Reinvention of Intimacy* (Cambridge: Cambridge University Press, 2011), pp. 4–5.
12. Richardson, *Pilgrimage*, vol. 3, p. 405.
13. Ibid. p. 428.
14. Gloria G. Fromm, *Dorothy Richardson: A Biography* (Champaign, IL: University of Illinois Press, 1977), p. 189.

15. With thanks to Eilidh Ruthven for this observation.
16. Richardson, *Pilgrimage*, vol. 3, p. 403.
17. While Bell provided the best-known expression of this theory, he by no means originated nor had the monopoly on its formulation. For a detailed examination of the emergence and legacy of the term, see Mark Hussey, 'Case Study: Clive Bell and the Legacies of Significant Form', in Derek Ryan and Stephen Ross (eds), *The Handbook to the Bloomsbury Group* (London: Bloomsbury, 2018), pp. 60–74. I have thus far found no evidence that Richardson engaged with the term 'significant form' (in her letters, for example), and therefore am not proposing we read it as a direct influence on her writing. It is, nevertheless, reasonable to assume that Richardson, given her social context and interest in contemporary developments in art and culture, may have come across the notion, either directly or indirectly.
18. Clive Bell, 'Post-Impressionism and Aesthetics', *Burlington Magazine*, 22.118 (January 1913), p. 227.
19. Ibid. p. 226.
20. Ibid. p. 227.
21. Jane Bennett, *Vibrant Matter: A Political Ecology of Things* (Durham, NC: Duke University Press, 2010), p. 99.
22. Ibid. p. 99.
23. See, for example, Bill Brown, 'The Secret Life of Things (Virginia Woolf and the Matter of Modernism)', *Modernism/modernity*, 6.2 (April 1999), pp. 1–28; and Brown, *A Sense of Things* (Chicago: University of Chicago Press, 2004).
24. Bennett, *Vibrant Matter*, p. 5.
25. Brown, 'The Secret Life of Things', p. 3.
26. Mary Beth Combs, '"A Measure of Legal Independence": The 1870 Married Women's Property Act and the Portfolio Allocations of British Wives', *The Journal of Economic History*, 65.4 (December 2005), p. 1031.
27. Rebecca Bowler notes that '"light" [...] is ever Richardson's word for joy in knowledge, or knowledge in joy' and later that sunlight is specifically associated with 'joy in existence' (*Literary Impressionism: Vision and Memory in Dorothy Richardson, Ford Madox Ford, H.D. and May Sinclair* (Edinburgh: Edinburgh University Press, 2016), pp. 45, 115).
28. Richardson, *Pilgrimage*, vol. 3, p. 406.
29. Bill Brown, 'Thing Theory', *Critical Inquiry*, 28.1 (2001), pp. 4–5.
30. Richardson, *Pilgrimage*, vol. 3, p. 407.
31. Ibid. pp. 417–18. In the first edition of *The Trap*, each chapter is broken up into numbered sections; these sections were removed in the 1938 reprint, then used as the basis for the Virago edition in which most current readers encounter *Pilgrimage*. It is worth noting, then, that in the first edition,

both this paragraph and the one beginning 'The new furniture' (see note 41 below) mark the start of a numbered section. This paragraph begins section 7 of chapter 1.
32. Agnes Heller, *Everyday Life*, trans. G. L. Campbell (London: Routledge & Kegan Paul, 1984), p. 239.
33. Ibid. p. 239.
34. Bill Brown, 'The Secret Life of Things', p. 2.
35. Richardson, *Pilgrimage*, vol. 3, pp. 401–2.
36. May Sinclair, 'The Novels of Dorothy Richardson', *The Egoist*, 5 (April 1918), p. 58.
37. 'intimate, adj. and n.', *OED Online*, available at < https://www.oed.com/view/Entry/98506> (accessed 12 July 2019).
38. Ibid.
39. Brown, 'The Secret Life of Things', p. 2; my emphasis.
40. Berlant, 'Intimacy', p. 286.
41. Richardson, *Pilgrimage*, vol. 3, p. 403.
42. Ibid. p. 410. See note 32 above; in the first edition, this paragraph begins section 4 of chapter 1.
43. Richardson, *Pilgrimage*, vol. 3, pp. 410, 411.
44. Richardson, *Pilgrimage*, vol. 4 (London: Virago, 1992), p. 265.
45. Bryony Randall, *Modernism, Daily Time and Everyday Life* (Cambridge: Cambridge University Press, 2007), p. 71.
46. Bennett, *Vibrant Matter*, p. 5.
47. Richardson, *Pilgrimage*, vol. 3, p. 404.
48. Ibid. p. 406.
49. Ibid. pp. 406–7.
50. Hobhouse, 'Women Workers', p. 475. For the unpopularity of cubicles, see Gee, 'Where Shall She Live?', p. 41.
51. Mulholland, *British Boarding Houses*, p. 29.
52. Richardson, *Pilgrimage*, vol. 3, p. 436; my emphasis.
53. Ibid. p. 406.
54. 'indispensable, B. n.' *OED Online*, available at < https://www.oed.com/view/Entry/94574> (accessed 18 September 2019).
55. Dorothy Richardson, Letter to Bryher, 3 October 1925, Bryher Papers. General Collection, Beinecke Rare Book and Manuscript Library.
56. Richardson, *Pilgrimage*, vol. 3, p. 407.
57. Henry James, *The Ambassadors* (Oxford: Oxford University Press, 1985), pp. 42, 41.

58. See Fredric Jameson, *Marxism and Form: Twentieth-Century Dialectical Theories of Literature* (Princeton: Princeton University Press, 1971), p. 167; David Lodge, *The Year of Henry James: The Story of a Novel: With Other Essays on the Genesis, Composition and Reception of Literary Fiction* (London: Vintage, 2014), p. 42; and Lodge, *The British Museum is Falling Down* (London: Vintage, 2011), p. 123.
59. Richardson, *Pilgrimage*, vol. 3, p. 406.
60. Ibid. p. 411.
61. Ibid. p. 412.
62. Ibid. p. 412.
63. Ibid. pp. 417, 441.

5

An Occasion of Intimacy: Duncan Grant, Paul Roche and a Jesus that Bloomsbury Could Live With

Todd Avery

In *Bloomsbury, Modernism, and the Reinvention of Intimacy* (2011), Jesse Wolfe shows how, as a 'subculture [...] organized around loves that had dared not speak their name in the nineteenth century', the Bloomsbury Group represented one of many early twentieth-century 'signs that an old order was crumbling' and a new one emerging from the rubble.[1] For Wolfe, Bloomsbury's engagements with intimacy in the first decades of the twentieth century place the group at the heart of British modernity and modernism alike. 'As much as any early-twentieth-century movement', he writes, 'Bloomsbury made intimacy central to its work, interrogating its meaning and imagining [new] models [...] of intimate relations.'[2] Wolfe focuses on Bloomsbury's writers, but his claim regarding the centrality of intimacy to their work applies equally well to that of the group's artists. The characteristic quality of the art of Vanessa Bell, Duncan Grant, Roger Fry and Dora Carrington is intimacy. In addition to sexuality, which it naturally conjures, 'intimacy' suggests the everyday and the domestic – the inmost individual and social interiority and the ordinary familiarity of the term's etymological origins. These regions of experience, as Christopher Reed has shown in *Bloomsbury Rooms: Modernism, Subculture, and Domesticity* (2004), functioned as workshop and synecdoche for Bloomsbury's vision of a transformed socius. For Reed, 'Bloomsbury made the conditions of domesticity its standard for modernity.'[3]

Domesticity implies intimacy: with the possible exception of parturition, no kind of labour is more intimate than the 'housework' that Reed locates at the core of Bloomsbury's 'avant-garde domesticity'.[4] Indeed, a great part of the work produced over a sixty-year span by Bloomsbury's artists centres on the intimate regions of domestic spaces, from interior design to still lifes, nudes, portraits and, most strikingly, the *hortus inclusus* of Charleston farmhouse, the

Sussex home and haven to Vanessa Bell, Duncan Grant and their many friends and family from the First World War years into the 1970s. Charleston is the place where Bloomsbury most vigorously practised its axiomatic commitment to flexibility in the realm of intimacy – where they lived and loved in various geometric configurations. But far from remaining sequestered in domestic intimacy, Grant and Bell imported their commitment to 'the conditions of domesticity' with its complex, nontraditional intimacies into the larger world. In the 1940s and 1950s, Bloomsbury's artists smuggled their commitment to alternative intimacies into the most public and traditional of spaces. They imported the values they cultivated in their domestic spaces into the *sancta* of an institution that, they believed, had long embodied the force of ideological and moral repression under the banner of a transcendent heteronormativity.

In short, in the 1940s and 1950s, Bloomsbury's artists took loves that dared not speak their names – to church. In the context of intimacy in modernism, the church murals painted by Bloomsbury's artists are chiefly important as the most visible examples of how the Bloomsbury Group promoted the individual and social desirability – the private and public *goodness* – of nontraditional intimacies through an inventive counter-interpretation of religious tradition. To a person, the Bloomsburyans thought that sexual freedom was a necessary precondition of social improvement. They vigorously contested beliefs and institutions that hampered individual self-determination in sexual matters, and they promoted sexual freedom as both an intrinsic good and a means of individual, social and political betterment.

That Bloomsbury's artists should have turned to church decoration – at first glance such an uncharacteristic Bloomsbury activity – speaks, ultimately, to a jointly critical, creative and ideological commitment that both subverted conventional values of the institution, the Church of England, that sponsored their work, and imagined alternative interpretations of the Church's theological convictions. It is in this turning that Duncan Grant and his occasional co-conspirators made the condition of avant-garde domesticity – together with what his American contemporary, the openly bisexual social critic, founder of gestalt therapy and leading figure in 1960s counterculture Paul Goodman calls the generative, integrative and therapeutic 'act of love' characteristic of advance-guard art – their standard and model for a new type of 'intimate community'.[5]

Bloomsbury Does Berwick

The Bloomsburyans were vigorous agnostics. Of course, given their cultural inheritance, it was Christianity that loomed largest in Bloomsbury's religious consciousness. They deplored Christianity as a form of social organisation, and derided its supernatural pretensions as the expressions of a 'primitive' worldview.[6] They did not ignore Christianity, however. Like so many fin-de-siècle and modern writers and artists, they were fascinated by the elaborations of Roman Catholic and High Church ritual whose complex sensuousness appealed to their aesthetic sensibilities and offered a language for the articulation of queer eroticism.[7] As with their aestheticist and decadent forebears, the Bloomsbury painters understood the continuing reality of Christianity in the increasingly secular twentieth century as a discourse that might redeem the utilitarianism, commercialism, materialism and positivism of modernity – while also providing a source of homoerotic expression. Bloomsbury's understanding of Christianity as an opportunity for the expression of intimacy, in conjunction with their understanding of intimacy as an everyday occasion that might find embodiment in Christian imagery, attains its visually most striking illustration in several works by Duncan Grant. Grant's explorations of intimacy in church spaces were offered in explicit service to a conventional religious institution. His approach to religious imagery in these cases, however, bespeaks a countercultural commitment to intimacy typical of Bloomsbury. Ultimately, Grant availed himself of the occasions to produce religious work for religious settings as opportunities to explore the spiritual complexities of queer intimacy.

Grant's explorations of connections between intimacy and Christianity began in the early 1940s in one church, at Berwick, near his home in Sussex, and achieved a climax a decade later in another, at Lincoln Cathedral, in artistic Bloomsbury's visually most coherent and thematically most carefully conceived engagement with Christianity as itself an expression of both physical and spiritual intimacy; a formalised expression of infinite love and devoted care. In late 1941, Charleston farmhouse 'found itself plunged into religious drama'.[8] As Vanessa Bell told her and Grant's daughter, Angelica: 'The house is chaotic, and all a dither with Christianity.'[9] The occasion for this dither was the commissioning of Grant by the Bishop of Chichester to decorate the interior of Berwick Church as part of a wartime scheme to celebrate England's rural churches and the local life centring on them. Grant recommended that the commission be extended to Bell, her and Clive Bell's son Quentin, and Angelica.

Their images represent conventional Christian themes – a Christ in Glory; an Annunciation and a Nativity; a Supper at Emmaus; illustrations of the sacraments of Baptism, Confirmation, Confession, Holy Communion, Marriage and Last Rites; the parable of the Wise and Foolish Virgins and a Crucifixion. The painters approached their subjects from an unorthodox perspective, given their being agnostics who also reflexively balked at the claims of patriotism, even in wartime. So, for example, 'it is characteristic of Vanessa's approach', Simon Watney writes of Bell's Annunciation, 'that the incarnation is effected not by the intervention of the Holy Spirit in the form of a dove, or by similarly miraculous rays of divine light, but simply by the wintry light falling on her right side'.[10] More generally, as Watney observes, 'the entire decorative scheme at Berwick shares with Charleston a sense of the intimate relationship between a building and its immediate surroundings, in this case the local Sussex landscape'.[11] In the Berwick murals the spiritual and everyday realms interpenetrate; they include, for instance, representations of the pond at Charleston farmhouse and of the South Downs that surround the church.

Through their celebration of the Sussex countryside and their use of sitters drawn from family and friends, and especially through Grant's depictions of both the crucified Christ (modelled by Grant's sometime lover the painter Edward le Bas, who had posed tied to an easel) and the Christ Triumphant as open-armed, welcoming, live and inviting fleshly figures, the decorations at Berwick Church ground spirituality in the intimate details of the everyday – in the details of the immediate geographical and agricultural surroundings and in the details of lovers' bodies – and invest the ordinary with a spiritual significance. Despite Bloomsbury's general superciliousness toward Christianity, such details embody, Watney writes, 'a Christianity that Bloomsbury could understand and respect'.[12] Grant himself so respected the Bishop of Chichester's commitment to a revivification of the tradition of church decoration – which included the Bishop's willingness to pose for long hours for the portrait of him that Grant included in his Christ in Glory mural above the chancel arch – that he agreed to join the Sussex Churches Art Council founded by the Bishop in 1942 as a way 'to overcome the estrangement between the Church and modern movements in the arts'.[13]

Together with the decoration of Berwick Church itself, Grant's willingness to join this Council challenges the conventional understanding of Bloomsbury as a collection of artists and thinkers for whom religious belief was merely a sign of intellectual decrepitude, and for whom organised Christianity constituted an intrinsic and necessary bulwark of sex and gender inequality and a force of political reaction. Beyond the financial benefit of the Berwick commission, Grant's participation in these endeavours may be understood in several ways: as a wholehearted embrace of Anglicanism; as a sentimental celebration of English rural life during a time of national trauma; or as an opportunity to begin promoting, under cover of official sanction, an innovative take on Christian ethics. There is no evidence of Grant's religiosity. Nor does he appear to have held particularly strong views about the virtues of Englishness or Britishness. He was, however, committed to individual freedom in the realm of intimacy. Did Grant consciously see, in the Berwick commission and in membership in the Sussex Churches Arts Council, a convenient invitation to put a queer foot through the door of an intellectually dubious and ethically pernicious institution, one so many of whose core values, from the time of Saint Paul, ran directly counter to the Bloomsbury Group's most cherished beliefs? Grant was by all accounts too sincere, generous and tolerant to have acted with such disingenuous intentions. He was also too honest not to paint consistently with his deepest convictions, those that found expression in all of his intimate homoerotic drawings and paintings, in his decoration of Charleston and in his openness to fluidity in sexual preference. And so, in his second major church commission, Grant gave free pictorial rein to these beliefs.

A Vessel of Honour: Enter Paul Roche

Decorative murals had long been a generic interest of Bloomsbury's painters; these works had found happy hosts in domestic and secular spaces – homes and schools – since the 1910s. The Berwick enterprise inspired Grant to pursue religious themes further. At the turn into the 1950s, for example, he sent to the first exhibition of the lately formed Society of Mural Painters three paintings, a *Resurrection*, a *Deposition* and a *Last Supper*.[14] Shortly thereafter, a commission for another church mural project came Grant's way that would occupy most of the 1950s; in it he gave shape to a vision of queer desire that celebrates Christian intimacy – that is, his insight that conventional, homophobic Christianity might be thematically subverted by a homoerotic image of Jesus the Good Shepherd. This commission also allowed Grant to memorialise, in a bold conflation of identities, his close friendship with a poet, translator and Catholic priest named Paul Roche.

Charleston had been all a dither with Christianity in the early 1940s; later in the decade, Grant himself was all a dither with this particular Christian. His relationship with Paul Roche began fortuitously one summer day in 1946 when, crossing the road at Piccadilly Circus, he exchanged cruising appraisals with a handsome young man in a sailor's uniform passing in the opposite direction. A casual exchange of words turned into an invitation to Grant's studio, where began Roche's education in modern art and ideas and his introduction to a world that, in its celebration of physical beauty, lay beyond the theological and philosophical abstractions and the ecclesiastical discipline to which he had submitted himself over many years. Later, in his semi-autobiographical *Bildungsroman Vessel of Dishonor* (1962), Roche would preserve a record of

Grant's influence. He would attribute this influence to Grant's understanding of intimacy as a celebration of the spiritual possibilities of physical life.

In this novel, which spans the late 1930s into the post-war years, the scrupulous life of the young English priest modelled on Roche, Father Martin Haversham, is ruptured and reshaped by a sexual, artistic and ethical awakening. Weeks before his scheduled ordination, Martin travels to Italy and experiences a sensual epiphany, in part through his friendship with Douglas Asherton, a late-middle-aged English expatriate painter and sensualist modelled on Grant. In Douglas's company, Martin remembers a simple spiritual truth about Jesus that lay deeper than any ecclesiastical or theological orthodoxy – namely, 'that the Christ-God was human'.[15] Martin's residual commitment to conventional Christianity grows complicated by his awakening paganism; his realisation of the corporeal indwelling of the spirit is sparked by Douglas Asherton's

> face of the 'good pagan': too immediately ravaged both by compassion and pleasure. Its obvious humanity was slightly shocking to the naïve young Catholic eye, used only to the pure aseptic rays of grace. Then it struck him that this face of humanity was like the face of Christ – utterly committed to the painful, often scandalous and always twisted reality of human existence.[16]

Eventually, Martin suffers an attack of religious scruples. In a scene that recalls the short fiction of E. M. Forster, himself an enthralled explorer of pagan sensuality and the clash of national temperaments in Italy,[17] Martin panics; he flees to England, to ordination and to his responsibilities as a parish priest in London.

But his Italian interlude continues to exercise a subversive influence on Martin's psyche. In time he succumbs to the needs of the flesh: he begins an entirely sexual relationship with a young American woman named Vanessa, meets and poses for Douglas Asherton when the latter returns to London for an exhibition of his paintings, rents a small flat in Bloomsbury, and on his days off explores the city in a sailor's uniform. Eventually, through a series of melodramatic plot twists, Martin ends up trading the vocation of soul-saving for that of mind-shaping. Despite the novel's bombastically heteronormative ending – Martin and Vanessa marry; she joyously embraces motherhood and domesticity – Martin's transformation from priest to philosophy professor (by way of a harrowing descent into 'bankruptcy mental and moral'[18] and subsequent ascent through a baptism in the senses) is impelled by a conversion that Roche attributes partly to the inner demands of a conflicted personality striving to overcome its ambivalence, and partly to the external influence of Bloomsbury and, specifically, of Duncan Grant and Virginia Woolf.

Both Grant and Woolf teach Martin important lessons in intimacy. Grant, in fact, has a dual role in the novel; he appears as the fictional Douglas Asherton and as himself, a famous artist with a talent for still life painting and for capturing, in portraiture, the intimate nuances of personality revealed by a sitter's face. Martin's father owns a portrait of Martin's late mother painted by Grant in which she 'leaned out toward the world with warmness and mischief, a teasing lovableness both positive and poetic'.[19] As his vocational crisis deepens, Martin consults his mother's portrait, which draws him into a tender remembrance because of the sensitiveness with which the artist had captured her inmost qualities:

> Her steady gaze, smoldering but brimming upon him with tenderness, drew him into all the enchantment of the past [...] He held up his head toward the picture. She was only nineteen when the great Anglo-Scottish master, Duncan Grant, had painted it. He had caught everything about her: not her beauty only but that amalgam of resilience and softness, of simplicity and naughtiness [...] which made her character so amiably rare.[20]

The portraitist's sure grasp of his subject's personality centres on her 'steady gaze'. It is the intimate understanding shown by both artist and sitter that causes a re-enchantment, however fleeting, of Martin's increasingly desperate life.

Grant's name carries a totemic power, betokening the approach of intimacy. Several key details in Martin's journey are only lightly fictionalised versions of Roche and Grant's relationship. As Father Martin's vocational crisis approaches ever nearer, he goes to the cinema dressed in his sailor's uniform, picks up a young woman and brings her to a coffeehouse, where they sit beneath a reproduction of a 'superbly painted' still life by Grant of a 'watermelon lying opened on a plate'.[21] Afterwards, he bargains with God for a moment of licence, for just '"one week of natural pleasure – please, just that" [...] His whole being wanted her; his body burned for her.'[22] Immediately thereafter, Martin runs into Douglas Asherton, returned for 'the opening of his show at the Leicester Galleries'.[23] He poses for Asherton, hoping to be immortalised in the flesh, while realising with increasing clarity 'how unfitted for the priesthood he was'.[24] Martin is confirmed in this realisation when he repeatedly returns to Douglas's exhibition portrait of the young woman (and friend of Douglas) with whom Martin had fallen in lust, and love, in Italy: 'How it moved him! It undermined the fabric of his tottering vocation.'[25] He returns on the final day of the exhibition for a last look at this portrait; it recalls a sojourn that appears now marked by fate. 'Could Providence', he thinks, 'have given him clearer indications in those golden days that something other than the priesthood was what he was intended for?'[26]

An aestheticist 'pleasure and beauty had been prime motives in [Martin's] ascent to the priesthood'.[27] The same motives, translated into sensualist terms, lead him to abandon what he had believed to be his religious vocation in order to embrace a life of natural, intimate physical and emotional pleasures. Duncan Grant plays, as himself and as Douglas Asherton, a catalytic role in Martin's transformation, which is in its essential qualities as well as in specific details that of Paul Roche – the sailor's suit, the flat in Bloomsbury, the Catholic priesthood, the physical beauty of the protagonist. So, too, does Virginia Woolf, who strikes a chord that resonates through Father Martin's life. Even as his moral and sensual disquietude intensifies, Martin caringly ministers to his parishioners in London. After an especially exhausting series of bombings, he escapes into the city, sees a movie, lunches at the legendary Oddenino's restaurant near the Café Royal on Regent Street,[28] and finally goes to bed intending to 'blank religion out of his mind'.[29] He haphazardly grabs a book from his bedside table and experiences an epiphany – or, perhaps more precisely, a 'moment of being' – in Woolf's deep plunge into the intimate thoughts of her characters so vitally alive on that one June day. For Martin, these thoughts compose a reality more vital than the religious. 'Ah!' he thinks, reading *Mrs Dalloway*,

> there were other realities besides the religious, and the human spirit must try to grasp them. Life was the context of religion and not the other way round. Life was the only stuff of which religion could be made; there was no such thing as religion without life.[30]

Vessel of Dishonor is a semi-autobiographical work of spiritual transformation that centres thematically on complexities of physical, emotional and spiritual intimacy. In it Paul Roche expresses his indebtedness to Bloomsbury, whose commitment to the sacredness of the everyday helped him to reimagine the place and purpose of human intimacy in his own life, and who offered him visual and literary languages through which to make sense of his spiritual and ethical development. Roche's testament to intimacy as an ethical end in itself and as both cause and effect of spiritual insight renders *Vessel of Dishonor* a quintessentially Bloomsburyan text. It is no accident that, feeling the imminent collapse of the foundations of his religious belief, Martin retreats to his flat in Bloomsbury; there, 'the world [. . .] seemed new with hope'.[31] Published in 1962, this novel looks backward in history, subtly locating – through its invocations of aestheticist values and locales: 'pleasure and beauty', a restaurant next to a favoured haunt of Wilde and Whistler – the origins of Bloomsbury's belief in the ethical value of intimacy in an art for art's sake tradition. It also affirms the continuing relevance of Bloomsbury values deep into the post-war years and into a decade that would come to be defined by countercultural and liberatory agitations which were themselves often expressive of spiritual desires, and which did so much to reinvent intimacy with far-reaching and long-lasting social, cultural and political consequences.

A Better Shepherd: Taking Paul Roche to Lincoln

Bloomsbury influenced the young priest Paul Roche into a pursuit of physical pleasure and intimacy that he understood in spiritual terms. The friendship between Grant and Roche also reciprocally influenced artistic Bloomsbury's grandest public representation of queer Christian intimacy, which Grant envisions in terms of an ethics of care inspired by the ancient Christian motif of the Good Shepherd. In the early 1950s, Grant used the private intimacy of his relationship with Roche as the inspiration for a painting that celebrates the eroticised body of the Saviour as a 'youthful male beauty' in a way that recalls pagan representations of the god Mercury,[32] and that, by so doing, carries on the Victorian countercultural tradition of queer Hellenism into the post-war years, at a time when Grant was directing a good part of his creative energies to the drawing and painting of nude male bodies by way of shaping what Simon Watney calls 'a world of Arcadian fantasy and reverie'.[33]

Watney's comment has been further developed by Darren Clarke, who offers a useful critical frame for understanding Grant's intentions in his engagements with Christianity. Clarke places Grant's painting in the specific domestic location of Charleston, which he calls

> a stage set for queerness [...] for Grant often used his art to re-imagine Charleston as a queer, homo-edenic place, to code queer representations in the permanence of paint. Grant created a visionary rural idyll in Sussex that was an arcadia of sexual dissidence and homosexual society, a utopian, private space.[34]

Clarke's characterisation of Charleston also applies to the murals that Grant painted at Lincoln Cathedral in the 1950s. The occasion for these murals was the awarding to Grant of a commission in 1952 to decorate the Russell Chantry, a small room dedicated to St Blaise, patron saint of the wool trade.[35] Three murals compose the Chantry walls. The west wall features an Italianate scene of medieval Lincoln: at its centre a group of muscular young men in tight shorts load wool onto ships beneath the city on its hill. The north wall contains scenes of sheep shearing and banners crowded with flowers and birds. The east wall, the focal point of the room, depicts a young, beardless Jesus as the Good Shepherd: standing in a golden mandorla with a sheep cradled over his shoulders, he looks towards the windows that form the south wall with an expression of confident benignity.

The model for Grant's Jesus was Roche, who explains the thematic significance of, and the contemporary official and public reaction to, the beardless Christ:

> Some people were and are at first disconcerted to see a young, beardless and undeniably athletic Christ instead of the usual more solemn portrayal, but [...] this is historically correct in the sense that this is indeed the Christ of the catacombs, the Greekified Christ that edged out the god Mercury (the Greek Hermes) in the conception of the early converts to Christianity in Rome. The gradual passing off of the gods of antiquity for Christian realities certainly eased the transition of paganism to Christianity. To see Hermes carrying a sheep must have been reassuring to those Romans of the first three centuries who were being weaned away from their old beliefs and enabled to accept a Good Shepherd they could relate to.[36]

If Grant's intention was to smuggle an eroticised gay Jesus into church then he could hardly have chosen a more appropriate motif than that of the 'Greekified' Christ. Perhaps the surest evidence that Grant's murals were disconcerting may be found in the fact that, shortly after the murals' unveiling, the Russell Chantry was turned into a storage room, a function it served for decades, the unseen paintings mouldering. It may have been reassuring to Romans in the proto-Christian era to see Hermes carrying a sheep on his shoulders; but the 1950s were not the fourth century AD. It was slightly less reassuring to the Lincoln Cathedral authorities to see the fresh-faced, muscular Paul Roche in the same posture. Of these murals Edward Mayor writes that Grant, 'in effect, painted the world of Charleston onto the walls of the Russell Chantry'.[37] By doing so, Mayor explains, Grant attempted to reconcile the competing aesthetic aims and ideological claims of home, Bloomsbury and Church. Grant's murals in Lincoln 'mix life, art, and religion'.[38] Grant never spoke or wrote in detail about his formal or ideological intentions in the Lincoln murals, and despite evidence to the contrary he denied any knowledge of Christian iconography. 'The fact', he said, 'that I chose to represent Christ as a youth was due to the whole spirit of the subject, chosen to combine scenes of everyday life in the sheep country with the issue of the Good Shepherd.'[39]

Might Grant not be being just a little bit coy? What does he mean by pointing to 'the whole spirit of the subject' as the reason for deciding 'to represent Christ as a youth'? What indeed is the whole spirit of the subject of Grant's Christ as the Good Shepherd? And what is 'the issue' of Christ the Good Shepherd? What is the fundamental issue here at all? Grant's cousin, erstwhile lover and Bloomsbury original Lytton Strachey had two decades earlier adopted the persona of the crucified Christ as a way to celebrate, in the spirit of the figure he was apparently mocking, the ecstasies of sadomasochistic experiments and the ethical legitimacy of same-sex love.[40] For his own part, in picturing Jesus as a muscular, blond, beardless young man carrying the body of his vulnerable charge and presiding over a host of fit, half-naked sheep shearers and dockworkers, many of them also modelled on Roche, Grant recovers a paganised, 'Greekified' Jesus. Further, just as he helped to transform Charleston into a queer Arcadia, so too, through a homoerotic Jesus who radiates his embracing care in the Russell Chantry, Grant transforms a corner of Lincoln Cathedral, of the Bishopric of Lincoln and of the Church of England itself into 'a queer, homo-edenic place'.[41] Grant is very much following in his cousin Lytton Strachey's footsteps here. Strachey had once defended his commitment to a religion of difference – a religion 'that admits of so much that is varied, and ridiculous, and strange'.[42] In his own representation of Christ as an object of erotic desire that is also an intimate portrait of Paul Roche, Grant paints a defence of meaningful sexual difference onto the panels that decorate the walls of the Russell Chantry.

Grant's painting represents his close friend without shame as Christ, and in so doing it celebrates the intimacy inherent in the 'issue' of the Good Shepherd. In Grant and Roche's friendship, and in Grant's Lincoln Cathedral murals, Bloomsbury's commitment to intimacy achieved a particularly sacred intensity. In 'The Story of Narcissus' (1950),[43] an unpublished *novella-à-clef* that Grant wrote to make sense of his feelings for Roche in the early years of their relationship, the older Patroclus (Grant) thinks, of his feelings for the younger Narcissus (Roche), that they had 'an understanding of a purely human nature. They loved one another.'[44] In a short paragraph marked by repetition of the term 'friend', Patroclus also thinks that he 'was only happy with his friend. While they were together everything every thought was shared. The truth is that Patroclus loved Narcissus.'[45] Grant's keen appreciation of the bond of intimacy shines through that phrase, 'everything every thought was shared', just as it shines through the aureole surrounding his Good Shepherd. Grant wrote 'The Story of Narcissus' as an exploration of friendship and love. 'What relation', one of the characters asks, 'did friendship bear to love?'[46] Expressive of a personal love, Grant's own Good Shepherd, recalling the earliest painted images symbolic of a new religious order, also embodies a more general care for human well-being, as expressed in the first Gospel. 'When he saw the multitudes', Matthew writes, 'he was moved with compassion on them, because they fainted, and were scattered abroad, as sheep having no shepherd.'[47] In Lincoln Cathedral, Grant's commitment to friendship and intimacy as the foundation stones for a Christianity that admits of sexual variety joins with his personal love for Paul Roche and finds its ideal image in the Good Shepherd. In this image, Grant announces a universal compassion for the lost and scattered, those who, like all the sick and sinners in the ninth chapter of Matthew, receive the same gift of care. In this, Grant exemplifies the artistic advance-guard as theorised by Paul Goodman in the early 1950s, contemporaneously with Grant's church murals. For Goodman, the essential role of the advance-guard is to aid in the creation of 'intimate community' through works that function as 'acts of love'.[48] Through their works, sometimes 'embarrassing in their directness', advance-guard writers and artists generate an integrative sense of 'meaning' and 'excitement' among the 'alienated', 'dis-integrated' members of an 'estranged society'.[49] 'The chief aim of integrated art', Goodman continues, 'is to heighten the everyday; to bathe the world in such a light of imagination [...] that the persons who are living in it without meaning or feeling suddenly find that it is exciting and meaningful to live in it.'[50]

In Grant's painting of the Good Shepherd, as in the equally unashamedly bisexual Paul Goodman's conception of the advance-guard, both the enjoyment and representation of personal intimacy carry political weight. For Goodman, 'acts of love' and 'intimate community' do not imply same-sex intimacy; but they allow for it, queering the heteronormative space of the dominant heterosexual culture in the interest of a more generous – a more Grantly Christian – embrace. Over the course of the 1950s, while Duncan Grant sketched and planned and painted and, finally, at the end of the decade, attached his finished panels to the walls in Lincoln Cathedral, gay men in Britain suffered under a severe government crackdown. In this decade, more than a thousand men were incarcerated for homosexual offences. The commission for the Lincoln murals came Grant's way at the same time as Alan Turing was convicted of gross indecency; Turing's death in 1954 coincided with the sensational trials of Lord Montagu, Michael Pitt-Rivers and Peter Wildeblood, which happened at the very moment when Grant was working through 'the spirit of the subject' in his studio at Charleston. These trials also generated a progressive reaction that led to the formation of the Wolfenden Committee in September 1954 and the publication of the Wolfenden Report in 1957, and eventually to the passage of the Sexual Offences Act of 1967. Duncan Grant's Good Shepherd stands, like Grant himself, unashamed, a symbol of hope to those suffocating in political and legal closets filled with what Lytton Strachey had called, in writing of Christian homophobia, 'the atrocious fog of superstition that hangs over us and compresses our breathing and poisons our lives'.[51]

The intimate friendship with Paul Roche that inspired Grant's Good Shepherd resulted in the artistic expression of a simultaneously aesthetic, ethical, spiritual and political commitment to a love the speaking of whose name had long been a source of legal and social danger in Britain. Grant did not believe in the divinity of Christ. That he devoted so much of his creative energy to church decoration in the 1940s and 1950s, however, and that he should so heartily have embraced the Good Shepherd as his theme in Lincoln, shows how he discovered in religious settings and, like Lytton Strachey, in the image of Christianity's founder, an ideal occasion to represent, in Mark Doty's aching phrase, 'love, by which I mean a sense of tenderness toward experience, of being held within an intimacy with the things of the world'.[52] When Paul Roche later fictionalised Grant in *Vessel of Dishonor*, this sensitivity is precisely what he had in mind. In Roche's novel, Grant, the model for Douglas Asherton, possesses the face of a 'good pagan', which also, 'ravaged both by compassion and pleasure', recalls that of Christ.[53] Roche is Grant's 'Greekified' Good Shepherd in the 1950s, just as he had embodied both 'Pagan' and 'Christian' qualities in equal measure in Grant's 1950 'Story of Narcissus'. The following decade, in an act of reciprocal generosity, Roche, the former Catholic priest, returned the tribute to his friend, by representing him as a pagan Christian and a Christian pagan. Even while working on the Lincoln murals, Grant, who saw Roche as 'a creature Pagan to the bottom of his soul',[54] was encouraging Roche to queer his religion. Thinking of Algernon Charles Swinburne's lament on the rise of Christianity, the 'Hymn to Proserpine' (1866), Grant suggested to Roche the title of his first novel, *O Pale Galilean* (1954). 'Thou hast conquered, O pale Galilean', writes Swinburne: 'the world has grown grey from thy breath.'[55] In Lincoln, Grant's gentle subversion restores vibrant colour to the drab world of Swinburne's Christ. In this queer gospel, the porter openeth,[56] and the Galilean arrives, compassionate and sexy and proud. He steps forth from the east wall of the Russell Chantry into the mid-twentieth century, bringing a breath of fresh air and the promise of a more abundant life. This conquering Christ is one that Bloomsbury could live with.

Notes

I wish to thank Elsa Högberg for the smart, generous editing that enabled this chapter finally to take shape, and for a few fine phrases that I have incorporated with her permission into the final product.

1. Jesse Wolfe, *Bloomsbury, Modernism, and the Reinvention of Intimacy* (Cambridge: Cambridge University Press, 2011), p. 1.

2. Ibid. p. 3.
3. Christopher Reed, *Bloomsbury Rooms: Modernism, Subculture, and Domesticity* (New Haven, CT: Yale University Press, 2004), p. 5.
4. Ibid. p. 5.
5. Paul Goodman, 'Advance-Guard Writing, 1900–1950', *The Kenyon Review*, 13.3 (Summer 1951), p. 376.
6. Dora Carrington, *Carrington's Letters*, ed. Anne Chisholm (London: Chatto & Windus, 2017), p. 112.
7. See, for example, Ellis Hanson, *Decadence and Catholicism* (Cambridge, MA: Harvard University Press, 1997); and Dominic Janes, *Visions of Queer Martyrdom from John Henry Newman to Derek Jarman* (Chicago: University of Chicago Press, 2015).
8. Frances Spalding, *Duncan Grant: A Biography* (London: Pimlico, 1997), p. 382.
9. Cited in ibid. p. 382.
10. Simon Watney, *The Art of Duncan Grant* (London: John Murray, 1990), p. 66.
11. Ibid. p. 66.
12. Ibid. p. 80.
13. Spalding, *Duncan Grant*, p. 384.
14. Ibid. p. 409.
15. Paul Roche, *Vessel of Dishonor* (New York: Signet, 1963), pp. 60–1.
16. Ibid. p. 68.
17. See E. M. Forster, 'The Story of a Panic', in *The Celestial Omnibus and Other Stories* (New York: Vintage Books, 1976), pp. 3–38.
18. Roche, *Vessel of Dishonor*, p. 157.
19. Ibid. p. 24.
20. Ibid. pp. 155–6.
21. Ibid. p. 177.
22. Ibid. p. 179.
23. Ibid. p. 179. This happens in the novel in 1944; Duncan Grant had an exhibition at the Leicester Galleries in June and July 1945.
24. Ibid. p. 181.
25. Ibid. p. 182.
26. Ibid. p. 186.
27. Ibid. p. 96.
28. Long a haunt of the famous and the Aesthetic, the Café Royal was the location of a meeting in 1895 in which Frank Harris advised Oscar Wilde to drop his libel suit against the Marquess of Queensberry. A story of same-sex intimacies in London might well centre on this location.
29. Roche, *Vessel of Dishonor*, p. 143.

30. Ibid. p. 143.
31. Ibid. p. 189.
32. Watney, *The Art of Duncan Grant*, p. 71.
33. Ibid. p. 69.
34. Darren Clarke, 'Duncan Grant and Bloomsbury's Queer Arcadia', in Brenda Helt and Madelyn Detloff (eds), *Queer Bloomsbury* (Edinburgh: Edinburgh University Press, 2016), p. 153.
35. Spalding, *Duncan Grant*, p. 418. See also the video 'Lincoln and Duncan Grant Murals' by Richard Warren and Phil Revels for a lovely tour through the Cathedral and the Grant murals, available at <https://www.youtube.com/watch?v=TnQsUMYjYcI> (accessed 27 January 2020).
36. Paul Roche, 'Reminiscences' (Appendix II), in Edward Mayor (with Archival and Visual Research by Judith Robinson), *The Duncan Grant Murals in Lincoln Cathedral* (Lincoln: Lincoln Cathedral Publications, 2000), pp. 50–1.
37. Mayor, *The Duncan Grant Murals*, p. 12.
38. Ibid. p. 9.
39. Duncan Grant, 'Statement about the Murals' (Appendix I), in ibid. p. 49.
40. See Todd Avery, 'Nailed: Lytton Strachey's Jesus Camp', in Helt and Detloff (eds), *Queer Bloomsbury*, pp. 172–88.
41. Clarke, 'Duncan Grant', p. 153.
42. Lytton Strachey, 'Should We Have Elected Conybeare?', in *Unpublished Works of Lytton Strachey: Early Papers*, ed. Todd Avery (London: Pickering & Chatto, 2011), p. 73.
43. Duncan Grant, 'The Story of Narcissus', an unpublished story located in a notebook held in the Berg Collection of British and American Literature at the New York Public Library: Grant, 'Notebook containing autograph notes and heavily emended autograph draft for obituary essay on Virginia Woolf; followed by Grant's "The Story of Narcissus" and two lengthy diary entries, with detached diary leaf laid-in; with 5 pages of detached notes for essay in separate folder; with two letters to Grant from Stephen Spender; and with copy of Horizon (June 1941)'. Berg Coll+ Cased Grant V57 1941. The Henry W. and Albert A. Berg Collection of English and American Literature, The New York Public Library, Astor, Lenox and Tilden Foundations.
44. Ibid.
45. Ibid.
46. Ibid.
47. Matthew 9:36.
48. Goodman, 'Advance-Guard Writing', p. 376.

49. Ibid. pp. 375–6.
50. Ibid. p. 376.
51. Lytton Strachey, *Letters of Lytton Strachey*, ed. Paul Levy (London: Viking, 2005), p. 594.
52. Mark Doty, *Still Life with Oysters and Lemon* (Boston: Beacon Press, 2001), p. 4.
53. Roche, *Vessel of Dishonor*, p. 68.
54. Grant, 'The Story of Narcissus'.
55. Algernon Charles Swinburne, 'Hymn to Proserpine', in *Poems and Ballads & Atalanta in Calydon*, ed. Kenneth Haynes (London: Penguin, 2000), p. 57, l. 35.
56. *John* 10:3.

6

Cold Intimacy: Compassion, Precarity and Violence in Nathanael West's *Miss Lonelyhearts*

Elsa Högberg

Nathanael West's 1933 novella *Miss Lonelyhearts* depicts with trenchant brutality the close and mutually sustaining relationship between vulnerability and violence in capitalist modernity. The text critically features the advice column as one central site, in Depression-era United States, for the production of sympathetic and moral images of a resilient people. Such images served political projects from communism to the New Deal to racist conservatism, but West's novella shows how they ultimately worked to depoliticise a ubiquitous precarity caused by capitalism. While West did not explicitly write his radical leftist convictions into his satirical fiction, *Miss Lonelyhearts*, published in the darkest year of the Great Depression, arguably stages a conflict between conspicuously absent yet massively needed political responses to poverty and precarity (such responses would only materialise a few years later with the New Deal) and an intra-textual world whose 'superrealist' absurdity[1] revolves around the compassionate, male advice columnist Miss Lonelyhearts being held ethically responsible for alleviating the material causes of his correspondents' acute vulnerability: 'Are you in trouble? – Do-you-need-advice? – Write-to-Miss-Lonelyhearts-and-she-will-help-you.'[2]

The letters persistently reveal an exacerbation of physical and mental suffering by social precarity and a blatant lack of educational, medical and economic support structures, all of which becomes unbearable for the columnist, who, on meeting a presumably tubercular man in a scene to which we shall return,

> felt as he had felt years before, when he had accidentally stepped on a small frog. Its spilled guts had filled him with pity, *but when its suffering had become real to his senses, his pity had turned to rage* and he had beaten it frantically until it was dead [. . .] he took [the old man's] arm and twisted

it [...] He was twisting the arm of Desperate, Broken-hearted, Sick-of-it-all, Disillusioned-with-tubercular-husband.[3]

How are we to understand the violent disgust, and disgusted violence, triggered throughout the novella by compassionate encounters with vulnerability? As a manifestation of uneasy slapstick comedy breaking with a fundamental convention of burlesque humour: that the staged pain and suffering remain unreal?[4] Or as an instance of the 'fascist' humour of which the anti-fascist West claimed to have been accused by the literary left?[5] The scene above certainly strikes a chilling resonance with the far right's mobilisation of violent repulsion directed at vulnerable individuals and groups in the wake of the ongoing financial crisis and continuing dismantling of state welfare. Despite, or rather because of, its explosive violence (modelled on the comic strip form and the burlesque stage) and West's notion that the American novel of the 1930s cannot be psychological or allow 'emotional description' if it is to capture the pervasive violence of that era,[6] *Miss Lonelyhearts* sketches an incisive psychology of the swift turns between compassion and disgust, care and aggression in a society where moral responsibility replaces political measures to prevent precarity and the exposure to violence it entails. In this, it lucidly depicts the affective dimensions of an enduring predicament: a clash between structural vulnerability requiring political intervention, and vulnerability perceived as a problem for ethics rather than politics.

I propose, in this chapter, that the text's frequently violent refusal of compassion as a response to vulnerability marks a conflict between twentieth- and twenty-first-century capitalism's use of such humanising, ethical emotions precisely to prevent (class) conflict and socio-economic equality, and a diegetic political vacuum that makes the novella's anti-capitalist politics all the more forceful. Paradoxically perhaps, given that violent disgust and disgusted violence tend to be expressed and exercised primarily by the (far) right,[7] I shall locate West's leftist textual politics in the moments where negative emotions triggering repulsion clash violently with positive emotions sustaining desire, attraction and love – that is, the realm of intimacy. The novella's foreclosure of intimacy – with oneself (as in the capacity to feel and communicate a spectrum of affective states) and with others (from erotic love to Christian *agape*) – amounts to far more than the alienation Cold War critics ascribed to West's presumed humanist diagnosis of a vaguely defined modern condition;[8] a powerful historicist critical lineage of the 1990s politicised this diagnosis, rightly viewing it as central to West's anti-capitalist, avant-garde aesthetic.[9] More recently, Seth Moglen has described literary expressions of a crisis of intimacy, and the capacity to love in particular, as a 'wound' inflicted by early twentieth-century capitalism, and manifest in

American modernism through political aesthetic practices variously mournful and melancholic.[10] However, while Moglen mentions West only glancingly in this context,[11] we would do well to re-examine West's treatment of affect *and* intimacy in *Miss Lonelyhearts* (the intimacies created as well as foreclosed) from a political angle.

In *The Great Depression and the Culture of Abundance* (1995), Rita Barnard reads *Miss Lonelyhearts* as a Benjaminian tale of the intimate bonds lost in capitalist modernity, where West's protagonist embodies 'the agonies of the agony columnist who has no counsel for his confused readers'.[12] However, Barnard also offers an intriguing counter-perspective, briefly considering West's ironic treatment of the 1930s advice column and the comic strip ad (both expressive forms shaped the novel) as key loci for new, mass-mediated forms of intimacy.[13] By imitating the intimate speech of the 'heart-to-heart' exchange, the advice column soared in popularity during the Depression through a strategy shared with the advertisement industry: the friendly provision of solace and easy, commercialised solutions to intimate matters relating to material as well as emotional precarity. As Barnard notes, 'copywriters did not hesitate to insert the solutions offered by their products into emotional situations only slightly less violent and embarrassing than those described by [Miss Lonelyhearts'] desperate clients'.[14] And West's response to this capitalist production of intimacy? It is, Barnard intimates, to be found in his revolutionary poem 'Burn the Cities', published in the same year as *Miss Lonelyhearts*, in which Karl Marx '"performs" the very trick Miss Lonelyhearts could never pull off: [...] giving the masses not the "stones" that [his editor] Shrike always urges him to deliver in his column, but bread'.[15]

While Barnard's alignment of *Miss Lonelyhearts* with West's communist poem remains controversial, her intimation that the novella's leftist politics was sparked, at least partly, by his reaction against capitalist intimacy remains compelling. In this chapter, I take up this vital but unfinished inquiry by reading West through the perspective of politicised twenty-first-century accounts of the ways in which different structures of intimacy and affect work to either maintain or resist the violence and vulnerability caused by capitalism. Specifically, I engage sociologist Eva Illouz's claim that since the emergence of therapeutic culture and the American advice industry in the inter-war years, capitalism has thrived on the 'cold intimacies' sustaining it – the intimacies, notably, stemming from emotional expression received with empathy and care in the therapeutic encounter.[16] I also take on board Lauren Berlant's theory of cruel optimism: optimistic desires and attachments nourishing fantasies of 'the good life' of 'job security, political and social equality, and lively, durable intimacy', fantasies that have become increasingly impossible with the past decades' withdrawal of social democracy.[17] Optimistic attachments are cruel, Berlant explains, when the object of desire is an obstacle to flourishing and a liveable life, so that adjustment to crisis, frequently in the form of violence and socio-economic precarity, becomes ordinary. We shall see how the 'systemic crisis or "crisis ordinariness"'[18] inscribed in the optimistic faith (shared by Miss Lonelyhearts and his correspondents) in therapeutic advice as a preventive to material precarity makes Berlant's work as relevant for Depression-era United States as for our present. West's novella may just be most politically forceful in moments when intimacy and optimism are revealed to be blatantly cold and cruel, in scenes where cold intimacy and cruel optimism are resisted through cold affective repulsion and cruel acts or fantasies of violence.

I will unpack this admittedly provocative claim by turning for an instant from intimacy to affect. The emotions that West's columnist strains with increasing compulsion to feel for his suffering correspondents are, variously, pity, sympathy and compassion, of which a culminating expression is Christian *agape* in the injunction 'to love the whole world with an all-embracing love'. On this injunction, Miss Lonelyhearts plainly reflects: 'It was excellent advice. If he followed it, he would be a big success. His column would be syndicated and the whole world would learn to love.'[19] It is no historical coincidence that Miss Lonelyhearts refers to his enterprise as 'the Christ business'.[20] As West's biographer Jay Martin observes, *Miss Lonelyhearts* satirises the flourishing of Christianity as a business ethos in the 1930s and the ways in which, in a time of staggering material insecurity, 'religion had become either a guide to business success or the consolation for missing it'.[21] What has yet to be fully appreciated, however, is West's exacting exposure of all-inclusive love as capitalism's fuel, and his novella's violent refusal of love and compassion as feelings stimulating cold intimacy and cruel optimism. Berlant's trenchant observation that 'projects of compassionate recognition have enabled a habit of political obfuscation of the differences between emotional and material (legal, economic, and institutional) kinds of social reciprocity'[22] could have been West's. Reflecting on her edited volume *Compassion*, Berlant notes that in this book's archive,

> scenes of vulnerability produce a desire to withhold compassionate attachment, to be irritated by the scene of suffering in some way. Repeatedly, we witness [...] an aversion to a moral claim on the spectator to engage [...] I thought about calling this volume *Coldness and Cruelty* [...] What if it turns out that compassion and coldness are not opposite at all but two sides of a bargain that the subjects of modernity have struck with structural inequality?[23]

This last question, too, could have been West's. *Miss Lonelyhearts* repeatedly stages scenes where the moral claim on the privileged spectator to respond compassionately to suffering triggers precisely irritation and aversion, scenes where such 'ugly feelings', in Sianne Ngai's sense of the term, appear to erupt when ethical and private compassion is revealed to be not only a deficient response to structural vulnerability, but 'part of the practice of [social] injustice'.[24]

Among the contributors to Berlant's volume, Marjorie Garber and Lee Edelman offer illuminating perspectives on West's insight that compassionate love, Christian as well as erotic, is 'all-embracing' because it sustains an unequal distribution of material privilege (Garber) and because it is impossible to imagine a community that would *not* be founded, compulsively, on loving compassion (Edelman).[25] The novella's anti-capitalist politics arguably crystallises as Miss Lonelyhearts becomes 'one who refuses compassion's compulsion as if he had taken to heart [...] the doctrine of "just say no"'.[26] When West's protagonist says 'no' to compulsive compassion, this refusal takes the form of violent aggression towards others whom he strains to love (his sweetheart Betty; his correspondents). Moreover, his aggression erupts when he can no longer master negative feelings such as irritation and disgust – affects seemingly triggered by these others' vulnerability – by compulsively transforming them into the positive feeling of love. Before turning to these scenes of explosive violence, I want to home in on an episode foregrounding this inner struggle, but where love momentarily prevails: Miss Lonelyhearts' first, intimate encounter with the physically disabled worker Peter Doyle. In the novella's final scene, West casts compassionate, all-embracing *agape* as absurd by having Doyle visit the delirious Miss Lonelyhearts not to return his embrace, but to shoot him:

> Doyle was carrying something wrapped in a newspaper [...] He shouted some kind of warning, but Miss Lonelyhearts continued his charge. He did not understand the cripple's shout and heard it as a cry for help from Desperate [...] Broad-shoulders, Sick-of-it-all, Disillusioned-with-tubercular-husband. He was running to succor them with love [...] the gun inside the package exploded and Miss Lonelyhearts fell, dragging the cripple with him. They both rolled part of the way down the stairs.[27]

Here it is Doyle who 'just say[s] no', but the novella's violent ending reads as a direct outcome of their first meeting and the strained intimacy of that episode, 'Miss Lonelyhearts and the Cripple'. The involuntary embrace closing the novella creates a morbid echo of that encounter, which ends with Miss Lonelyhearts unwillingly holding Doyle's hand.

At the speakeasy Delehanty's, the columnist is introduced to a man who has sought him out to hand over a letter in person. As soon as the two are left alone, a bond of compassion is forged between them:

> Miss Lonelyhearts was still smiling, but the character of his smile had changed. It had become full of sympathy and a little sad.
> The new smile was for Doyle and he knew it. He smiled back gratefully [. . .] They sat staring at each other until the strain of wordless communication began to excite them both. Doyle made vague, needless adjustments to his clothing. Miss Lonelyhearts found it very difficult to keep his smile steady.[28]

The columnist's sympathy emerges as an emotion compulsively assumed to overcome what seems like an initial feeling of disgust on seeing the vulnerability of the approaching stranger: 'He used a cane and dragged one of his feet behind him [. . .] As he hobbled along, he made many waste motions, like those of a partially destroyed insect.'[29] But the strain of the compassionate bond is broken by a verbal outpouring in which 'Doyle was making no attempt to be understood. He was giving birth to [. . .] a jumble of the retorts he had meant to make when insulted and the private curses against fate that experience had taught him to swallow.'[30]

Doyle's word flow recalls the catharsis or relief of pure communication that Illouz theorises as a fundamental principle of an emergent interwar therapeutic culture in which the advice industry played a central part.[31] Illouz traces the origin of 'emotional capitalism' – a persistent 'culture in which emotional and economic discourses and practices mutually shape each other'[32] – to the widespread use, by the 1920s American corporation, of clinical psychologists who would listen empathetically to and thereby validate the workers' emotions, no matter what was said. The aim of such listening was 'eliciting uncensored speech and emotions and [. . .] building trust'.[33] I suspect Illouz uses the adjective 'cold' about these intimate sessions because they were designed to reduce legitimate anger and prevent labour unrest about deficient work conditions in order to maximise productivity and profit.[34] When Doyle eventually hands his letter to Miss Lonelyhearts, it turns out that his grievances are about his low pay and excruciating physical pain as an inspector of gas meters. And when West makes Miss Lonelyhearts first listen to, then read Doyle's emotionally charged words, he brings together two major sites of cold intimacy: the advice column and one-to-one therapeutic encounters such as that between worker and the psychologist hired to ensure the smooth running of the corporation, in which a semblance of equality – or, rather, the substitution of socio-economic equality for emotional reciprocity – would pacify averse emotions and thereby preclude class conflict.[35]

This dynamic becomes fully apparent when Miss Lonelyhearts is given Doyle's letter to read. Therapeutic cold intimacy merges here with compassion as a moral feeling that, as in Garber's scrutiny of compassion's ethical and political work, operates to keep the needy sufferer and the privileged observer in their socially assigned places:[36]

> *Dear Miss Lonelyhearts [. . .] I am a cripple 41 yrs of age which I have been all my life and I have never let myself get blue until lately when I have been feeling lousy all the time on account of not getting anywhere and asking myself what is it all for. You have a education so I figured may be you no. What I want to no is why I go around pulling my leg up and down stairs reading meters for the gas company for a stinking $22.50 per while the bosses ride around in swell cars living off the fat of the land. Don't think I am a greasy red. I read where they shoot cripples in Russia because they cant work but I can work better than any park bum and support a wife and child to [. . .] It aint the job that I am complaining about but what I want to no is what is the whole stinking business for [. . .] Please write me an answer [. . .] Yours truly, Peter Doyle*
>
> While Miss Lonelyhearts was puzzling out the crabbed writing, Doyle's damp hand accidentally touched his under the table. He jerked away, but then drove his hand back and forced it to clasp the cripple's. After finishing the letter, he did not let go, but pressed it firmly with all the love he could manage. At first the cripple covered his embarrassment by disguising the meaning of the clasp with a handshake, but he soon gave in and they sat silently hand in hand.[37]

This is a striking exposition of the capacity of intimacy – broadly conceived as the realm of desire, attraction and attachment – and compassionate love to create a fantasy of equality; diagetically, physical proximity and affective reciprocity as expressed by the two men holding hands, a gesture affirming the seeking and giving of compassion, emerge here as a satisfying resolution to a problem of socio-economic inequality at the same time as they soothe and pacify a political anger quickly suppressed.

West's reader, however, must resist this lure of compassion, love and intimacy. In exaggerating the letter writer's illiteracy, something he appears to have done repeatedly in his literary transformation of the actual letters for the 'Susan Chester' advice column that spurred him to write the novella,[38] West creates a darkly comic effect ('*I am a cripple 41 yrs of age which I have been all my life*') that distances the reader from Doyle's earnest, deferential faith in Miss Lonelyhearts' answer as a satisfying solution to his problem. For all his protesting ('*Don't think I am a greasy red*'), Doyle's anger about staggering social inequality is plain to West's reader, not least in the telling, repeated rendering of 'know' as 'no': '*It aint the job that I am complaining about but what I want to no is what is the whole stinking business for.*' Doyle allegedly wants not better pay and more humane working conditions, but the columnist/therapist's answer to an existential problem that, once resolved, would restore meaning and happiness to his life; he also desires intimacy with his therapist. This is an instance of cruel optimism as defined by Berlant, who sees 'the subordinated sensorium of the worker' as 'an effect of the relation between capitalism's refusal of futurity in an overwhelmingly productive present and the normative promise of intimacy', this promise being the compelling idea that 'looking longingly at someone who might, after all, show compassion for our struggles, is really where living takes place'.[39] The logic by which Doyle's imagined way to a liveable life goes not through class struggle and an egalitarian, political redistribution of resources, but through intimacy with an advice columnist displays an optimism that is cruel because the objects of desire and attachment – therapeutic advice and the therapist himself – perpetuate the capitalist system that is the root and cause of his suffering. This is plain for West's reader to see each time Doyle's '*know*' becomes '*no*' ('*what I want to no*'): it is as if the residue of averse, 'ugly' feelings in his 'crabbed writing' explodes into a protest – '*no!*' – with each deferential address of his want to the columnist. '*No!*' to '*the whole stinking business*' of wearing body and soul down for lousy pay and then expecting *intimacy* (the superior knowledge about your predicament provided by the therapist who holds your hand[40]) to make you happy again. As in Ngai's formulation about 'disgust's unambiguous "No!" to its object',[41] the repulsion that clashes with cold intimacy in this episode appears to be mutual; it surfaces as much in Doyle's political '*no*' as in Miss Lonelyhearts' instinct to withdraw his hand when the other man reaches for it.

It needs to be said that West's penetrating insights into cruel optimism and cold intimacy made him explore, not dismiss, their affective foundations. As Martin points out, West's deeply felt compassion for the writers of the letters on which the fictional letters are based was a source of inspiration that came to decisively shape his artistic development and *Miss Lonelyhearts*.[42] Martin implies that this compassion prompted West's aesthetic intensification of the correspondents' pain and suffering in his fictional letters.[43] For Jonathan Veitch, West makes 'the sentimental clichés of American culture – home, marriage, and true love' – replace class consciousness as his correspondents' imagined remedy for their pain, thereby showing how these clichés 'create the suffering they are supposed to answer'.[44] We could add that the letters betray 'the kinds of unraveled life to which *Cruel Optimism* points: impasses in zones of intimacy that hold out the often cruel promise of reciprocity and belonging'.[45] Berlant's inquiry into intimacy as a desired way to flourishing in the absence of a welfare state is immediately relevant for West's novella. His letter writers' desire for love and a thriving home is matched by a shared faith in the mutual benefits of intimacy between columnist and correspondents, in which fellow feeling – the giving and receiving of compassion – is imagined as a sustaining answer to problems of emotional and material precarity. At every turn, such faithful attachments emerge as obstacles to a good life, and indeed as 'instruments of suffering'.[46] Nowhere is this clearer than in the letter signed 'Broad Shoulders' – the most horrifying of these testimonies to Depression-era 'crisis ordinariness', that is, *systemic* crisis as a series of traumatic, yet ordinary events that engender strategies of resilient adjustment to precarious living conditions.[47] This correspondent relates in painstaking detail her efforts *'to be mother and housekeeper and wage earner etc'* in the midst of a life shattered by her abusive husband's subjection of his family to poverty and psychic trauma, and writes towards the end:

> *Every woman is intitiled to a home isnt she? So Miss Lonelyhearts please put a few lines in your column when you refer to this letter so I will know you are helping me. Shall I take my husband back? How can I support my children?*[48]

In thus politicising intimacy and compassion, West's novella complicates a persistent privileging of sincerity – a kind of sincerity bias – manifest in the idea that faithful literary transcriptions of the human voice and authentic affects form a precondition for ethical and political writing. This idea, which informed the documentary turn serving various political causes during the Depression,[49] has gained momentum with this century's focus on affect and ethics in literary and modernist studies. For Jonathan Greenberg, who perpetuates a tension manifest in West's own reflections on his writing, *Miss Lonelyhearts* and *The Day of the Locust* oscillate between an inhuman, anti-sentimental satire insensitive to suffering and socio-economic injustice (the realm of an apolitical and amoral aesthetic, manifest in Shrike's laughter), and literary expressions of genuine feeling – compassionate and sympathetic responses to suffering in particular – as the privileged locus for ethico-political commitment.[50] Justus Nieland, however, argues that *Miss Lonelyhearts* resists the protagonist's (compassionate) 'desire to feel the pain of his mass readership', and provocatively casts Shrike's dismantling of this desire as a model for 'an ethical publicness on the other site of sentimentalism'.[51] Both critics diverge from a Cold War tradition of reading West's comedy as humanist and humanising but not political, as springing from his sincere compassion and moral compass; this casting of West's fiction as moral and compassionate but apolitical was clearly part of a wider effort to depoliticise American modernism.[52] However, neither parses the affect of compassion or examines West's grappling with its ethical and political complexities. In either perpetuating (Greenberg) or resisting (Nieland) the sincerity bias, these influential scholars leave the following questions largely unaddressed: if West was driven by compassion in his aesthetic heightening of pain and suffering – his stylistic transformation of the original letters to make their affects and sensations appear *more* real or genuine – how do we account for the many scenes in the novella where intense suffering and the vulnerability it exposes trigger not compassion but repulsion in the more privileged observer? With regard to West's uncertain place as a leftist writer in relation to Mike Gold and other communists, does not his defiance of their realist bias through his own 'superrealism' foreground socio-economic precarity (manifest as illiteracy and bodies whose pain is exacerbated by this precarity) in ways that problematise the ethical aims of compassion as well as its political uses and limits?

One key to these questions is no doubt the absurd contrasts West creates between his correspondents' material predicaments and their optimistic faith in the solutions of cold intimacy, contrasts veiled in the original letters' comparably polite expression. In highlighting the absurdity of cruel optimism (*'please put a few lines in your column when you refer to this letter so I will know you are helping me'*), West also shows with cutting clarity how capitalist intimacies make the ethical telos of compassion difficult to realise because they overburden the compassionate individual. That is to say, Miss Lonelyhearts probes deeply the ways in which 'compassion measures one's value (or one's government's value) in terms of the demonstrated capacity [...] to embrace a sense of obligation [...] to become involved in a story of rescue or amelioration', and shows how, in the absence of a government committed to social justice, 'the aesthetics of compassion [...] opens a hornet's nest of problems about what responses should be desired and when private responses are not only insufficient but a part of the practice of injustice'.[53] The overwhelming weight of the columnist's ethical mission is signalled from the first page in the desperate, silent cry inserted into Shrike's formulaic mock prayer – 'Help me, miss L, help me, help me.'[54] Reverberating throughout the letters, this cry disrupts Miss Lonelyhearts' initially light task:

> A man is hired to give advice to the readers of a newspaper. The job is a circulation stunt and the whole staff considers it a joke [...] but after several months at it, the joke begins to escape him. He sees that the majority of the letters are profoundly humble pleas for moral and spiritual advice, that they are inarticulate expressions of genuine suffering [...] For the first time in his life, he is forced to examine the values by which he lives.[55]

Through the text's many-layered satirical mediations, the letter writers' suffering emerges as an unanswered ethical demand. Reading West, we are compelled to face vulnerability as a socio-economic rather than merely existential or ontological condition, and to ask whether the creation of a caring society is primarily an ethical or political responsibility. In this regard, the most striking target of West's dark satire is not the letters' sincerity or Miss Lonelyhearts' messianic task of providing relief, but, rather, the absurdist Depression era reality in which the advice columnist becomes morally responsible for mitigating the socio-economic causes of the letter writers' extreme vulnerability: 'Are you in trouble? – Do-you-need-advice? – Write-to-Miss-Lonelyhearts-and-she-will-help-you'; '*Shall I take my husband back? How can I support my children?*'[56]

The absurd discrepancy between the correspondents' cry of suffering and the complete inadequacy of Miss Lonelyhearts' strained compassion and moral advice as responses to this cry makes the novella 'superrealist' in the sense of a specifically American 'excessive realism'.[57] This conflict also shapes its politics, and complicates Nieland's claim that West dismisses sympathetic identification with suffering through an anti-humanist ethics. Compassion is repeatedly refused or blocked in *Miss Lonelyhearts*, though arguably for political reasons. We have seen how physical repulsion becomes a form of affective resistance to the capitalist operations of cruel optimism and cold intimacy, but why does the ethical mission to relieve vulnerability repeatedly trigger aversion and aggression in the columnist? What do such reactions say about the political limits of compassion, love and intimacy, and about vulnerable-making capitalism? Ngai's theory of ugly feelings may help illuminate these questions. Among the affects Ngai is mapping, irritation and disgust erupt persistently as Miss Lonelyhearts faces acute vulnerability and its moral claim on him.[58] When he can no longer turn these negative feelings into positive affects such as compassionate love (as he barely managed in the first encounter with Peter Doyle), they fuel his violent aggression towards – what exactly? Manifestations of vulnerability as such, a vulnerable individual, or the countless vulnerable individuals that person comes to represent? As we shall note next, these all appear to be objects of (the columnist's) violent disgust, but there are others too, which arguably shape the novella's leftist orientation. In particular, West targets as objects of aversion – an aversion instilled in his reader – the moral burden of compassion placed on the individual in a society where the advice industry substitutes for political measures to prevent socio-economic precarity, as well as the ethical and political betrayal inflicted by such business ventures.

If compassion and love can work to eliminate class conflict and an egalitarian redistribution of resources through cold intimacy's pretence of equality, then the ugly feelings in West's novella prove central to its leftist politics because they disrupt the positive affects sustaining capitalist intimacies. Ngai observes that literature, criticism and theory tend to favour desire and attraction while often overlooking the critical and political potential of disgust and repulsion. The all-inclusive language of desire, she argues, is coextensive with the language of capitalism and with ethical theories privileging positive feelings such as sympathy and compassion. But disgust blocks these hegemonic languages along with their affects and ethical claims.[59] With regard to West, Miss Lonelyhearts' revolted and violent reactions to vulnerability and suffering emerge as futile attempts to renounce his compassionate enterprise; these reactions are not unlike the columnist's unsuccessful attempt to get fired by recommending suicide to his readers (Shrike's response: 'Remember, please, that your job is to increase the circulation of our paper. Suicide [...] must defeat this purpose'[60]). Throughout the novella, such acts and their attendant affects highlight the futility marking any effort to resist the capitalist order of positive feelings. In this, they illustrate strikingly Ngai's observation that ugly feelings frequently index suspended agency and political inaction within a literary text, but also the powerlessness of literature itself to disrupt the workings of capitalism. While such emotions can be mobilised by the right as they can by the left, they are critically productive, Ngai argues, because of their exceptional diagnostic capacity. Unlike 'morally beatific states like sympathy', ugly feelings are '*a*moral and *non*cathartic, offering no satisfactions of virtue [...] nor any therapeutic or purifying release'.[61] These feelings are also 'organized by trajectories of repulsion rather than attraction, by phobic strivings "away from" rather than philic strivings "toward"'.[62] In this, ugly feelings, and particularly disgust, defy the intimate manifestations of desire[63] and, we could add, the 'philic strivings "toward"' that structure love and compassion.

In 'Miss Lonelyhearts and Mrs. Shrike', West's columnist perceives his heart as 'a congealed lump of icy fat' when taking Shrike's wife for a date at a South American restaurant, and enduring 'irritation [...] too profound for him to soothe' marks an affective revulsion vis-à-vis the Depression-era 'business of dreams' disseminated by mass culture which West politicised, as Barnard has shown.[64] If *Miss Lonelyhearts* explores how the hugely popular, commercialist advice column claimed to offer real ways out of violence and precarity,[65] a key to the protagonist's irritation here is given later, in the episode where he observes the crowds in the Bronx slums:

> he was overwhelmed by the desire to help them, and because this desire was sincere, he was happy despite the feeling of guilt which accompanied it.
> He saw a man who appeared on the verge of death stagger into a movie theater that was showing a picture called *Blonde Beauty*. He saw a

ragged woman with an enormous goiter pick a love story magazine out of a garbage can and seem very excited by her find [...]

Men have always fought their misery with dreams. Although dreams were once powerful, they have been made puerile by the movies, radio and newspapers. Among many betrayals, this one is the worst.

The thing that made his share in it particularly bad was that he was capable of dreaming the Christ dream. He felt that he had failed at it.[66]

The columnist's guilt seems to stem from his part in fuelling his correspondents' cruel optimism, but also from an ethical betrayal manifest in the knowledge that his compassionate 'desire to help them' – 'dreaming the Christ dream' – cannot lead them out of precarity any more than a love story magazine. The passage, like each of the letters he receives, prompts the following questions about compassion's moral task:

When we want to rescue X, are we thinking of rescuing everyone like X [...]? When a multitude is symbolized by an individual case, how can we keep from being overwhelmed by the necessary scale that an ethical response would take?[67]

Contra Nieland's notion of 'the letters' ontological ambiguity (are they material manifestations of singular ills or codified abstractions of universal suffering?)',[68] we could read them as plain manifestations of what Berlant terms 'crisis ordinariness': the staggering ordinariness of crisis fuelled by socio-economic precarity during the Depression. Such a reading may help explain why West's protagonist responds to his impossible ethical mission with irritation that entails cold renunciation of love; indeed, this ugly feeling erupts persistently when he feels '*overwhelmed* by the desire to help' (my emphasis).

On returning from the country via the Bronx slums to his office, Miss Lonelyhearts finds the long letter from 'Broad Shoulders' waiting on his desk: 'he picked up a bulky letter in a dirty envelope. He read it for the same reason that an animal tears at a wounded foot: to hurt the pain.'[69] Far from the commodity suggested by the columnist's initial idea of the letters as 'stamped from the dough of suffering with a heart-shaped cookie knife',[70] this letter appears to be swelling like a monstrous dough threatening to rip open the skin of the grimy envelope containing it (and by which the letter could be categorised simply by its envelope-skin, as betraying the grime of poverty), while the reading of it is likened to scratching open a wound in Miss Lonelyhearts' skin. The image of tearing at a wound suggests irritation as defined by Ngai: 'a conspicuously weak or inadequate form of anger [...] an affect that bears an unusually close relationship to the body's surfaces or skin' and to 'soreness, rawness, inflammation, or chafing'.[71] Back in his office reading letters, the columnist's irritation slides into nausea.[72] This also happens during the date with Mary Shrike, who soon after the following remark begins reiterating how her mother died from breast cancer in terrible pain made worse by an abusive husband: "'Every one wants to be gay – unless they're sick". Was he sick? In a great cold wave, the readers of his column crashed over the music, over the bright shawls and picturesque waiters, over her shining body.'[73] To avoid literally being sick, Miss Lonelyhearts compulsively tries to arouse them both and thereby 'bring his great understanding heart into action again'.[74] 'Listen to me', says Mary Shrike, 'We can't stop talking. We must talk', whereupon she frantically retells her mother's story while he kisses her body and tears open her dress.[75] Here again, West deploys his absurdist 'superrealism' to political ends, exposing capitalism's chillingly real joining of compassion and erotic desire as fuel on which cruel optimism thrives. There is resonance here with Barnard's and Illouz's inquiry into capitalist intimacy, and an echo of William Shrike's ironic remark: 'I adore heart-to-heart talks [...] It's better to make a clean breast of matters than to let them fester in the depths of one's soul.'[76] But in *Miss Lonelyhearts*, the festering wound of irritation keeps the 'matters' of material and experienced precarity festering, thereby preventing their superficial resolution in the communicative contract of cold intimacy.

In the two episodes preceding 'Miss Lonelyhearts and Mrs. Shrike', it seems to be manifestations of vulnerability that spur not only irritation ('Miss Lonelyhearts and the Fat Thumb') and disgust ('Miss Lonelyhearts and the Clean Old Man'), but also their culmination in violent aggression. These two scenes chart an escalating breakdown of intimacy, where Miss Lonelyhearts' aggressiveness infuses the reader with a repulsion directed at least partly at the columnist's compulsive compassion. In the first episode, the protagonist's growing irritation with his girlfriend Betty is triggered by her happy exemption from compassion's moral compulsion: "'I've got a Christ complex [...] All the broken bastards ..." He finished with a short laugh that was like a bark.'[77] This unsettles Betty's serenity,

> But his anger was not appeased. 'What's the matter, sweet-heart?' he asked, patting her shoulder threateningly [...] Instead of answering, she raised her arm as though to ward off a blow. She was like a kitten whose soft helplessness makes one ache to hurt it.[78]

In the next scene, on his way to Delehanty's, the columnist 'felt as though his heart were a bomb, a complicated bomb that would result in a simple explosion, wrecking the world'.⁷⁹ But rather than exploding in cathartic, anarchist anger (one of the politically effective affects that Ngai opposes to ugly feelings), 'Miss Lonelyhearts' anger grew cold and sodden like the snow' on leaving the speakeasy with a friend.⁸⁰ They find a man with effeminate manners seeking shelter from the cold:

> 'If you can't get a woman, get a clean old man', Gates sang.
> The old man looked as if he were going to cry, but suddenly laughed instead. A terrible cough started under his laugh, and catching at the bottom of his lungs, it ripped into his throat. He turned away to wipe his mouth. [. . .]
> The snow had stopped falling and it had grown very cold. The old man did not have an overcoat, but said that he found the cold exhilarating.⁸¹

Then follows a scene at a cellar bar where Miss Lonelyhearts and Gates, impersonating sexologists Havelock Ellis and Richard von Krafft-Ebing, try to force the man into an intimate and therapeutic exchange:

> 'When did you first discover homosexualistic tendencies in yourself?' [. . .]
> 'How dare you . . .' He gave a little scream of indignation.
> 'Now, now', Miss Lonelyhearts said, 'he didn't mean to insult you. Scientists have terribly bad manners . . . But you are a pervert, aren't you?'
> The old man raised his cane to strike him. Gates grabbed it from behind and wrenched it out of his hand. He began to cough violently and held his black satin tie to his mouth. Still coughing he dragged himself to a chair in the back of a room.
> Miss Lonelyhearts felt as he had felt years before, when he had accidentally stepped on a small frog. Its spilled guts had filled him with pity, but when its suffering had become real to his senses, his pity had turned to rage and he had beaten it frantically until it was dead.
> 'I'll get the bastard's life story', he shouted, and started after him [. . .]
> Miss Lonelyhearts put his arm around the old man. 'Tell us the story of your life', he said, loading his voice with sympathy [. . .] 'Tell it, damn you, tell it'.
> When the old man still remained silent, he took his arm and twisted it. Gates tried to tear him away, but he refused to let go. He was twisting the arm of all the sick and miserable, broken and betrayed, inarticulate and impotent. He was twisting the arm of Desperate, Broken-hearted, Sick-of-it-all, Disillusioned-with-tubercular-husband.
> The old man began to scream. Somebody hit Miss Lonelyhearts from behind with a chair.⁸²

If we follow Edelman's theory of compassion's compulsion, this sequence brings out the sadism and disavowed callousness underlying the fantasy of loving compassion as a humanising, ethical feeling, and gestures towards violent 'malignant *jouissance*' as the privileged observer's primordial response to another's vulnerability and suffering.[83] By such a reading, Miss Lonelyhearts would embody the queer figure of the *sinthom*-osexual; one who substitutes the intimacies of love, desire and compassion with 'access to their surplus of *jouissance*'.[84] But it is on this figure that the reading of West with Edelman founders; despite the explosive, comic strip violence ending the episode, such violence is never cathartic in West's novella, nor does it provide the erotic, sadistic *jouissance* that Edelman's *sinthom*-osexual experiences in making another's pain worse. The non-cathartic, ugly feelings of irritation and disgust persist, and block the protagonist's access to any erotic pleasure. In this, they stubbornly oppose the capacity of positive affects to be 'all-embracing' and hence to absorb resistance to a capitalist order sustained by cold intimacy.

Ultimately, what West and his columnist take seriously but Edelman's *sinthom*-osexual scorns is compassion's ethical claim on the individual to relieve the suffering they witness, and one object of disgust in the 'Clean Old Man' episode is arguably cold intimacy's intensification of vulnerability already exacerbated by socio-economic precarity, and which compassion utterly fails to mitigate. His 'Christ complex' merging with the 'Christ business' of the advice column, Miss Lonelyhearts must inflict and aggravate suffering, as these scenes reveal. The columnist's aversion and ensuing aggression seem directed not only at the old man's effeminacy and sickening cough (the latter made worse by precarity), but also at his affective resilience; the way he turns the impulse to cry facing a threat of violence into laughter, and his lack of adequate clothing into the positive feeling of exhilaration. Such resilience is also what makes therapeutic cold intimacy possible, and Miss Lonelyhearts appears to sense his complicity with capitalism's affective-political regime of resilience, here an object of his loathing, when he forces the man into a distorted session where the therapist's physical violence against one man becomes systemic violence against a multitude lacking the material means for subsistence. As we shudder at the episode's most arresting image, we infer that the man's terrible cough has acted on the protagonist like his correspondents' cry – 'Help me, miss L, help me, help me':

> Miss Lonelyhearts felt as he had felt years before, when he had accidentally stepped on a small frog. Its spilled guts had filled him with pity, but when its suffering had become real to his senses, his pity had turned to rage and he had beaten it frantically until it was dead.[85]

It is only when 'its suffering had become real to his senses' that the frog triggers Miss Lonelyhearts' rage and violence. Could it be that in this moment, pity (a near-synonym for modern (capitalist) compassion as 'an emotion felt *on behalf of another who suffers* [...] from high to low [...] a kind of emotionally gratifying condescension') gives way to compassion in the pre-modern sense, as '*suffering together with one another*'?[86] And might it be this feeling of the frog's suffering that spurs him to kill it, either to expel this unbearable emotion or to relieve the frog from its pain, or both? In prompting such questions, the passage points to a betrayal of compassion's original affective composition and ethical mission, whereby compassion in capitalist modernity is more likely to perpetuate suffering than mitigate it.

Read in correlation with the coughing man who triggers this memory, the figure of the suffering frog condenses the novella's inquiry into the ethics and politics of compassion. West's advice columnist has come to (1) realise his violent complicity with capitalism's exacerbation of vulnerability intensified by socio-economic precarity ('he had accidentally stepped on a small frog'), (2) sense, in moments of 'fellow feeling', that pity is a crushingly inadequate (because private and ethical) response to the acute and widespread suffering this vulnerability entails, and (3) turn increasingly to violence as the only viable way of handling this dilemma. The disgust that is bound to fill most readers of these lines is no doubt directed at this entire sequence (1–3), and not only or even primarily at the frog's 'spilled guts', in response to which the columnist himself reportedly felt only pity (a politically ineffective emotion in the context of anti-capitalist resistance, if we follow Ngai), then a rage that also seems void of critical insight. Miss Lonelyhearts' non-cathartic anger may well exemplify the anti-capitalist melancholia that Moglen detects in American modernism – a melancholia manifesting itself as (self-)destructive aggression that is displaced because the cause (capitalism) of object losses (the lost objects being, for instance, the ability to love and 'stalled emancipatory movements [...] crushed by the Red Scare') remains blocked from consciousness.[87] However, West arguably makes his readers alert to these submerged connections when he mobilises disgust as an ugly feeling, one that furthers a textual politics channelled through the rejection of cold intimacy. While this politics might not consist in imagining a more equitable social order, it nonetheless remains powerful in its diagnostic capacity. Indeed, Ngai's insights into capitalism's 'democratization of averse emotion'[88] raises intriguing questions about the paucity of sustained critical engagements with West's incomparable representations of repulsion. If the recent turn to ethics and affect in West studies has seen a renewed privileging of positive feelings like compassion,[89] it seems fair to speculate that West's novella continues to undergo the fate of objects (notably art and literature) rendered politically harmless by capitalism's 'taming' of disgust that becomes tolerance – this affective transfer Ngai correlates with the ways in which even radical leftist literature tends to be tolerated and absorbed by the capitalist system it critiques, rather than enabling revolt against it.[90]

In contrast, attending to West's problematisation of ugly feelings and cold intimacy, themselves indexing a diegetic absence of political consciousness or commitment, reveals how an anti-capitalist politics nonetheless materialises in *Miss Lonelyhearts*. The most topical and thought-provoking conflict in this novella may not be the frequently observed clash between West's unsentimental, modernist satire and the ethico-political appeal of his earnest depiction of so-called humanising feelings such as sympathy and compassion, but a literary and political opposition, distilled by West but generally obscured in West scholarship, between positive and negative affects as contending sites for resilient versus resistant responses to the forces causing socio-economic precarity and the vulnerability it entails.

Notes

1. On 'superrealism' as an American, political form of surrealism – an 'excessive realism' – see Jonathan Veitch, *American Superrealism: Nathanael West and the Politics of Representation in the 1930s* (Madison: University of Wisconsin Press, 1997), pp. 15–22.
2. Nathanael West, Miss Lonelyhearts and The Day of the Locust (hereafter cited as *ML*) (New York: New Directions, 2009), p. 1.
3. Ibid. pp. 17–18; my emphasis.
4. See Jay Martin, 'Nathanael West's Burlesque Comedy', in Ben Siegel (ed.), *Critical Essays on Nathanael West* (New York: G. K. Hall, 1994), pp. 161, 167; and Justus Nieland, 'West's Deadpan: Affect, Slapstick, and Publicity in *Miss Lonelyhearts*', *NOVEL: A Forum on Fiction*, 38.1 (Autumn 2004), pp. 58, 64–5.
5. Nathanael West, Letter to Edmund Wilson, 6 April 1939, in *Novels and Other Writings*, ed. Sacvan Bercovitch (New York: The Library of America, 1997), p. 793.
6. See Nathanael West, 'Some Notes on Miss L.' (1933), in *Novels*, pp. 401–2; and West, 'Some Notes on Violence' (1932), in *Novels*; quote from 'Some Notes on Violence', p. 399.
7. See Sianne Ngai, *Ugly Feelings* (Cambridge, MA: Harvard University Press, 2005), pp. 338–40.
8. See, for instance, W. H. Auden, 'West's Disease', in Jay Martin (ed.), *Nathanael West: A Collection of Critical Essays* (Englewood Cliffs, NJ: Prentice-Hall, 1971),

pp. 147–53; and Daniel Aaron, 'Late Thoughts on Nathanael West', in Martin (ed.), *Critical Essays*, pp. 161–9.
9. See especially Rita Barnard, *The Great Depression and the Culture of Abundance: Kenneth Fearing, Nathanael West, and Mass Culture in the 1930s* (Cambridge: Cambridge University Press, 1995), pp. 188–213.
10. Seth Moglen, *Mourning Modernity: Literary Modernism and the Injuries of American Capitalism* (Stanford: Stanford University Press, 2007).
11. Ibid. p. 237n10.
12. Barnard, *The Great Depression*, p. 195.
13. Ibid. pp. 202–4.
14. Ibid. pp. 191–2; see pp. 188–204.
15. Ibid. p. 212.
16. Eva Illouz, *Cold Intimacies: The Making of Emotional Capitalism* (Cambridge: Polity Press, 2007).
17. Lauren Berlant, *Cruel Optimism* (Durham, NC: Duke University Press), p. 3.
18. Ibid. p. 10.
19. West, *ML*, p. 8.
20. Ibid. p. 3.
21. Jay Martin, *Nathanael West: The Art of His Life* (London: Secker & Warburg, 1971), p. 181; see pp. 180–1.
22. Berlant, *Cruel Optimism*, p. 182.
23. Lauren Berlant, 'Introduction', in Berlant (ed.), *Compassion: The Culture and Politics of an Emotion* (New York: Routledge, 2004), pp. 9–10.
24. Ibid. p. 9.
25. See Marjorie Garber, 'Compassion', in Berlant (ed.), *Compassion*, pp. 15–27; and Lee Edelman, 'Compassion's Compulsion', in Berlant (ed.), *Compassion*, pp. 159–86.
26. Edelman, 'Compassion's Compulsion', p. 160.
27. West, *ML*, pp. 5–8.
28. Ibid. p. 45.
29. Ibid. p. 44.
30. Ibid. pp. 45–6.
31. See Illouz, *Cold Intimacies*, pp. 5–24.
32. Ibid. p. 5.
33. Ibid. p. 13.
34. These strategic experiments, which remained successful during the late 1920s recession, were premised on the finding that 'productivity increased if work relationships contained care and attention to workers' feelings' (ibid. p. 12; see pp. 10–24).
35. See ibid. pp. 17–18.

36. See Garber, 'Compassion', pp. 20–4.
37. West, *ML*, pp. 46–7.
38. See Martin, *The Art of His Life*, pp. 109–10, 186–7.
39. Berlant, *Cruel Optimism*, p. 189.
40. Cf. 'intimacy, n.', 1.c. 'Closeness of observation, knowledge, or the like', *OED Online*, available at <https://www.oed.com/view/Entry/98503> (accessed 27 September 2020). Illouz stresses the emergent therapists' and advice literature's air of scientific authority and expertise (*Cold Intimacies*, pp. 10–11).
41. Ngai, 'Afterword: On Disgust', in *Ugly Feelings*, p. 350.
42. Martin, *The Art of His Life*, pp. 110, 139, 166.
43. Ibid. p. 187.
44. Veitch, *American Superrealism*, p. 74.
45. Berlant, *Cruel Optimism*, p. 21.
46. Berlant, 'Introduction', p. 5.
47. Berlant, *Cruel Optimism*, p. 10.
48. West, *ML*, pp. 42, 43.
49. See Veitch, *American Superrealism*, pp. 67–9; and Gavin Jones, *American Hungers: The Problem of Poverty in U.S. Literature, 1840–1945* (Princeton: Princeton University Press, 2008), pp. 106–47.
50. Jonathan Greenberg, 'Nathanael West and the Mystery of Feeling', *Modern Fiction Studies*, 52.3 (Autumn 2006), pp. 588–612.
51. Nieland, 'West's Deadpan', pp. 58, 60; see pp. 66–7, 74–7.
52. See, for instance, Norman Podhoretz, 'Nathanael West: A Particular Kind of Joking', in Martin (ed.), *Critical Essays*, pp. 154–60. In his only mention of West, Moglen lists him among American modernists of whom a Cold War 'critical whitewashing often took place as a condition for canonization [. . .] [in] the longstanding critical evasions of the[ir] anticapitalist commitments' (*Mourning Modernity*, p. 237n10).
53. Berlant, 'Introduction', pp. 7, 9.
54. West, *ML*, p. 1.
55. Ibid. p. 32.
56. Ibid. pp. 1, 43.
57. Veitch, *American Superrealism*, p. 15.
58. See Ngai's discussion of West in relation to the affect she names 'stuplimity' (*Ugly Feelings*, pp. 249–50, 252, 254–7).
59. Ngai, 'Afterword', p. 332.
60. West, *ML*, p. 18.
61. Ngai, *Ugly Feelings*, p. 6.
62. Ibid. p. 11.

63. Ngai, 'Afterword'.
64. West, *ML*, pp. 18, 22; Barnard, *The Great Depression*, pp. 166–87.
65. Barnard, *The Great Depression*, pp. 191–2.
66. West, *ML*, p. 39.
67. Berlant, 'Introduction', p. 6.
68. Nieland, 'West's Deadpan', p. 68.
69. West, *ML*, p. 39.
70. Ibid. p. 1.
71. Ngai, *Ugly Feelings*, pp. 35, 21.
72. West, *ML*, p. 39.
73. Ibid. p. 23.
74. Ibid. p. 23.
75. Ibid. p. 24.
76. Ibid. p. 21.
77. Ibid. p. 13.
78. Ibid. p. 13.
79. Ibid. p. 13.
80. Ibid. p. 16.
81. Ibid. p. 16.
82. Ibid. pp. 17–18.
83. See Edelman, 'Compassion's Compulsion'.
84. Ibid. p. 163.
85. West, *ML*, pp. 17–18.
86. Etymology from Garber, 'Compassion', p. 20. See also 'pity, n.', I. 2.b., *OED Online*, available at <https://www.oed.com/view/Entry/144814> (accessed 27 September 2020): 'Tenderness and concern aroused by the suffering, distress, or misfortune of another, and prompting a desire for its relief; compassion, sympathy.'
87. Moglen, *Mourning Modernity*, p. 24; see pp. 3–25.
88. Ngai, 'Afterword', p. 339.
89. See especially Greenberg, 'Nathanael West'; and Stefanie Stiles, 'A Philosophy of Suffering: Redemption, Rorty, and Nathanael West's *Miss Lonelyhearts*', *Interdisciplinary Literary Studies*, 16.2 (2014), pp. 239–64.
90. Ngai, 'Afterword', pp. 333–4, 339–42.

7

'Me you—you—me': Mina Loy and the Art of Ethnographic Intimacy

Sanja Bahun

At an early point in her 1915 (1917, 1923) sequence of poems 'Songs to Joannes'/'Love Songs', Mina Loy complains about 'the casual vulgarity of the merely observant' which reduces observation to 'a clock-work mechanism' and an engagement with time-space-self that lacks profundity and purpose – one to which her lyric subject is both unaccustomed and principally opposed.[1] This complaint forays the reader into what might appear as its exact opposite: a string of poems vividly describing the lyric subject's sexual encounter with a certain excessively rationalistic, 'merely observant' Joannes. Replete with tongue-twisters and cerebral games, and shrouded in images whose explicitness shocked Loy's contemporaries, the poetic sequence doggedly scrutinises acts and processes that necessitate physical intimacy and/or are perceived as too intimate to share with the reader, such as sexual intercourse, orgasm, abortion, and bodily functions like sweating and urination. Inaugurally published in 1915, and in its fuller, thirty-four-part long version in 1917, 'Songs to Joannes' presents itself as an ethnographic report written by a consciously involved anthropologist: a comprehensive and unsentimental look at sexual intimacies, their dynamics, causes and consequences, and the 'souvenir ethics' we cloak them in.[2] It is neither the first nor the last case of such concentration in Loy's poetic opus. Loy is known for hybridising genres into linguistically exuberant poems that navigate the terrain of conflicting emotions, emotional postures and bodily reactions at the site of convergence of the public and the private spheres: sexual interest, empathy, attraction, uncanniness, disgust, contempt, shame, sorrow. While also profoundly spiritual and often analytical, Loy's poetry is customarily experienced as excessive in its haptic imagery and challenging content. It is a world without respite, wherein the sharing of bodily intimacy is the *modus operandi* through which the constituents of meaning are constellated; to understand it, the reader must subject themselves to an often uncomfortable observation of intimate content and intimate acts – an observation that, Loy's wager has it, will enable us to move beyond 'the merely observant'.

Mina Loy was creating in a context marked by the open and dynamic traffic between literary and scientific discourses, especially literature and sciences like sexology, psychology and anthropology. The interaction between literature/art and anthropology was particularly close: anthropologists often acted out and commented on their creative-author function (Bronisław Malinowski, for one, famously exclaimed: 'I will be the Conrad [of anthropology]') and writers as different as W. B. Yeats and Robert Frost reconceived themselves as ethnographers.[3] Loy's approach to intimacy was shaped by the insights and methods of all these swiftly developing disciplines, but the interanimations between literature and ethnography were particularly inspiring for her. As I shall argue in this chapter, Loy's poetic practice specifically explores the variants of 'participant observation', an ethnographic method contemporaneously developed and celebrated by anthropologists like Malinowski and Nels Anderson. The operational premises of participant observation are *proximity* and *immersion*, and its ultimate aspiration is to produce a joint record of the observed subjects' behaviour and of the observing subjects' rapport to that behaviour. In practice, the approach could include various levels of involvement, from being a bystander to complete integration in the population of study beforehand (often also called 'observing participation', where the researcher could also produce an autoethnography). In all these modes, however, participant observation challenges the binaries of proximity and distance, attachment and detachment, the inside and the outside, and, for this reason, transforms the ways in which we conceive of intimacy. It does so in a multipronged way, all aspects of which are relevant to our understanding of how modernist literature (re-)engaged intimacy. First, it is worth noting that, like other ethnographical approaches, participant observation strives to document the undocumented, in as much detail as possible, while avoiding external ideological pressures and internal psychological mechanisms (such as denial or 'selective perspective'); the ambition is to produce a record of as many acts, actions and processes occurring within the observed group as possible, including the most intimate ones. As a scientific method, participant observation relies on the belief that we have to relate intimately to a certain behavioural content and the network of signification it generates in order to understand them, and we can achieve this level of closeness only by being part of the content itself. The method thus abrogates the heuristic privileges of 'objective distance' in favour of physical proximity and involvement. Furthermore, it postulates that the observer must be a self-conscious participant, a positionality that verges on a paradox: the ethnographer needs to be intimately involved yet sufficiently self-aware and ethically responsible to be able to record that very involvement; to be inside a relation and to record the same relation as if from the outside; to be the subject and the object. Such a multi-focal record, where the distribution of affects, control and authority is multidirectional, and the form itself invites simultaneous empathy and distancing, inevitably provokes a disoriented response in the audience. Participant observation accounts are often uncomfortable to read, and the dialogue they establish between the author, the text and the reader is entangled in affective and cognitive conundrums.

In Loy's hands, this practice has some additional – and additionally unsettling – twists. She deliberately scrutinises social behaviours and populations that may disquiet the audience, often because of the deep structural embeddedness of their marginalisation. As an ethnographer, she is attracted to content that is experienced as a social taboo (like sexual intimacy) and acts that are seen as violating social expectations or even infringing legal regulations (in the range from abortion to peddling), and to subjects that she believes have been consistently marginalised (from women to the homeless, and their diverse intersections). She cloaks these close observations in a reader-challenging but forceful poetic idiom that purports to relay the affective stakes of participant observation itself: Loy's poetry is highly naturalistic, emphatically haptic, and imbued with the shifting sensual and emotional experiences of the researcher-writer; overly inclusive, it disregards pre-selection, but is peppered throughout with cognitive gaps. Thus Loy's is a complex economy of intimacy: the reader is made to be intimate with content they might rather avoid (including content that involves personal intimacies) through a method that challenges our preconceptions about intimacy and in the print medium that foregrounds it.[4] Her poetry is uncomfortable and it inspects precisely the sources of the writer/ethnographer's and the audience's discomfort. Highly self-conscious and often with open political agendas, though, Loy's engagement with participant observation sometimes discloses the ethical limitations of ethnography as such. This chapter focuses on a few poetic works encircling Loy's career, where the dynamics of intimacy and the participant observation method interact closely: her early 'Songs to Joannes' and her mature poems 'Hot Cross Bum' (1949) and 'Photo after Pogrom' (c. 1945). While shaped by dissimilar vicissitudes of production, these texts all partake in Loy's ethnographic project of capturing the realities of obscured, taboo body matter and investigating the interaction between the author, the artwork and its receiver that such a transgressive record engenders; and they all have indirect yet distinct social missions.

It is appropriate, then, to start this inquiry with a contemporary reader's remembrances. Writing with hindsight, Alfred Kreymborg recalled the audience's outrage when they read the first four parts of 'Songs to Joannes' in the inaugural issue of *Others: A Magazine of the New Verse* in 1915.[5] The first readers, Kreymborg (the journal editor) relates, felt deceived by the romantic title that goaded them into reading the notorious opening lines, 'Spawn of Fantasies / Silting the appraisable / Pig Cupid his rosy snout / Rooting erotic garbage';[6] they detested the poem's guiding image, an amalgam of kitsch sentimentality and coarse lust, and were infuriated by the nonchalant precision and disregard for the rules of grammar with which Loy addresses the most intimate contents of physical desire. They felt incarcerated in Pig Cupid's habitat of 'sophistry', 'clinical frankness' and 'sardonic conclusions', and could not decide what was more disturbing, the content or the form: 'To reduce eroticism to the sty was an outrage, and to do so without verbs, sentence structure [was] even more offensive.'[7] Tellingly, the early audience's response also vocalised the accelerated pulse of anxieties surrounding female and feminist agency – a circumstance which Loy the ethnographer may have cherished. Had a man written these poems, he might have been tolerated with comparative comfort, Kreymborg writes; but the problem was that 'a woman wrote them, a woman who dressed like a lady and painted charming lamp-shades'.[8] While sexologists, psychoanalysts, anthropologists, health practitioners and indeed writers increasingly addressed sexual desire and practice in print in the 1910s, female contributions to these explorations of sexual intimacies were rare. This is one of the reasons why Loy visibly structures her poem as an autoethnography, written by a highly involved participating observer. The last line of Loy's poem, 'Love – – – the preeminent litterateur', specifically confirms the status of the text not as a private confession for the ears of a certain Joannes, but as an ethnographic account of sexual love, as experienced by women (who, the paradox of expansion notwithstanding, constitute Loy's marginalised ethnographic group subject).[9]

Not incidentally did Kreymborg describe the experience of reading 'Songs to Joannes' for the first time in terms of bodily functions, metabolising and readerly endurance: 'It took a strong digestive apparatus to read Mina Loy.'[10] Veiled in the tone of both unapologetic proximity and reinforced exteriority, Loy's poem foregrounds questions of gaze and touch, and the possibilities, or limits, of intersubjective bodily intimacy, as experienced by someone who is simultaneously inside the sexual exchange and observing it from the outside – an uncertain positionality which sustains disquietude in the reader. This account of bodily intimacy is clinically frank and disturbing: as we follow the trajectory of sexual intercourse and its aftermath in close-up detail, we discover that bodies can be not only fused and amalgamated, but also parcelled, split, dissected and uncomfortably slit open in the sexual exchange, and that the outcomes of sexual union can further violate the body. As a true ethnographer, Loy does not evaluate the rightness or wrongness of the actions she records or implies. But she does pass judgement on something else. Her ethnographic record is underwritten by a profoundly cynical commentary on the male-dominated tradition of being inspired by love, writing about love and 'authoring' love. This undertone reveals the political and ideological interpellations in the act of sexual exchange: the specific repercussions that our need for and treatment of sexual intimacy have for the identification of and interaction between the sexes (and human beings as such), evolution 'fall[ing] foul of / Sexual equality' and 'similitude' being 'prettily miscalculated'.[11] Loy's poem evolves into a public message on equality, objectification, asymmetrical relations and gendered desire.

'These are   suspect places',[12] both socially and poetically. In terms of contemporary politics, the poem gave voice to a certain New Woman subjectivity – energetic, investigative and committed to addressing the realities of woman's experience, including her sexuality and the politics of reproduction.[13] Challenging the very language in which early twentieth-century women made claims for equality, however, Loy's poetic idiom, Paul Peppis notes, was also at odds with the language of liberal rights feminism of the day.[14] Rachel Blau DuPlessis has pointed out that Loy's poetic sequence presents an early precursor of the feminist refigurations of heterosexual and homosexual intimacy in the cultural production of the 1920s – the daring poetic utterances of Edna St. Vincent Millay, Gertrude Stein and others – which targeted the patriarchal repression of the corporeal.[15] Loy's 'Songs to Joannes' is, then, a scandal in the most productive sense of this word, that is, a text that changes the course of the orientation of cultural signs; here, the cultural signs with which we represent and evaluate sexual intimacy. It is important to note, however, that, while some of its lines are body-euphoric and many of them address the dynamics of desire with excitement, the poem cannot be understood solely as a celebration of the body and its processes. The corporeal and affective currents are continuously undercut by a more sombre, scrutinising, and occasionally sardonic tone, which parcels and reassembles the bodies in the poem with the aim to articulate the anxieties that attend to the (scientific, religious, artistic) penetrations and revelations of the body. As such, 'Songs to Joannes' both expresses and *comments on* what Susan McCabe has termed the modernist 'crisis of embodiment': a gradual shift in which the body ceased to be perceived as the self-contained temple housing anything, and became a malleable site, co-formed with and reshaped by the environment, other bodies and objects (from medical instruments to radio waves), permanently open to both violation and pleasure.[16]

The split focalisation that enables such dual operation of the poem, as both expression of an experienced content and the socio-scientific commentary on that content, is paired with an equally complex poetic utterance. The latter was contemporaneously hailed by Ezra Pound as the idiom of 'arid clarity'.[17] Pound's assessment is both insightful and limited. Loy's images are often austere, bared to their semantic core, precise and sincere; but they are not arid.[18] Her poetic utterance is, simultaneously and without cancelling its opposite, linguistically exuberant and excessive in emotion, her images being often uncontainable in their affective bifurcations. The real attraction of Loy's poetic language resides precisely in the fusion of the ethnographer's and the sensual poet's writing drives, and of the modes of obtaining and conveying knowledge they articulate. Hers is an intensive expression that tackles the most intimate content of desire; it dwells on the body – its tectonics, its penetrable and violable boundaries, its processual nature, and its responses to the impulses from 'within' – but, guarded by the ethnographer's impulse, it never collapses into interiority.[19] The scientific and quasi-scientific discourses of contemporary biology and sexology, manifest in phrases such as 'mucous-membrane', 'skin sack', 'spermatozoa' and 'cymophanous sweat', warp the text, posited in contradistinction and relation to other types of utterance, and typographic and expressive ambivalences.[20] This interaction also signals and facilitates the analogical relationship Loy establishes between the body and language. For Loy, language is a body in itself, to be dissected and probed in its capacity to relate to a human body. Taking seriously F. T. Marinetti's advice to de(con)struct syntax,[21] Loy omits commas and full stops to accelerate pace, compulsively uses dashes to articulate fusions and splits of the bodies, and most liberally spaces her text, using gaps to signal exhalations, supressed moans, silent movement of body and mood, or affective and cerebral inexpressibles.[22] Here, as in a proper account of fieldwork, the interplay between accumulated images and gaping interstices generates insight.

But Loy's linguistic and para-linguistic choices also gesture to the wider anthropological aspirations of 'Songs to Joannes'. One of the poem's organising props, the dash, is particularly illuminating in this respect. John Lennard has described poetic dashes as uniquely versatile: 'dashes are used in pairs to create dash'd off parentheses, or singly in (infinite) sequence – to chop sentences up – and change subjects – to anything – even dragons – without the inconvenience of grammatical stops'.[23] Mina Loy – who 'was able to understand without the commas', as Gertrude Stein once put it – loved the dash and used it, together with the hyphen, excessively and irreverently.[24] 'Songs to Joannes' is replete with multi-functional hyphens, dashes and their occasional substitutes, blank spaces. Loy's dashes and hyphens operate syntactically, lexically and narratively, in pairs or individually, articulating, as Alex Goody writes, the 'unbounded potentiality' of language.[25] They concoct neologisms ('Wire-Puller', 'shuttle-cock and battle-door'), estrange familiar words ('eye-lids'), alter the grammatical status of words ('mucous-membrane'), accentuate the coming words and phrases ('I bring the nascent virginity of / —Myself'), individualise syntagms in parentheses, juxtapose statements to create an alternative narrative-line (for instance, a series of dashed-off sentences related to cleaning in poems IV and V), substitute commas and full stops, mark the unspeakables that punctuate the poetic sequence, and conclusively make the poem into both a cogitation on the constructedness of language and a visual object in its own right.[26] Thus unremittingly cutting, stapling, pasting and montaging the constituent parts (and depicted bodies) in 'Songs to Joannes', Loy's dashes and hyphens establish relations and signal relatedness. They dialogise the interaction between the antithetical Joannes and the participant-observer by alternatively fusing them and differentiating between them. This practice receives its verbal embodiment in the dash-ridden, difference-driven compound suggestive of the orgasmic union: 'Me you—you—me'. The lyric subject being wary of 'tumbl[ing] together / Depersonalised / Identical / Into the terrific Nirvana', the compound reads not only as the verbal equivalent of the synchronic (or differentially timed) orgasm but also as an inverse of Hegelian dialectic: the difference results from, rather than being sublated by, synthesis.[27] Both philosophically and anthropologically, their union is preservable only as polycentric and differential, intuitively inductive rather than rationally deductive, and pointedly unresolvable.

The purpose of such relational practice is political, as Loy's 1918/1920 'International Psycho-Democracy: A Movement to Focus Human Reason on the Conscious Direction of Evolution' manifesto suggests.[28] In this text, Loy argues that, with the help of strategically activated intuition, we can learn to relate, conquer the obsolete destructive impulses that eventuate in war, and change international politics. It is the task of 'intellectual heroes', distinguished by their 'originality of conception' and creative strength, to scrutinise the evolution of the body-psyche and develop 'a new social symbolism, a new social rhythm, a new social snobism'.[29] This innovative (aesthetic) frame to our social interactions would be able to challenge the dominance of militarism and help us relate through our differences, she maintains. This transformation of collective consciousness would entail the corresponding transformation of obsolete social institutions and education. Thus conceived, intuition, in Loy's interpretation, does not generate a sense of 'intuitive belonging' to a group, an affect often abused by quasi-democratic mob-psychology or individualist masculinism for the purpose of war, but a capacity to coexist democratically in a 'life-amplifying' way.[30] Loy the amateur-ethnographer is brazenly subjective, and the limitations of her idiosyncratic blend of individualism and collectivism as a political and aesthetic praxis are obvious, as Rachel Potter correctly observes.[31] But Loy's aspiration to foreground relation as a vital political and living practice and a key component of ethical artwork in 'Psycho-Democracy' also provides an answer to the question of why she lays bare sexual intimacies so persistently, clinically, meticulously, in 'Songs to Joannes'. The continuity between anti-war politics, ethics of relation and expression of intimacy is foregrounded here. Loy relays intimacies precisely in order to incite – intimacy: to force readers to relate (socially, politically) by involving them in an intimate exchange with the text. Yet, to *force* the reader into an encounter with physical intimacy in order to espouse relational ethics is inherently paradoxical and I shall return to this contradiction towards the end of this chapter. Let me note here only that the political viability of Loy's early poetics and her use of the participant observation may be circumscribed: in its forcefulness and un-mediacy, her early poetry actually hosts too little dialogical space for the more complicated dynamics of intimacy between the author, the text and the reader to develop.

Loy never abandoned the project of using the body-proximate, multi-sensual utterance to emphasise the political necessity of relational knowledge and the obstacles in its way. It re-emerged, with particular force, in her production of the late 1940s, marking a new stage in Loy's effort to negotiate the economy of intimacy. At the time, Loy lived and worked in increasing obscurity in the Bowery, a semi-segregated urban space that was the central habitat of the impoverished, homeless and dispossessed population struggling to survive in New York City. The Bowery homeless population was estimated to be more than 15,000 in the late 1930s, and, as the 1940s and 1950s progressed, the area gradually hosted fewer vagrants and a more static, long-term unemployed, 'often disabled population of down-and-outers, averaging over fifty years of age'.[32] Loy, who spent much of these two decades moving from one cheap flat or communal rooming house to another, grew to become a participant-observer of this cohort: she scavenged the back streets of the area, accumulated trash in her room in a cheap boarding house, and transformed it into (mostly destroyed) collages-assemblages and poems. Loy's take on intimacy meets a social concern again in this period, carrying forward the ethnographic work that she started in her early poetry, but further specifying its social dimension and public relevance. Her Bowery artwork and prosodic poetry engage, almost compulsively, the subjects at the margin of what the ideologically habituated eye sees: dilapidated housing, rags and heaps of trash; a homeless woman resting at the foundation corner of a department store, an overworked seamstress, a ticket-seller imprisoned in a box office, a straying nun, a mentally handicapped child clutching at a fire-escape staircase, and a drunkard copulating with the pavement; pigeons, together with their excrement; and, in a distinct response to World War II, corpses. The observing participant is on the task to record all these; her eye, Loy writes in 'Mass Production on 14th Street', is 'the commodious bee' gathering evidence.[33] The record of this observation is harsh: the eyes of the child in 'An Idiot Child at a Fire-Escape' are uncompromisingly vacant; the bodies of the homeless are infested by parasites, dirt and alcohol; the pigeons' song is punctuated by their frequent production of excrement; the corpses putrefy unredeemed. While Loy's 'eye/I' occasionally intimates beauty in unlikely places and some abject figures temporarily procure spiritual uplift, no real relief is provided for this cognitive and visceral discomfort. The reader is repeatedly reminded that this is not a sentimental salvaging of the excluded: their appearance is emphatic but transitory, and the poet underscores their ephemerality and disposability.

Discomfort created by this representational practice functions as both a punctum which binds the author, the text and the reader, and an investigative tool whose purpose is to examine precisely our reactions to being lacerated by the unhomely and disposable 'other'.[34] Lingering on these transient figures thus has a specific target, which Loy's unremitting prolongation of the reader's intimate, cognitive and visceral discomfort attempts to both acknowledge and overcome: the range and adaptability of our strategies of denial. This objective is most visible in Loy's poems on the Bowery homelessness, and, especially, her long parodic poem 'Hot Cross Bum' (1949). The poem should be read against the background of various social and representational trends that accompanied the global increase in inadequately housed populations and their clustering in metropolitan centres in the early twentieth century: derogatory stereotyping but also eulogising of vagrancy and attitudinal homelessness ('hobohemia'); the rise of both philanthropy and academic disciplines like urban anthropology; and the modernist artists' tendency to recast homelessness as transcendental and symbolic. Loy, once a proponent of heroic itineracy, now regarded all these attitudes and discourses as neglectful of the physical reality of homelessness.[35]

Wary of both sentimental and realistic depictions of homelessness, Loy, like in 'Songs to Joannes', strategically uses multi-sensual imagery and dialectical tension between participation and observation to draw readers into what could be described as a forced dialogue on the socially obscured and the discursively manipulated. The poem opens with an establishing shot of the Bowery as the city's underbelly – 'Beyond a hell-vermilion / curtain of neon / lies the Bowery'[36] – and unfolds into a linear ekphrasis that takes stock of the various increasingly disquieting gestures of homelessness. The participant observation of these indices to disposability both invokes and challenges our capacity for intimate relation. The poem finishes with a shocking inversion of the preceding death-drive-ridden narrative, with a tableau of a bum 'still savor[ing] the favor of Eros' through a coitus with the city street, 'a folly-wise scab of Metropolis / pounding with caressive jollity / a breastless slab / [...] lovin' up the pavement – interminable paramour / of horizontal stature / Venus-sans-vulva –'.[37] Loy warps this undecided image of delirium tremens/masturbation into a verbal play – 'of ocean / of inhalation / of coition' – as if to remind us at the end, and perhaps tongue-in-cheek, that poetry's primary function is still to sound ideas and images rather than evaluate them.[38]

Our anchors and guides through this semiosphere of destitution are the voices of two participant-observers who could be described as the (disillusioned, realistic) ethnographer/narrator and the (redeeming, romanticising) poet/spiritualist. These positionalities disagree on a few fundamental questions: how much the Bowery bums are to be blamed for their condition of lingering homelessness, what form of social help would be most appropriate to their situation, and whether the plight of the homeless can eventuate in their spiritual renovation. The clashing dialogue of the two voices draws in Loy's readers and keeps them fastened to the text under the chimera that they, too, will be able to take sides. Engulfed in corporeal, excessive, often painfully satirical imagery, however, the reader soon realises that all the attempts to alleviate homelessness (through philanthropy, political and artistic measures) and/or square it in a comprehensible narrative are 'abortive oculars'[39].

As the undated drafts of 'A Hard Luck Story' and poetry fragments like 'Crowd Soul' suggest and 'Hot Cross Bum' evinces by its challenging modalities, Loy was intensely aware of the dangers inhering in the representation of homelessness: those that accost the interactive space between the observing artist and the homeless person, and those that characterise the rapports between the recipient (reader/viewer) and the represented. She sees the psychological and socio-political mechanisms of denial as informing both philanthropic sympathy (which accentuates the distance between the philanthropist handing out hot cross buns and those that receive them) and empathy (which purportedly breaks down the barrier between the empathising and the empathee but risks invading, or appropriating, the only property left to the homeless subject, namely, their thoughts[40]), and chastises both. All routes to affective or cognitive intimacy with the homeless seem to be questioned in Loy's poem: precisely because no discourse is immune to Loy's relentless relativisation of our impulses, noble or otherwise – including the desire to kindle our eyes on the intimacies of those who are less fortunate than we are as well as the opposite but related impulse not to describe the visceral plights of other humans in too much detail – *and* because the reader must have partaken in one of these discourses in their own lifetime, 'Hot Cross Bum' is uncomfortable reading. However, this production of uneasiness paradoxically foregrounds discomfort as the only mode of intimacy that cannot be relativised and that is shared between the writer, the observing subject and the reader. Loy's poem is disquieting because of the simultaneous and consistent operation of three distinct planes of affective signification in them: the subjects put on display are in physical and emotional discomfort, their representation incites discomfort in the reader, and the artwork obstinately scrutinises the sources of the observers' (the writer's and reader's) discomfort. Once inside this zone of discomfort, we are tempted by various strategies of denial: we would like to celebrate the potential of the homeless figures to be or become urban angels; or we would wish to commend Loy for doing some restorative work for the city on a practical basis in highlighting the plight of the marginal. But the poem's lengthy format, inexorable transparency and unremitting pace soon make us realise that both responses are missing the point: it is only through the affect of discomfort, provoked by differently ordered triggers and experienced in individual ways but with an ultimately shared emotive structure, that we may relate.

These ethical stakes are even higher in the final poem I would like to engage here.'Photo after Pogrom' brings the reader to a site of abject intimacy that is even more emotionally challenging than the one hosted by the unsettlingly disposable homeless cohort, and to the figure that Julia Kristeva has described as 'the utmost of abjection', indeed 'the most sickening of wastes' – the corpse.[41] The poem's eight diminutive stanzas revolve around the lyric subject's attempt to describe and give meaning to an image of a field of corpses, 'human rubble' 'arrang[ed] by rage'.[42] It may appear unclear at first how Loy can be a participant-observer in the cohort she is describing – until we realise that she is intent on (self-)scrutinising not the victims' corpses but their audience, of which she is a member. Written in response to the images that flooded the US media in the wake of the liberation of Europe's concentration camps, the poem noticeably engages photographic tools and the increasingly popular genre of the photo-essay – a dominant mode in which the historical reality of the war was conveyed in the 1940s.[43] As in a photo-essay, the poem first takes up an inclusive photo-perspective (an establishing shot), which, at a narrative turn, suddenly converts into a close-up of the corpse of a woman 'tossed on a pile of dead', her face attaining 'the absolute smile / of dispossession' by rigor mortis.[44] This image zooms out quickly, as if apprehensive of too much lingering on an individual body, of poetic reification. The perspective reverts to the collective of corpses, to which death has finally imparted lack of fear and 'unassumed composure', the poetic voice concluding that 'corpses are virgin' – blank bodies, impenetrable even to violation by our eyes and the meanings we may impose on them.[45]

The language of the poem is terse, generating an *imagetext* that is both impersonal and materially specific. The dual voicing typical of Loy's poems of discomfort now appears compact: the poet's labour to find 'utter beauty' in the woman's corpse is instantaneously destabilised by a voice reminding us of the 'false-eternal statues of the slain / until they putrify' and the 'purposeless[ness]' of their 'peace' in the context of an 'extinct haven'.[46] The poem addresses this aporetic condition, and the ethico-political responsibilities it entails for the one who represents it, contemporaneously pondered by one Theodor Adorno.[47] 'Photo after Pogrom' purposefully equilibrates between materiality and aestheticisation. The genocidal victim's corpse is divinised just enough for the aesthetic residues and the question of their status to continue to haunt the reader. The latter is forced to re-read 'Photo after Pogrom', becoming ever more uncomfortably proximate to/intimate with the text and to interrogate, inconclusively, the dynamics of representation, appropriation and complicity. Discomfort functions here, once again, as both an ethical imperative and an affect that connects the writer, the reader and the represented subject.

To place this audacious project in its writer-reader context of heightened ethical demands, it is appropriate to invoke an incident that marked its publication history. When, in 1947, one of Loy's poems on homelessness, 'Chiffon Velours', was first published in *Accent: A Quarterly of New Literature*, part of the run of the journal's issue contained the last twelve lines of 'Photo after Pogrom' beneath a pasted-down sheet on which lines 19–23 of the contemporaneously written 'Chiffon Velours' appeared. Loy did mention the error in her response to the copyeditor, but seems not to have been troubled by it. She simply exclaimed 'How surrealist!', apparently treating this emotionally and ethically puzzling superimposition as a propitiously derived index to a conflated history. This reaction led Colbey Emmerson Reid to interpret the case as an unintentional but welcome intervention, a palimpsest – an artistic practice with which Loy was more than familiar.[48] I applaud such recontextualisation because it allows for some complex new routes of interpretation to emerge. As the stiffness of the aged woman, compared to a skeleton in 'Chiffon Velours', blends with the rigor mortis of the female corpse in 'Photo after Pogrom', this conflation of two kinds of dispossession and disposability becomes illuminating of both. The juxtaposition retrains our eyes to recognise what escapes the habituated vision and admission: that the living could be dead for society and that the dead could (indeed must) live on the pages of a witness, both a participant and an observer. Such practice suggests that an ethically vigilant writer should create intimate spaces for the articulation of both conditions and will bind the reader to those spaces – inescapably, inexorably. The crucial value of Loy's early and mature work alike lies in the fact that the poet explores not only her liminal subjects and the ideological narratives eclipsing them, but also our intimate responses to them. What makes her art both disquieting and spellbinding is not the subjects themselves, but Loy's creation of an interactive space through which the artwork operates, a space that is simultaneously exteriorised and unthinkably intimate.

Mina Loy does not grant us an effortless passage: to engage with her art means to be captured in a world with no relief, where (feeling and creating) discomfort is instated as the only genuine, unappropriable mode of intimate relation between humans, and humans and texts. Here, one is bound to object to this practice of forced dialogue by raising the issue of the reader's relative freedom vis-à-vis the multi-sensual creative act: how free or constrained is the reader in this relationship? What are the unsigned but binding contracts we enter into when we read a work that foregrounds intimacy and the shifting sensual and affective experiences of the writer? The issue of the reader's rights is a more general question relating, on the one hand, specifically to modernism and its poetic politics, and, on the other hand, any literature which engages intimacy. All reader-response criticism, from Hans Robert Jauss and Wolfgang Iser through Umberto Eco and Roland Barthes, to Norman Holland and Stanley Fish and onwards, exults the role of the reader as an agent that constitutes the meanings of the text, forging out of semantic apertures left by the writer a narrative that is unique to a reading individual or a reading group, and, as a rule, liberatory of authors and authorial power. Yet, Loy's case defies such theories: she plants semantic gaps, even an excess of them, and makes them typographically visible, but, rather than liberating her readers, she makes them captives to a world into which they would rather not enter. Surely, the recipient can opt out of such engagement altogether, one surmises – yet not before she or he has already experienced what the artwork is about; not before she/he has been unsettled, intimately provoked, that is, not before his or her own intimate sphere has been reconstellated into the gestures of either a disquieted opening or a convulsive retreat.

Loy's poetic practice relegates the question of the reader's response and his or her relative freedom vis-à-vis the creative act from the matters of co-structuring interaction to the plane of affects and the unfree circulation of desire. Generally speaking, an emphatic relay of the intimate, or body-proximate, content curbs the readers' potential to make independent interventions in the text, as their engagement with the text is premised on being implicated in a flow of desire (the currents ranging from revolting abjection to erotic attraction) – a flow from which they cannot easily extricate themselves. Loy's practice thrives on this dynamic but also deploys it strategically. Exercising the prerogatives of the writer to command affects and steer the motion of desire, and the power of the ethnographer to record minute details of physical reality, she uses them to expose us to an uncomfortable and unsentimental intimate content and reorient our vision to what she calls 'the forms of entities hitherto visually illimitable'.[49] Her hope is to induce a genuine relationship with subjects, objects and phenomena which we would rather deny or poeticise. The freedoms we might be given as readers are contingent on our acceptance to enter and remain in this zone of unpleasant ethnographic records and inconclusive dialogues. In the crevices of this gesture one may still forge one's own vision of her artwork – or one will decide that the ultimate vision imparted by these works is that we must learn to relate in such a way that we feel the 'others' (humans, texts), even viscerally so, but do not appropriate them in any interpretation.

Notes

1. Mina Loy, 'Songs to Joannes', in *The Lost Lunar Baedeker* (hereafter cited as *LLB*), sel. and ed. Roger L. Conover (New York: Noonday Press, 1996), p. 53.
2. Ibid. p. 67.
3. See Paul Peppis, *Sciences of Modernism: Ethnography, Sexology, and Psychology* (Cambridge: Cambridge University Press, 2014); Sean Heuston, *Modern Poetry and Ethnography: Yeats, Frost, Warren, Heaney, and the Poet as Anthropologist* (New York: Palgrave Macmillan, 2011); and Marc Manganaro, 'Introduction: Textual Play, Power and Cultural Critique: An Orientation to Modernist Anthropology', in Manganaro (ed.), *Modernist Anthropology: From Field-work to Text* (Princeton: Princeton University Press, 1990), pp. 3–49.
4. See Jane Goldman's chapter in this volume (Chapter 3, pp. 52–73).
5. See Alfred Kreymborg, *Troubadour: An Autobiography* (New York: Liveright, 1925), pp. 235–6; and Kreymborg, *A History of American Poetry: Our Singing Strength* (New York: Coward-McCann, 1929), pp. 488–90. Loy's poem first appeared in an abbreviated form as 'Love Songs', *Others: A Magazine of the New Verse*, 1.1 (July 1915), pp. 6–8, and then in its full version as 'Songs to Joannes', *Others*, 3.6 (April 1917), pp. 3–20.
6. Loy, *LLB*, p. 53.
7. Kreymborg, *History*, p. 489.
8. Ibid. p. 489.
9. Loy, *LLB*, p. 68.
10. Kreymborg, *History*, pp. 488–9. When Loy published the sequence in her 1923 book *Lunar Baedeker*, the tone was softer, the imagery less explicit, the typographic excesses were mediated, and the organisation of the whole was simpler. This move reflected not only her desire to rethink the matters of economic balance in representation, but also her fear of censorship: Loy closely followed the confiscation of the four issues of *The Little*

Review serialising James Joyce's *Ulysses* and the US ban on the import and publication of the novel. Roger Conover argues convincingly for treating the 1917 version as definitive (in Loy, *LLB*, p. 191) and my discussion is based on this version.
11. Loy, *LLB*, p. 65.
12. Ibid. p. 53.
13. On Mina Loy and Marie Stopes, see Peppis, *Sciences of Modernism*, pp. 148–95.
14. See ibid. pp. 152, 169–92.
15. Rachel Blau DuPlessis, '"Seismic Orgasm": Sexual Intercourse and Narrative Meaning in Mina Loy', in Maeera Shreiber and Keith Tuma (eds), *Mina Loy: Woman and Poet* (Orono, ME: National Poetry Foundation, 1998), p. 45. See also Leslie Hall, 'Feminist Reconfigurations of Heterosexuality in the 1920s', in Lucy Bland and Laura Doan (eds), *Sexology in Culture: Labelling Bodies and Desires* (Hoboken: Wiley, 1998), pp. 135–51.
16. Susan McCabe, '"Delight in Dislocation": The Cinematic Modernism of Stein, Chaplin, and Man Ray', *Modernism/Modernity*, 8.3 (2001), p. 430. Laura Frost's *The Problem with Pleasure* (New York: Columbia University Press, 2013) describes the modernist form more generally as an art of difficult or un-pleasure.
17. Pound's praise originally appeared in 'A List of Books', *The Little Review*, 4.11 (March 1918), pp. 54–8.
18. On Pound and Loy, see Peter Nicholls, '"Arid Clarity": Ezra Pound and Mina Loy', in Rachel Potter and Suzanne Hobson (eds), *The Salt Companion to Mina Loy* (Cambridge: Salt Publishing, 2010), pp. 129–45.
19. However emphatic the use of the 'lyric I' and the depiction of instinctual impulses may be in her poems, Loy was never the poet of concentrated interiority, one who only '[looks] within and not without' (Virginia Woolf, *A Letter to a Young Poet* (London: Hogarth Press, 1932), pp. 15, 18).
20. Loy, *LLB*, pp. 53, 53, 56, 64.
21. F. T. Marinetti, 'Destruction of Syntax—Untrammeled Imagination—Words-in-Freedom' (May–June 1913), in *Critical Writings*, ed. Günther Berghaus, trans. Doug Thompson (New York: Farrar, Straus and Giroux, 2006), pp. 120–31.
22. Loy's typographic ambitions (almost never honoured in print) were even wider: to have the poem 'printed on one side of each page only – & a large round in the middle of each page – & one whole entirely blank page with nothing on it between the first and the second parts' (Mina Loy, letter to Carl Van Vechten, n.d., 1915, cited by Conover in Loy, *LLB*, p. 191).
23. John Lennard, *The Poetry Handbook* (Oxford: Oxford University Press, 2006), p. 132.

24. Gertrude Stein, *The Autobiography of Alice B. Toklas*, in *Selected Writings*, ed. Carl Van Vechten (New York: Vintage Books, 1972), p. 124.
25. Alex Goody, 'Gender, Authority and the Speaking Subject, or: Who is Mina Loy?', *How 2*, 1.5 (March 2001), available at <https://www.asu.edu/pipercwcenter/how2journal/archive/online_archive/v1_5_2001/current/in-conference/mina-loy/goody.html> (accessed 25 November 2018).
26. Loy, *LLB*, pp. 55, 56, 56, 58.
27. Ibid. p. 58.
28. Mina Loy's 'International Psycho-Democracy: A Movement to Focus Human Reason on the Conscious Direction of Evolution' was drafted in 1918, and published as a pamphlet in 1920 and then as an article in *The Little Review*, Brancusi Number (Autumn 1921), pp. 14–19. All further references in the notes below are to the 1921 article.
29. Ibid. p. 18. On Loy and intuition, see Ellen McWhorter, 'Body Matters: Mina Loy and the Art of Intuition', *European Journal of American Studies*, 10.2 (2015), pp. 1–25.
30. Loy, 'Psycho-Democracy', p. 19.
31. Rachel Potter, *Modernism and Democracy: Literary Culture, 1900–1930* (Oxford: Oxford University Press, 2006), p. 182.
32. David A. Snow and Leon Anderson, *Down on Their Luck: A Study of Homeless Street People* (Oakland: University of California Press, 1993), pp. 14–15.
33. Loy, *LLB*, p. 111.
34. Here I use the term 'unhomely' – a gloss on both Freud's use of 'Unheimlich' and a physical and attitudinal descriptive 'not homely' – in order to register the continuities between the reality of homelessness, its psychological effects, and its social codification. It correlates with the continuities between material world and psychic space that Julia Kristeva underscores in her own discussion of abjection in *The Powers of Horror: An Essay on Abjection* (New York: Columbia University Press, 1982).
35. For a more extensive account of Loy's engagement with homelessness, see Sanja Bahun, 'Against "Selective/Perspective": Mina Loy, Homelessness, and the Economy of Discomfort', in *Modernism and Home* (forthcoming).
36. Loy, *LLB*, p. 133.
37. Ibid. pp. 143, 144.
38. Ibid. p. 144.
39. Ibid. p. 134.
40. On Loy's attitude towards this risk, see Rachel Potter, 'At the Margins of the Law: Homelessness in the City in Mina Loy's Late Poems', *Women: A Cultural Review*, 10.3 (1999), pp. 253–65.

41. Kristeva, *The Powers of Horror*, pp. 3–4.
42. Loy, *LLB*, p. 122.
43. Linda A. Kinnahan, *Mina Loy, Twentieth Century Photography, and Contemporary Women Poets* (London: Routledge, 2017), p. 172.
44. Loy, *LLB*, p. 122.
45. Ibid. p. 122.
46. Ibid. p. 122. For an opposite reading, see Maeera Shreiber, 'Divine Women, Fallen Angels: The Late Devotional Poetry of Mina Loy', in Shreiber and Tuma (eds), *Mina Loy*, pp. 463–82.
47. Theodor W. Adorno, 'Cultural Criticism and Society' (1949), in *Prisms* (Cambridge, MA: MIT Press, 1983), pp. 17–34.
48. Colbey Emmerson Reid, 'Mina Loy's Design Flaws', *Florida Atlantic Comparative Studies*, 10 (2007–8), pp. 79–106. On the material context of this incident, see ibid. pp. 92–3; and Conover in Loy, *LLB*, pp. 211–12. Loy submitted both poems to the journal and the editors' final choice was 'Chiffon Velours' – a poem about a homeless woman leaning on a corner of the department store, which was perceived as 'safer' in the immediate aftermath of the Nuremberg trials.
49. Mina Loy in response to the question 'What do you see in the stars?', *The VIEW* (February–March 1942), p. 10.

8

The Intimacies of the Modernist Diary

Laura Marcus

The conceptual relationship between the diary or journal and intimacy is a close one, as is revealed in the French 'journal intime'.[1] For the life-writing theorist Philippe Lejeune, 'the true *journal intime* [is] intimate in its content and above all in its function'.[2] In the English term 'diary', as in the German *Tagebuch*, the semantic link is also with the temporality of the day, though many diaries have gaps where 'nothing happened' or the diarist was otherwise occupied, and some entries are focused on longer periods of time. Diaries of major events such as wars or, in the personal sphere, an illness, have the further property that the outcome (peace, cure or death) and its timing are unpredictable. Whether or not the diary is a daily one, its future use is also open: it may be unread after the event even by the author, shared with selected 'intimates' or, in some instances, published and widely read.

The history of the diary as a mode of writing could never be traced fully, as the majority of examples remain unpublished and a very large proportion of these will not have survived. Yet the research undertaken to date into histories of the diary form has been highly revealing of shared conventions in particular periods – shaped by such cultural tropes as the values placed on introspection or on everyday life – as well as of national differences. Lejeune's exhaustive studies, published and unpublished, have revealed, for example, the importance of 'self-address' in French diaries from the eighteenth-century onwards, with the diary or journal becoming, in one diary-keeper's words, 'the most intimate and secret confidant of my thoughts, whom I leave and come back to without the slightest complaining from you [...] You bring me insight and experience.'[3]

In the early decades of the twentieth century, which is the focus of this chapter, the writer's diary or journal (as a sub-set of diaries and journals more broadly) bears an important relationship to literary modernism. The mode of the late nineteenth-century *journal intime* continued to exert its fascination on diarists such as Katherine Mansfield and Julien Green (whose diaries, running from 1928 to 1954, were published in six volumes).[4] The fragmentary form of the diary was also a central feature of much modernist writing, as was the fascination with the temporalities of dailiness; these elements were central to the work of Virginia Woolf, who also created, over her lifetime, one of the most sustained diaries in existence. The diary, in both private and published realms, has also been very fully associated with women's writing (as modernism has been substantially defined, in recent years, through the shaping contribution of women authors and artists) and as, in the words of Elizabeth Podnieks in her important study *Daily Modernism*, 'a significant literary space for women authors'.[5]

The emergence of psychoanalysis, from the late nineteenth century onwards, opened up a new understanding of self-analysis which found its way, directly or obliquely, into diaristic conventions. At the same time, the political contexts of decades which saw two world wars created a particularly charged relationship between the spheres of private and public life, including the perception of the writer's role in these situations. Was there a new imperative for the diarist to act as a historical witness in an age of crisis? In this chapter, I look at the ways in which three writers – David Gascoyne, Antonia White and Anaïs Nin – explored and negotiated this context in the 1930s.

*

The poet David Gascoyne, in his Afterword to the 1991 publication of his *Collected Journals*, described the ways in which his original journal notebooks, written in the 1930s, had re-emerged some thirty years after their disappearance. Their wholly unexpected restoration after decades was important to Gascoyne less, perhaps, because the journals allowed for a recovery of the past, than because the weight of words swelled an oeuvre whose relative slightness was such a source of distress and regret to him. Soon afterwards, Gascoyne added, he received through the post the exercise book in which he had written the first part of the Journal,

> starting soon after the International Surrealist Exhibition of 1936 and ending not long before my departure to live in Paris in 1937. This manuscript had been discovered among the papers of the recently deceased wife of a doctor friend I had known since my country childhood.[6]

The doctor had at one point shared a flat with Sonia Brownell Orwell, to whom Gascoyne must have lent the journal, though he had no recollection of doing so.[7]

To lose two journals might look like carelessness, but it indicates the ways in which Gascoyne, in the 1930s, had perceived his journal writing as something not to be hoarded but put into circulation. One text which was particularly important for Gascoyne was Lawrence Durrell's *The Black Book: An Agon*, a diaristic novel, published in Paris in 1938 and strongly influenced by Henry Miller, which did not appear in Britain until 1973.[8] In *The Black Book*, the narrator, Lawrence Lucifer, describes his present-day London life in a London boarding house. He has found the diary – the 'Black Book' of a former boarder named Gregory – and intersperses this text with his own narrative. In the journal, Gregory emphasises the self-consciousness of his diary: 'It is artifice which dictates this form to me [...] All diaries have been written for an audience.'[9]

After reading *The Black Book*, Gascoyne sent his own diary to Durrell so that Durrell could see how closely the fictional diary resembled his own. He wrote to Durrell on 18 October 1937 (a letter which is included in the published journals):

> Dear Durrell
> After having read those horrifying journals in *The Black Book*, I feel even more diffident about showing you these pages than before. The first part of your book particularly made me feel the writing of journals to be such a miserable hole-in-the-corner game that I hardly dared to open this *cahier* again. Yet none the less there are still two reasons why I would rather present the foregoing to you than to almost anyone else, and they are 1) because I can see that you are engaged on a sort of adventure of experience to which documents of this kind are particularly relevant; and 2) because you are an expert on the English Death, and what I have written here seems to deal almost entirely in one way and another, even if not deliberately, with precisely that.[10]

At this point, Gascoyne describes whatever interest his journal might have in terms of its status as 'a photographic record of a small cross-section of the E.D. [the "English Death", defined as "the absolutely universal spiritual squalor or projection of the inhabitants of the British Isles"] at work in myself and in the lives of the people I know (I mean as near photographic as possible)', while the conflict within himself is imagined as the struggle between the part of the self implicated in the English Death 'and the other side, which somehow, blindly, is trying to struggle towards absurdity and life'.[11]

Durrell's response came in the form of a poem published as 'Paris Journal: For David Gascoyne (1939)', so that the connecting chain becomes that of Durrell's novel, Gascoyne's journal and Durrell's poem. The poem begins on

'Monday', which 'escapes destruction. / Records a vernal afternoon, / Tea on the lawn with mother', and continues:

> By the deviation of a hair,
> Is death so far, so far, no further.
>
> Tuesday: visibility good: and Wednesday.
> A little thunder, some light showers.
> A library book about the universe.
> The absence of a definite self.
> O and already by Friday hazardous,
> To Saturday begins the slow reverse.
> A Saturday without form. By midnight
> The equinox seems forever gone:
> Yet the motionless voice repeating:
> 'Bless the hills in paradigms of smoke,
> Manhair, Maidenhair meeting'
>
> But today Sunday. The pit.
> The axe and the knot. Cannot write.
> The monster in its booth.
> At a quarter to one the mask repeating:
> 'Truth is what is
> Truth is what is Truth?'[12]

The poem 'Paris Journal' articulates a relationship between dailiness, writing and death. Dailiness, which is also diary time, is a 'form' which guards against despair or madness, but the ability to record Monday or Tuesday seems also to be tied into the English Death.[13] This diary of a week is a weather report; a barometer of emotional and mental states. The formlessness of Saturday opens up to the surrealist imaginary – 'Bless the hills in paradigms of smoke' – which is also a psychic disturbance; Sunday is 'the pit' in which the self becomes a 'knot' but 'cannot write' (the 'axe' is on the writing block), and in which the voice becomes a mask which can only repeat a question without answer.

*

At around the time of his exchange with Durrell, Gascoyne met the writer Anaïs Nin (a friend of the Durrells) in Paris, and they exchanged diaries. Nin recorded this initial exchange in her journals: 'He leaves me his diary, full of reticences and evasions. I give him diary volumes thirty-one, thirty-two, thirty-three. Can I light the fire in him?'[14] 'At five o'clock', she wrote a week later, 'Gascoyne comes to see if he can catch his own image in the pool of my understanding, the volumes of the diary he read have enlarged the space of his prison.'[15] When they met again a few months later, Gascoyne recorded that Nin asked him 'when she would be able to see more of my journal, and I had to confess that there was nothing to see, as I had not written any more since the time when we first met and I read her own diary'.[16] The theme of lost diaries was continued when Gascoyne returned one of her early journals, which he had been typing out, to Nin by unregistered mail: 'a crazy destructive act for which I curse him', Nin wrote. 'And I am trying to find it. I feel the loss terribly, like a fragment of my life itself. The diary is too human, too close a thing. The loss of it is like my own death.'[17]

Both Gascoyne and Nin published fragments of their diaries in this period: Gascoyne in the November 1937 issue of *Booster* (an avant-garde literary journal which was ostensibly the house magazine of the American Country Club of France, and which became the short-lived *Delta* in April 1938, with a special poetry issue) and Nin in the 1938 summer issue of *Seven*. There was also discussion in this period of the publication of an abridged version of Nin's diaries.[18] In 1937, Miller launched a plan to publish the early diary *Mon Journal* in the original language and by subscription, in a limited edition of 250 copies. In the event there were not enough subscribers to make the project viable.[19]

During this same period, Gascoyne met the writer Antonia White, also a committed diarist and one for whom journal-writing was a way of compensating for her difficulties in writing fiction.[20] Writing a diary, as she states of her heroine in *The Sugar House* (1952), 'gave her the illusion that she was at least producing something'.[21] As in Gascoyne's case, substantial portions of White's diaries are given over to her problems with writing – in particular, the production of any creative literature that was not autobiographical. 'Suddenly tonight', reads the entry for 26 September 1935, 'I feel I must re-examine my life. This guilt about my writing; distaste for it: guilt at not doing it: fearful anxiety connected with it.'[22] The notebooks she used for her diary-writing were significant as both material and symbolic objects; in October 1935 the diary entry laments the loss of a green notebook which

> was a legitimate new beginning: I cannot help feeling the loss and the consequent break in continuity . . . it was my own fault for wanting to *show* it to anyone, though I think the unconscious was at work making me lose it because I was afraid of what I had written about my father . . . . What was in the green notebook was, I think, of some value to me.[23]

White's diary-writing also became bound into her periods of psychoanalysis, and in 1935 she started a separate 'Analysis Diary', in which she recorded, somewhat fitfully, the material arising out of the three years of her analysis with Dr Dennis Carroll, including dreams and fantasies.[24] The boundaries between the diary notebooks and the 'Analysis Diary' were, however, porous. In August 1938 White wrote, with reference to her reading of her previous year's notes:

> Somehow more truth and less distortion gets into these notebooks than into anything else. They are only a half-way house and a prop, I know. I think they will stop in their present subjective form when analysis is over and I eventually get going on work [...] They are still a sign of my distrust of myself: I look at them when I feel confused or lose my sense of identity. They are like a photograph of myself to which I refer [...] It is as if I kept my identity in these books. I become more anxious to show them to people – though still apprehensive ...[25]

In an entry in her 'Analysis Diary' two years earlier, White had interpreted her dreams and fantasies of 'nakedness' as 'morbid fear of exposure yet secret desire to be exposed',[26] a contradictory impulse which, she implied, related to the tension between the privacy of the diary/self and the desire to make it known. In an entry in her 'Analysis Diary' for 1939 she wrote (addressing herself in the second person) of the novel in progress, *The Lost Traveller*, with which she was struggling, of the contradictatory forces impelling both her wish 'to display yourself to people' and the fear both of being exposed to contempt and of the self's depletion in such display: 'And yet you want to get rid of it: I believe the book should be about my father. If some of the trouble comes from having my father inside me, I should get him out.'[27]

While it would seem that White suffered great anxiety about the publication and reception of her work, she did attempt to publish material from the 1935 diary in 1937, very possibly as a result of the publication of sections of Gascoyne's and Nin's diaries in this period. Both psychoanalysis (in which the subject opens him- or herself up to the analyst) and the charged historical and political conditions of the 1930s (in which the very terms of 'private' and 'public' selfhood were being altered in radical ways) would appear to have been shaping forces here, turning the 'inside out'.[28]

The relationships between psychoanalysis and diaries or journals are close and complex ones, not least in terms of the habitual temporalities of dailiness – full analysis, like regular diary-writing, happens on a daily basis – though analysis is normally suspended on Saturdays and Sundays, the days, we recall from Durrell's poem, in which there is a 'slow reverse', followed by 'the pit' in which writing becomes impossible. David Gascoyne started psychoanalysis with Blanche Reverchon-Jouve on 22 October 1938; three months later he wrote that he was finished with analysis – only two weeks after Mme Reverchon-Jouve had told him that he must come for analysis every day instead of every two days. He does not write a great deal about the experience of analysis, though in a journal entry written immediately after one analytic session he writes: 'Have been thinking it might be useful to put down a few notes about *sex*. Mme Jouve says I have an exceptional faculty of transformation.'[29] This Gascoyne links to his capacity for sublimating sex urges. He goes on to state: 'It no longer seems possible for me to make any reservations about accepting to be a homosexual', and the entries at this time do seem to acknowledge a greater degree of pleasure in sexual love: 'movements of strength and grace, slimness and smooth resistance of a defiant, pliant body discovered in its final secrecy'.[30] (His lover at this time was a Danish doctor, Bent von Müllen, murdered some years later by the Gestapo during the German occupation of Denmark.) But he also writes of having

> reached the same sort of check in analysis as I am accustomed to meeting in my life. Feeling that there is a barrier between my conscious mind and the part that is being analysed. Lay on the couch this evening associating words and images *around something that was hidden* and which I could not get at.[31]

Gascoyne's analyst Blanche Reverchon was married to the writer Pierre Jean Jouve, and in their professional and literary union psychoanalysis and poetry became closely connected. Jouve was an important influence on Gascoyne, who translated a number of his poems. It is also significant, in the light of Gascoyne's distancing of himself from surrealism[32] only a few years after the writing and publication of *A Short Survey of Surrealism* (1935), that Jouve rejected surrealism while sharing its project of absorbing psychoanalysis into literature. Elizabeth Roudinesco, in her study of psychoanalysis in France, *Jacques Lacan & Co.*, writes that

> Unlike the Surrealists and the *NRF* group, Pierre Jean Jouve's appeal was to a mystical vision of Freud's discovery. Blood, death, and culpable desire were the emblematic signs of a spiritual quest in which passionate love combined with the elaboration of a distinctive mode of writing. The encounter with psychoanalysis took place under the sign of conversion and repudiation.[33]

In 1931, Jouve had sent Freud his novel *Vagadu* (1930) (and probably also the earlier volume *Hecate* (1928)), which recounted the therapy of one 'Catherine

Crachat'; Freud wrote in return: 'Copious thanks for sending your engaging books which I read in a single sitting, not without some protest from my sober side.'[34]

In 1933, Jouve and Blanche Reverchon published a clinical study entitled *Moments d'une analyse*. This recounted the case history of Mademoiselle H., who consults a doctor in the hope of freeing herself from a 'vampire', a compulsion to reverie 'devouring' her days. 'The impression of strangeness', Roudinesco writes,

> stems from the fact that the tale is told by a couple taking itself for the object of the narrative and seeking its identity through a gallery of mirrors infinitely reflecting the image of a stroller lost in a labyrinth. If the girl so resembles a novelistic heroine, it is because the conditions of therapy allowed Jouve and Reverchon to transform analytic practice into a tale of devouring.[35]

The image of devouring – and of reverie or inanition 'devouring' days – emerges in Gascoyne's journals during the period of his analysis with Reverchon-Jouve in a section (echoed in Durrell's poem) which Gascoyne headed 'The Pit':

> I sink, I climb laboriously, I lose the thread, I fall . . . A sort of panic begins to rise. They were right to build the wall that I detest, the wall of caution and habit, blind prejudice and unconsciousness; when one has no wall to protect one, one sees that the world is at the bottom of an abyss, that it is dark and tumultuous here, that we are the helpless prey of an eternal, terrifying purposelessness, monster with staring empty eyes and all-devouring jaws.[36]

This spatialising of mental geography, and the images of movement – rising, falling – occur in many of Gascoyne's poems, as in his poem dedicated to Hart Crane and its playing out in spatial terms of Crane's suicidal leap. The image of devouring is also central to Gascoyne's poem 'The Fabulous Glass'[37] written, probably in 1938, for 'Mme. B. R-J', a poem which is also about the faculty of transformation, an ambivalence towards the Mother/analyst,[38] and a complex interplay between the mirror and the eye, in which self-regard becomes a kind of blindness.

Both mirroring and looking are represented by, and enacted in, the journal as a genre of writing and as self-analysis. Gascoyne situates his journals primarily in the French tradition of the *journal intime*. 'I belong to Europe before I belong to England',[39] he wrote in connection with his poetic affiliations and, in April 1937, 'How eternally thankful one should be for people like K.M. [Katherine Mansfield] and Barbellion, and Tchekov, and Baudelaire.'[40] One aspect that links these writers is the intensity of their writing in the face of death. Barbellion's

The Journal of a Disappointed Man (1919), an important model for White as well as for Gascoyne, was the diary of a young, self-educated naturalist (whose real name was Bruce Frederick Cummings) with a terminal illness. An extraordinary success on its publication, it closes with the statement that 'Barbellion died on December 31 – 1917', though its author in fact died on 22 October 1919 at the age of thirty-one. (A further journal was posthumously published in 1920 as *A Last Diary*.)

Gascoyne writes, after reading Barbellion's Journal and shortly after beginning his journal-writing:

> Now I feel as he felt when he read the Journal of Marie Bashkirtseff [who died in Paris of consumption at the age of twenty-five]. 'He feels as I feel. We have the same self-absorption, the same vanity and corroding ambition. He is impressionable, volatile, passionate – ill!' (not that, thank Heaven!) 'So am I. His journal is my journal' – but that's absurd, because I've hardly written more than 20 pages of journal in my life, though I intend to continue now, and to try and strip myself as Barbellion did in his.[41]

Commenting on his own difficulty in writing his journal every day, in the light of his reading of Marie Bashkirtseff's *Journal* (1887), Gascoyne

> noticed how she too was obsessed not so much by death, but by the fear that all her living and feeling might be wasted, that all her passionate days might pass and never leave a trace behind them ... I value all experience and want so much at least to record it.[42]

Later, he expresses disappointment at reading Gide's Journals: 'I think a journal should be a continual confession of an incurable passion for life.'[43] The epithet is transferred here – it was Mansfield's and Chekhov's tuberculosis, and Barbellion's multiple sclerosis, which were 'incurable' – but the assertion brings together in important ways questions of life, death (including an equation between romanticism and consumption) and journal-writing. It also suggests the importance of a community of, and communion between, the keepers of diaries or journals.

The question of the reader of the diaries is raised by Gascoyne at the very start: 'In order to be able to continue writing this one I have to have some imaginary audience in view. You are reading this? But I had to pretend that no one would ever read it!'[44] A few months later, the reader of the journal is projected as a future lover:

> That's what I'm writing these pages for: to make a record of what I am so that someone, perhaps only one or two people – someone with whom I may be in love in years to come – may know me as I was, may feel some sort of contact with a sensibility, a passion, an imagination, a restlessness ... Whoever you are like myself, we understand each other, we know each other, we touch hands somewhere.[45]

Here the ideal reader becomes a mirror image of the self, and is thus also to be identified with the journal, or the journal-self, as the mirror of the self as other.[46]

*

The published versions of Anaïs Nin's journals were later redactions of the many hundreds of notebooks she filled throughout her life, hand-writing their content before, in many instances, typing up the material.[47] From 1932 onwards, Nin wrote of her experience of psychoanalysis, first with René Allendy and then with Otto Rank (both of whom became her lovers): as with Gascoyne and White, psychoanalysis and diary-writing were both intertwined and counterposed. In an entry for 1932, Nin commented:

> Never have I seen as clearly as tonight that my diary-writing is a vice. I came home worn out by magnificent talks with Henry [Miller] at the café; I glided into my bedroom, closed the curtains, threw a log into the fire, lit a cigarette, pulled the diary out of its last hiding place under my dressing-table, threw it on the ivory silk quilt, and prepared for bed. I had the feeling that this is the way an opium smoker prepares for his opium pipe. For this is the moment when I relive my life in terms of a dream, a myth, an endless story.[48]

Nin's words here place the diary-writing in the contexts of an ambiguously gendered Decadence, but the phrase 'endless story' is also fully continuous with turn-of-the-century writings on female adolescence, the 'private theatre' (in Freud and Breuer's phrase),[49] daydreaming and an (auto)erotics of self-narration and of reading – as in Hugh Stutfield's account (written in 1897) of Marie Bashkirtseff's journal as 'a kind of secret Bible' in which 'the tired and discontented women of the time [...] read a few sentences every morning, or at night before going to sleep'.[50] Like Barbellion and Gascoyne, Nin expressed an identification with Bashkirtseff, writing in an early diary: 'I understand her [MB] so well that sometimes I wonder if I am like her.'[51]

In 1933, Nin recorded that her new analyst, Otto Rank, had asked her to give up the diary, which he saw as 'a shell' around her and as 'as a defense':[52] The diary 'is your last defence against analysis [...] I don't want you to analyze the analysis', she records him telling her.[53] 'Rank', she writes, 'wants me to see if I can keep a sketchbook, instead of being kept by a diary':[54] 'I will not give my all to the sketchbook. Is this what Rank wanted, to throw me into my novels, books, out of the intimacy of the diary?'[55] Being 'kept by a diary' (as a mistress would be 'kept' by a lover) is linked here to the time-boundedness, the calendrical nature, of the diary form. As Maurice Blanchot writes:

> The journal intime which seems so detached from forms, so compliant with the movements of life & capable of all liberties, because everything fits in, thoughts, dreams, fictions, self-commentaries, important and unimportant events, in the order or disorder desired, is subject to an apparently light, but in fact formidable clause: it must respect the calendar.[56]

In the case of Nin, or perhaps more accurately, for Rank, the sketchbook, with its impressionistic qualities, becomes identified not only as a preparation for her creative (rather than diaristic) writing but also with the more flexible and free-floating nature of memory. The distinction bears on the ways in which psychoanalysis (like the affair) negotiates temporality: its strict time-keeping (the analytic hour, the daily or twice- or thrice-weekly sessions) running in tandem with a resistance to calendrical time and a commitment to the very different temporalities, or atemporalities, of psychic life.

In Rank's (reported) perception of the diary as a 'shell', the 'intimacy of the diary' (in Nin's phrase) is rendered as (to use Jacques Lacan's term for the imbrications of interiority and exteriority) an 'extimacy' (*extimité*).[57] The hidden and secret dimensions of the diary represent intimacy (a word that Nin uses with great frequency) as, in its dictionary definition, the most interior; as Julia Kristeva notes, 'the word comes from the Latin *intimus*, the superlative of *interior*, thus "the most interior"'.[58] Yet this coexisted for Nin with its exterior qualities – she carried her current diary volume around with her, and wrote it in public. 'I carry away no secrets, as Henry reads the journal',[59] she wrote in one journal entry, but added a month later: 'That was an exception. There must always be a secret.'[60] In more complex ways, the diary was for her a second self, her only adequate auditor (the one who never tired of hearing her self-recountings) and the father, who left the family when Nin was ten, and for whom she began the practice of diary-keeping, as a form of letter to him in his absence. Describing these years after his abandonment of the family in a letter to Artaud, Nin wrote: 'I withdrew into myself and began a secret life in my diary. I turned away from real life.'[61]

This latter element becomes highly charged when Nin meets her father, Joaquim Nin, after a twenty-year absence, and they become lovers, for a period apparently lasting some months. She gave the unpublished diary volumes of this time in the early 1930s the title 'Incest' (with a possible nod to the 1912 study for which her analyst Rank was best known, *The Incest Theme in Literature and Legend: Fundamentals of a Psychology of Literary Creation*). 'All this unfolded itself as it should, gloriously', she writes, 'but without the ultimate spark of joy, because at certain moments he was the unknown lover [...] And at other times too intimate, too like myself.'[62] Here incest and intimacy start to share a highly troubling identity: one which is reinforced by her perception of the connection between 'the diary and my father'.[63] 'Diary thus originates', as Rank observed to her, 'in the need to cover a loss, to fill a vacancy. I call the diary, little by little, a personage; then I confuse it with the shadow, *mon ombre* (my Double!) whom I am going to marry...'[64]

In Nin's diaries, 'incest' becomes the most secret, the most intimate, of her diary's secrets, doubly transgressive in its defiance of the most fundamental of cultural proscriptions and because, as Mary Hamer notes, a taboo is also a prohibition against speaking (or writing).[65] 'I had wanted', Nin writes in an entry for 2 July 1933, 'the journal to die with the confession of a love I could not make. I had wanted at least my incestuous love to remain unwritten. I had promised Father utter secrecy.'[66] But she finds it impossible to observe this ordinance and to 'kill [her] journal off'.[67] 'This diary', she writes in an entry dated 21 July, 'proves a tremendous, all-engulfing craving for truth, since to write it I risk destroying all the edifices of my illusions, all the gifts I made, all that I created, Hugo's life [Nin's husband], Henry's life [Henry Miller]; everyone I saved from truth, I here destroy'.[68]

With the coming of war in 1939, Nin left Paris for New York. Her diaries make reference to the world situation, but often with the disclaimer that her proper role was to engage with the eternal structures of myth rather than with the transience of historical events. More interestingly, perhaps, Nin drew a connection between the drives and desires of the individual and the collective psyche in terms which bear some relationship to the wartime writings of Melanie Klein and other psychoanalysts of the period, in which the destructive impulses which lead to world conflict are perceived as externalisations and projections of psychic life. 'For the small diminutive figure of the child', Nin writes, with reference to her own past, 'the war between parents and division and separation are as great as the world wars of 1914 and 1940.'[69] Nonetheless, when Nin sought to publish her abridged diaries during this period, Houghton Mifflin rejected her proposal, on the grounds that it would be inappropriate to publish such introspective writings during wartime. Nin incorporated the rejection letter into her journal: 'Certainly the writing is extraordinary: the cadences, the ability to communicate an intensity of emotion. But I don't think this is the time to bring it out. Today such morbid preoccupation with one's inner life will seem trivial.'[70]

For other diarists of the time, the question, which became increasingly exigent in the 1930s, was that of whether the self should observe itself or the world. In June 1938, David Gascoyne wrote:

> Saw today in an English paper a notice of somebody's journal, recently published, containing a sort of daily account of the year's events described from a personal angle: which led me to reflect that, considering the extraordinary and momentous nature of 'the times' [...] these pages contain singularly little reflection of contemporary history. Demonstrations in London, Spain, the Anschluss, do appear, but only in passing [...] I've never been able to decide whether or not I wanted this book to be published some day [...] quite what its interest is I find it difficult to say: a record of the late 1930s, or a '*mon coeur mis à nu*' [my heart laid bare] sort of confession? [...] In the end, perhaps, the real reason for keeping a journal is vanity or narcissism, unless one is absolutely determined that no one shall read it; which I am not.[71]

Gascoyne expressed regret that he had failed to keep a record of his time in Paris during 1933, when he was most involved with the surrealists, and gathering together material for his study of the movement.[72] Editing his journals decades later, he added material about his experiences in Spain in 1936, during which time he broadcast in English for the Propaganda Ministry. In a diary entry from 1937, he had indicated that he felt his notes

> give only a very fragmentary idea of my actual existence and what's happened to me – At this point, for instance, a very full and important period has been left out – Barcelona, Valentine Penrose; the most difficult stages of my relationship with Antonia [White] – Roland Cailleux; Mass Observation and Charles Madge; a frightful month of depression following a visit to Antonia's analyst; and now, a sort of 'reawakening'. It is my intention to arrange all these notes one day, and those of previous notebooks, and to fill in the gaps with autobiographical reminiscences. I should hate anything to be lost! It's a curious thing that when anything is actually happening to me, I feel no inclination to record it until afterwards.[73]

There is a palpable tension in Gascoyne's journals between the desire to write a kind of philosophical autobiography, to become a 'subjective' thinker, in the Kierkegaardian sense, an 'existential' thinker (though Gascoyne also writes of 'the extraordinary objectivity of [Kierkegaard's] psychological genius'[74]), and his feelings of responsibility as historical witness. This conflict was, to a certain extent, more readily resolved, though undoubtedly at significant psychic cost, during the war years, when inner and outer crises – the intimate and the external – could be understood more clearly in relation to each other. In a journal entry for March 1940, a meditation to which he gave the title 'Tenebrae' – 'Night. "The stars look down . . . ."' – Gascoyne wrote of the black-out in London as a 'great motionless sea of darkness', which appeared to him as 'an exteriorization for that unwalled intimate dark space with which I am so familiar *within* myself [. . .] irresistibly I felt the outer and the inner night exchange themselves'.[75]

Notes

1. While the histories of the terms 'journal' and 'diary' are not identical – 'journal' precedes 'diary' in English by some two hundred years – the distinctions between them have become obscured, and theorists of the diary tend to treat them more or less interchangeably. See, for example, Judy Simons, *Diaries and Journals of Literary Women from Fanny Burney to Virginia Woolf* (London: Palgrave, 1990).
2. Philippe Lejeune, *Cher cahier* (Paris: Gallimard, 1989), p. 12; my translation.
3. Quoted in Philippe Lejeune, *On Diary*, ed. Jeremy Popkin and Julie Rak (Manoa: University of Hawaii Press, 2009), pp. 96–7. The diarist was Antoine Métral (1778–1839).
4. See Julien Green, *Journal* (Paris: Plon, 1928, 1939, 1946, 1949, 1951, 1955).
5. Elizabeth Podnieks, *Daily Modernism: The Literary Diaries of Virginia Woolf, Antonia White, Elizabeth Smart, and Anaïs Nin* (Montreal: McGill-Queens University Press, 2000), p. 5.
6. David Gascoyne, *Collected Journals 1936–42* (London: Skoob Books, 1991), p. 339.
7. Ibid. p. 339.
8. Anaïs Nin, discussed below, was introduced by Miller to Durrell and helped him type *The Black Book*.
9. Lawrence Durrell, *The Black Book: An Agon* (London: Faber, 1977), p. 78. This assertion of course raises the question of the intimacy of the *journal intime*.
10. Gascoyne, *Collected Journals*, p. 139.

11. Ibid. pp. 139–40.
12. Lawrence Durrell, 'Paris Journal: For David Gascoyne (1939)' (1943/1939), in *Collected Poems 1931–74*, ed. James E. Brigham (London: Faber & Faber, 2012), pp. 68–9. The ironic question 'What is Truth?' is attributed to Pontius Pilate in John's Gospel, chapter 18, verse 38, in response to Jesus' claim that he was born to 'bear witness to the truth'.
13. Compare Virginia Woolf's image of consciousness and modernist aesthetics: 'Examine for a moment an ordinary mind on an ordinary day. The mind receives a myriad impressions [...] as they fall, as they shape themselves into the life of Monday or Tuesday, the accent falls differently from of old' ('Modern Fiction', in *The Essays of Virginia Woolf*, vol. 4, ed. Andrew McNeillie (London: Hogarth Press, 1994), p. 160).
14. Anaïs Nin, *Nearer the Moon* (London: Peter Owen, 1996), p. 172.
15. Ibid. p. 177.
16. Gascoyne, *Collected Journals*, p. 142.
17. Nin, *Nearer the Moon*, p. 238.
18. Ibid. p. 173. See also Podnieks, *Daily Modernism*, p. 11.
19. See Anita Jarczok, *Writing an Icon: Celebrity Culture and the Invention of Anaïs Nin* (Athens, OH: Ohio University Press, 2017), especially ch. 1.
20. White's diaries have been published, in an abridged form, edited by her daughter Susan Chitty, who selected about a quarter of the original material (Antonia White, *Diaries 1926–1957*, ed. Susan Chitty (London: Constable, 1991)).
21. Antonia White, *The Sugar House* (London: Virago, 1979), p. 154.
22. White, *Diaries*, p. 56.
23. Ibid. p. 58.
24. White's analysis with Dr Dennis Carroll (1935–8) was followed in 1948/9 by therapy, strongly centred on dream analysis, with the untrained Dorothy Kingsmill. In the 1960s, White re-entered psychoanalysis/psychotherapy with Dr Philip Ployé; the motivation was again her concern about her writing block.
25. White, *Diaries*, p. 149.
26. Ibid. p. 68.
27. Ibid. p. 168. In her detailed discussion of White's diaries, Podnieks, like many other writers on White, points up the connection White herself drew between her writing block and the occasion of her father's anger over the novel she had produced as a teenager (*Daily Modernism*, pp. 166ff.). Patricia Moran has also linked 'the primal scene of paternal prohibition' to two powerful frameworks in White's life, psychoanalysis and Catholicism, but has resisted the speculation that White was the victim of her father's sexual

abuse (*Antonia White and Manic-Depressive Illness* (Edinburgh: Edinburgh University Press, 2018), p. 100).
28. On this term, used for example by E. Stuart Bates and Adrian Stokes, see Laura Marcus, *Auto/biographical Discourses: Theory, Criticism, Practice* (Manchester: Manchester University Press, 1994), pp. 250–1. It conveys both the sense of looking out and that of the inversion of outside and inside, exposing the self, as in the trope of autobiography as self-dissection.
29. Gascoyne, *Collected Journals*, p. 203.
30. Ibid. p. 205.
31. Ibid. pp. 218–19.
32. For a nuanced discussion of the various elements behind this shift, see Robert Fraser, *Night Thoughts: The Surreal Life of the Poet David Gascoyne* (Oxford: Oxford University Press, 2012). These include the influence of the Romanian poet and critic Benjamin Fondane, Gascoyne's own unwillingness to be stereotyped and his later enthusiasm for existentialism.
33. Elizabeth Roudinesco, *Jacques Lacan & Co.: A History of Psychoanalysis in France, 1925–1985*, trans. Jeffrey Mehlman (Chicago: University of Chicago Press, 1990), p. 94.
34. Quoted in ibid. p. 95.
35. Roudinesco, *Jacques Lacan & Co.*, p. 99.
36. Gascoyne, *Collected Journals*, pp. 206–7.
37. David Gascoyne, *Selected Poems* (London: Enitharmon, 1994), p. 106.
38. In his journal Gascoyne writes: 'My unconscious appears to have a very hostile opinion of Mme. Jouve, representing her as a witch with a pointed hat, a beard and horns! I am too polite, of course, to tell her so to her face; but I imagine she is wise enough to realize that each part of this composite image refers to a certain extent to her' (*Collected Journals*, p. 205).
39. Ibid. p. 170.
40. Ibid. p. 72.
41. Ibid. p. 16.
42. Ibid. pp. 47–8.
43. Ibid. p. 56.
44. Ibid. p. 9.
45. Ibid. p. 53.
46. See, for example, Max Saunders, '"Fusions and Interrelations": Family Memoirs of Henry James, Edmund Gosse, and Others', in Adam Smyth (ed.), *A History of English Autobiography* (New York: Cambridge University Press, 2016), pp. 255–68; and Laura Marcus, 'Experiments in Form: Modernism and Autobiography in Woolf, Eliot, Mansfield, Lawrence, Joyce, and Richardson', in Smyth (ed.), *A History of English Autobiography*, pp. 298–312.

47. References in the notes below are sometimes to the first published editions and sometimes to the later, 'unexpurgated' versions, since the content differs in other respects too.
48. Anaïs Nin, *The Journals of Anaïs Nin*, vol. 1, 1931–1934, ed. Gunther Stuhlmann (London: Quartet, 1973), p. 97.
49. See Josef Breuer, 'Fräulein Anna O.', in Breuer and Sigmund Freud, *The Standard Edition of the Complete Psychological Works of Sigmund Freud, vol. 2 (1893–1895): Studies on Hysteria*, trans. from the German by James Strachey (London: Hogarth Press, 1955), p. 22.
50. Hugh Stutfield, 'The Psychology of Feminism', *Blackwood's*, 161 (January 1897), p. 109.
51. Anaïs Nin, *The Early Diary of Anaïs Nin*, vol. 2, ed. Rupert Pole (New York: Harcourt Brace Jovanovich, 1982), p. 291.
52. Nin, *The Journals of Anaïs Nin*, vol. 1, p. 290.
53. Ibid. p. 294.
54. Ibid. p. 299.
55. Ibid. p. 295.
56. See Maurice Blanchot, *Le Livre à venir* (Paris: Gallimard, 1959), p. 224; my translation.
57. See Jacques Lacan, *The Seminar of Jacques Lacan. Book VII: The Ethics of Psychoanalysis, 1959–1960*, ed. Jacques-Alain Miller, trans. Dennis Porter (London: Routledge, 1992), p. 139.
58. Julia Kristeva, *Intimate Revolt*, trans. Jeanine Herman (New York: Columbia University Press, 2002), p. 43.
59. Nin, *The Journals of Anaïs Nin*, vol. 1, p. 101.
60. Ibid. p. 107.
61. Anaïs Nin, *Incest: Unexpurgated Diaries 1932–1934* (San Diego, New York and London: Harcourt Brace, 1992), p. 199.
62. Ibid. p. 212.
63. Ibid. p. 297.
64. Ibid. p. 298. This also refers to Rank's study of *The Double* ('Der Doppelgänger'), first published in 1914 and translated into French in 1932 as *Don Juan. Une étude sur le double* (Paris: Denoël and Steele).
65. Mary Hamer, *Incest: A New Perspective* (Cambridge: Polity Press, 2002), p. 31.
66. Nin, *Incest*, p. 216.
67. Ibid. p. 217.
68. Ibid. pp. 232–3.
69. Anaïs Nin, *Mirages: The Unexpurgated Diary of Anaïs Nin* (San Diego: Swallow Press, 2013), p. 140, 19 January 1943.

70. Ibid. p. 101, 24 February 1942.
71. Gascoyne, *Collected Journals*, p. 158.
72. Ibid. p. 9.
73. Ibid. p. 47.
74. Ibid. p. 287.
75. Ibid. p. 292.

9

Leonora Carrington's Poetics of Listening

Anna Watz

Leonora Carrington's surrealist novel *The Hearing Trumpet* (written sometime in the 1950s but not published until 1974)[1] is at once a parodic quest narrative, a fictionalised transposition of Robert Graves's 1948 study *The White Goddess: A Historical Grammar of Poetic Myth* (which Carrington described as 'the greatest revelation' of her life[2]) and a utopian vision of an ethics of being and knowing. Narrated by its whimsical, anecdote-prone and near-deaf protagonist, the ninety-two-year-old Marian Leatherby, the novel chronicles six elderly women's search for the Holy Grail in a nursing home for the aged. As Jonathan P. Eburne has observed, *The Hearing Trumpet* 'serves as a kind of commonplace-book for Carrington's thinking during this period'.[3] Drawing on alchemical and esoteric narratives, revisionist theology, alternative knowledges, myth and fairy tale, *The Hearing Trumpet* is indeed shaped by the same interests that characterise Carrington's visual art at the height of her career.[4] Carrington's pursuit of an alternative spirituality through alchemy, goddess worship and other occult practices was in line with a broader surrealist interest in occultism,[5] just like her adoption of the quest structure harmonised, as Kristoffer Noheden has shown, with the way in which many of the post-war surrealists articulated their aesthetic and epistemological goals.[6] At the same time, *The Hearing Trumpet* is an intimately personal exploration of subjectivity and self-knowledge. Carrington's surrealist-feminist narrative quest for an alternative way of understanding the world and humanity's place in it ultimately suggests that self-knowledge will not be attained solely through introspection and the adoption of revisionist belief systems; without relational intimacy, these strategies to achieve self-knowledge will not fully work.

This chapter explores these socio-ethical dimensions of *The Hearing Trumpet* through a reading of the way in which the novel narrates the construction of self through the intimacy of listening. Whereas the fantastical surface plot closely follows the anti-patriarchal mythology outlined in Graves's *The White Goddess* (which posits that a prototypical ancient goddess cult preceded the inception of male-centred monotheism and patriarchy),[7] with a sprinkle of intertextual allusions to, for example, the Arthurian Grail legend, Hans Christian Andersen's fairy tale 'The Snow Queen' (1844), alchemy, the Kabbalah as well as autobiographical episodes from Carrington's own life, the novel's frequent references to listening and hearing reveal an underlying narrative that concerns the intimacies of the self's relationship to the other. More than just a meditation on the importance of friendship and relationality, however, Carrington's poetics of listening is predicated on something akin to Luce Irigaray's philosophy of love (which underpins her writings from the early 2000s onwards): as I will show, what is at stake in *The Hearing Trumpet* is a subject configured in close relation to the other (whether human, animal or vegetable), and a philosophy of intersubjectivity in which respect for and an acknowledgement of the other take precedence over coherent self-articulation.

While the novel parodically revisits the Grail quest narrative, the more important quest, as I have already suggested, is Marian's search for self-knowledge. Her adventures in the old-age home ultimately lead her to a subterranean cavern in which she meets another version of herself. In a bizarre scene rife with alchemical symbolism, Marian jumps into a cauldron of hot soup; her double proceeds to eat her (in the broth), and both of them are united in a new self, reborn and presumably wiser. But this apparent end-point of her mythical and alchemical journey is only a beginning; what Marian attains is not an epiphany regarding her own self, but rather a new understanding of subjectivity as founded on listening – not merely to human others, but to all living things. Thus, Marian's quest for self-knowledge is ultimately redirected away from the self and towards a relational intimacy achieved through listening to the other.

The hearing trumpet itself, which is given to Marian by her friend Carmella at the beginning of the narrative, functions as a symbol for Carrington's ethics of listening in the novel. The reader is alerted to its subversive qualities already from the novel's first two lines, in which Marian tells us that 'when Carmella gave me the present of the hearing trumpet she may have foreseen some of the consequences. Carmella is not what I would call malicious, she just happens to have a curious sense of humour.'[8] The most immediate consequence of the introduction of the hearing trumpet in Marian's life is that with it she overhears her family conspiring to send her to Lightsome Hall, an institution for the elderly run by the 'Well of Light Brotherhood'. Marian hears her unsympathetic grandson Robert exclaim: 'Grandmother [...] can hardly be classified as a human being. She is a drooling sack of decomposing flesh', to which his mother adds: 'those old people do not have feelings like you or I' (10). Marian's unempathetic family is so exaggeratedly mean that the scene becomes grotesquely humorous. But the family also serves a narrative function beyond dark comedy; they are the first in a line of characters in the novel that refuse to listen to others. Their violent denial of Marian's subjecthood stands in stark contrast to the intersubjectivity based on listening advocated by the novel, and which I will outline below.

The act of overhearing her family's devious plans does not stop Marian's transferral to the institution — fortunately, we might add, since this is where her quest for understanding begins. Soon, she finds herself installed at the old-women's home, housed in an ancient convent and run by a 'Sanctified Psychologist' by the name of Dr. Gambit. Dr. Gambit is committed to making the old women conform to his programmatic teachings, with the aim of revealing to them 'the key to the understanding of Inner Christianity' (28). As Georgina, another of the old women, wryly comments: 'The result is Holy Reason like Freudian table turning. Quite frightful and phony as Hell' (33). Georgina also delivers a biting dig at the patriarchal logic that underpins Dr. Gambit's institution: 'If only one could get out of this dump he would cease to be important, being the only male around, you know' (33).

Carrington herself admitted that Dr. Gambit was a caricature of the spiritual teacher and esotericist George Gurdjieff, whose writings she had studied together with her close friend and fellow surrealist, Remedios Varo, who in turn serves as the inspiration for the likeable character Carmella. As Eburne explains, although Carrington and Varo were sympathetic to Gurdjieff's and other esoteric thinkers' 'alternative epistemologies' and 'systems of discovery and understanding that suspend the ordering imperatives of classical reason', Carrington was simultaneously 'profoundly attentive to their limits as explanatory systems, which could so often become proscriptive in their universalising pretensions'.[9] As a surrealist, Carrington was of course wary of unthinking acceptance of any prescribed creed; as someone who had also intimately experienced the rise of fascism in Europe, robotic compliance with doctrine was for her associated with real evil. Although her parody of Gurdjieff in *The Hearing Trumpet* might be read as playful irreverence, the narrative nevertheless contains a profoundly serious warning about thoughtless acceptance of any dogma.

The trauma of the war, and the fear of the mindset that had led up to it, would continue to haunt Carrington's work for the rest of her career. In her post-war work, this anxiety about fascist indoctrination became inflected through distinctly post-war angst regarding impending nuclear devastation. As she explains in an artist's statement in 1975, the year after *The Hearing Trumpet* was published:

There are so many questions and so much Dogmaturd to clear aside before anything makes sense, and we are on the point of destroying the earth before we know anything at all. Perhaps a great virtue, curiosity can only be satisfied if the millennia of accumulated false data are turned upside down. Which means turning oneself inside out and to begin by despising no thing, ignoring no thing [...] and make some interior space for digestive purposes. Our machine-mentation still reacts to colossal absurdities with violence, pleasure, pain [...] automatically. Such as: I am, I am, I am. (Anything from an archbishop to a disregarded boot.) But is this so? Am I?[10]

Carrington's deconstruction of the self-assertive 'I am' in this excerpt (which echoes surrealism's conscious disruption of the notion of a coherent identity) is posited as the antipode – and possible antidote – to 'Dogmaturd'. This latter concept, as its name indicates, encapsulates Carrington's contempt for dogma and doctrine, which, as Eburne explains, 'reduced knowing to a totalising, totalitarian act of will'.[11] 'Dogmaturd' characterises not only the militaristic and nationalist logic of fascism or the cold-war nuclear arms race, but, more generally, also a Western rationalistic tradition that privileges the sovereign self. To turn 'oneself inside out' means to question such autonomy. More than that, as we shall see, in *The Hearing Trumpet* Marian finds that her digestion of herself in the alchemical broth (a quite literal subversion of the boundary between inside and outside) prompts a different kind of synaesthetic listening that enables an empathetical engagement with the natural, animal as well as human world.

While the totalising tendencies of esotericists such as Gurdjieff are parodied in *The Hearing Trumpet*, the novel simultaneously suggests that esoteric or arcane forms of knowledge may be repositories of valuable lessons regarding how to be in the world – resonant alternatives to the 'Dogmaturd' Carrington identifies in her contemporary political culture. Carrington's interest in myth and magical tradition is well known; as I have already suggested, her points of reference range from fairy tales and alchemy to the revisionary theology of Graves and the Kabbalah; in addition to these, she was also drawn to Celtic myth, Zen Buddhism, Aztec and Mayan hermetic knowledge, Gnosticism and the writings of Carl Jung. As the sheer diversity of influences suggests, Carrington did not espouse a single belief system or view of knowledge. Moreover, her ever-ironic stance, which permeates the narrative of *The Hearing Trumpet*, troubles any literal interpretation of the esoteric knowledges she presents in her work. As Eburne rightly points out, 'even at her most seemingly sincere, Carrington's tongue is always in her cheek; this ironic distance suspends the magical thinking of Carrington's use of esoterica and hermetic knowledges within an intertextual framework whose instabilities render it virtual rather than propositional'.[12] The intertextual web formed by magical and esoteric references in *The Hearing Trumpet*, I would add, also prompts an attitude of openness to contradiction and otherness. Without a single interpretative framework forced upon the text, or the world, we might hear things that would otherwise have gone unnoticed.[13]

Unsettling the Wor(l)d

As a narrative about self-knowledge, *The Hearing Trumpet* closely echoes *Down Below*, Carrington's autobiographical account of her mental breakdown in 1940; in many ways the novel can be read as a fictionalised version of her attempt to 're-establish contact between [her] mind and [her] self' in a psychiatric clinic in Santander, Spain.[14] The two texts differ dramatically in tone, however; while *The Hearing Trumpet* is marked by Carrington's surrealist humour, *Down Below* is a distressing text in which violence, alienation and isolation dominate both outer and inner reality. As Susan Rubin Suleiman notes, '*The Hearing Trumpet* can be read as a self-conscious, artistically controlled transposition and expansion of some of the delusionary constructions described in *Down Below* [...] with an accompanying change in mood and color from the tragic to the comic.'[15] Carrington's elaboration of the listening subject in *The Hearing Trumpet* is thus locked in dialogue with her search for a coherent subjectivity in *Down Below*; framed in relation to the latter, the novel's engagement with knowledge and self-knowledge emerges even more clearly. Before elaborating the novel's vision of an ethics of listening, I will therefore outline the main junctures of Carrington's failed quest for self-knowledge in her memoir.

Down Below begins as a journey of escape; after the capture by the Nazis of her lover Max Ernst (for his 'degenerate art') in May 1940, Carrington joins two friends travelling to Spain in order to escape the approaching Nazis and to try to organise Ernst's release. Once in Madrid, she succumbs to psychosis and is incarcerated in a psychiatric clinic in Santander.[16] The quest structure is present in the journey from the very beginning; Carrington tells us that she sets out on her expedition carrying a suitcase bearing her engraved name and a brass plate with the word REVELATION written on it. Simultaneously, the reader understands that this quest is doomed to fail; 'Revelation' was a British suitcase brand popular in the 1930s, and it is likely that the seemingly momentous brass plate is in fact merely the company's logotype. Carrington's misinterpretation of signs here characterises the pursuit of knowledge in the narrative as a whole as one of intense disconnection from the world of others. Indeed, Carrington's description of her madness seems to hinge precisely on the breakdown of language and signification. Her symptoms include alternately feeling omnipotent and able to control the outside world with her thoughts and able to understand languages she cannot actually speak, and at the same time feeling what she repeatedly describes as 'jammed';[17] a feeling of stasis and petrification in which she cannot speak or even move. This suspension outside language – a kind of freefall in which she alternately feels empowered and disempowered – is the key principle in Carrington's description of psychosis.

Carrington writes that in her delusion she believed that she was being tortured in the asylum in order eventually to 'attain Absolute Knowledge'.[18] 'Absolute Knowledge' is described as a truly psychotic space, in which linguistic signification has collapsed and Carrington herself has become the protagonist of all religious or mythological narratives: in her mind, when she reaches 'full lucidity', she will become 'the third person of the Trinity'.[19] Once she has achieved 'Absolute Knowledge', or the 'Whole Truth', she believes that she will be transferred to another building in the hospital, which she calls 'Down Below'.[20] In line with the religious transcendence fantasies that tinge her illness, this place is referred to as a heavenly 'paradise', a 'Jerusalem' where 'people lived [...] very happily'.[21]

Carrington's notion of 'Absolute Knowledge' is adopted from esoteric and alchemical discourses, which she would continue to explore and engage with for the rest of her career. In *Down Below*, however, Carrington's description of 'Absolute Knowledge' is 'framed', as Eburne points out, 'as a systematic delusion rather than as a lucid experience of comprehension'.[22] In the opening paragraphs of the memoir, the now 'recovered' Carrington comments that, at the time of her incarceration, she 'was not aware of [...] the necessity that others be with me that we may feed each other with our knowledge and thus constitute the Whole'.[23] Even though she still employs esoteric terms like 'Whole' and 'Absolute', her later understanding of 'Absolute Knowledge', as Eburne notes, 'demanded resisting its very claim to totality. To believe otherwise was to succumb to what she later called "Dogmaturd."'[24] Carrington's deluded quest for wisdom in isolation from others in the asylum is thus brought into juxtaposition, both by the framing of the memoir and in her subsequent work, with a conception of knowledge as both open-ended and relational.

Given the spiritual importance accorded to the place 'Down Below' in Carrington's memoir, it is not a coincidence that Marian's alchemical self-transformation in *The Hearing Trumpet* happens 'down below', in an underground cavern. After her rebirth, having digested herself in the soup, to which her alternative self has 'added a pinch of salt and some peppercorns' (138), Marian looks at herself in a mirror and sees a union not with the Christian Holy Trinity, but instead with various reincarnations of an Ancient Goddess. This scene, which clearly draws on the model of the triple female deity that Graves elaborates in *The White Goddess*, not only replaces a masculine Holy Trinity with a feminine one (the womb-like cave of course adds to this symbolism); it also unsettles the search for an apparently singular version of 'Absolute Knowledge', which seems to fuel Carrington in *Down Below*, and instead foregrounds a patchy, intertextual and even contradictory approach to wisdom, which is no sooner presented than it is called into question. Indeed, Marian adds after her description of the vision in the mirror: 'This of course might have been an optical illusion' (138). We are thus urged by Marian to take her alchemical transformation in the soup cauldron with 'a pinch of salt', both literally and figuratively. In this way, while the novel references alchemy and esoteric wisdom as much as, if not more than, *Down Below*, it simultaneously subverts these narratives' claims to totality or authority. As Eburne writes, 'rather than simply drawing upon hermetic traditions', Carrington's work 'engages actively and experimentally with them'.[25] Her ambition 'is not to follow hermetic or esoteric "traditions", but to turn them, and the world they envision, upside down'.[26]

Just like the pursuit of 'Absolute Knowledge' is interrupted in *The Hearing Trumpet*, so is the quest for a self that is capable of fully knowing itself. When Marian stands in front of her double by the cauldron, she knows that she is expected to ask her questions about herself, 'but [her] mind was as numb as a hunk of frozen mutton' (137). Her subsequent self-transformation, then, does not result in formulating answers or truths about the self; rather, the most significant thing that is attained after Marian's transmutation is a more profound connection with her friends (who, she learns, have similarly met themselves in the underworld) and harmony with the world around her. Emerging from the cavern, Marian finds the institution in ruins after an earthquake, which has also disposed of Dr. Gambit and the programmatic routine he represents. In their stead, we find the community of crones laughing and dancing around a fire to the sound of a tom-tom drum.

The Hearing Trumpet, as Suleiman observes, is indeed full of reworked scenarios originally introduced in *Down Below*. The foregrounding of the activity of listening in *The Hearing Trumpet* has a parallel in the menacing gaze in *Down Below*. The penetrating and phallic gaze in the latter text is connected to an overtly fascist violence. Strapped to a bed and injected with the drug Cardiazol, which causes intense convulsions, Carrington relates how she becomes petrified by the doctor's and guards' unified stare: 'Each of them got hold of a portion of my body', she narrates, 'and I saw the *centre* of all eyes fixed upon me in a ghastly stare.'[27] This gaze equals self-annihilation for Carrington; her doctor's eyes, she writes, 'were tearing my brain apart and I was sinking down into a well ... very far ... The bottom of that well was the stopping of my mind for all eternity in the essence of utter anguish.'[28] Later the menacing 'pinpoint pupils' of the doctor are, through a chain of associations, connected with Adolf Hitler.[29] In her delusion, Carrington believes that the convulsions caused by the drug are the effect of a kind of hypnosis practised upon her through the stare of the medical staff.

The hypnotic stare is also connected to the contemporary political climate; Carrington is convinced that the rise of Nazism and fascism in Europe is the result of a similar mass hypnosis. In a Madrid hotel, a few days before her incarceration, she had met a Dutch man, whom she believes to be Hitler's right hand. 'To me Van Ghent was my father, my enemy, and the enemy of mankind; I was the only one who could vanquish him', she states.[30] This realisation prompts her to visit the Consul at the British Embassy and to attempt 'to convince him that the World War was being waged hypnotically by a group of people – Hitler and Co. – who were represented in Spain by Van Ghent'.[31] The crippling fear of the gaze in *Down Below* is thus linked to an anxiety of being co-opted into the state of 'robots, of thoughtless, fleshless beings' that had already established itself – a community of people who have stopped thinking and who are just following orders, as if under hypnosis.[32] This blind acceptance of orders or 'facts' – a mindset that was ultimately responsible for the establishment of fascism in Europe – resembles what Carrington would later call 'Dogmaturd'. The same dogmatic understanding of the world is referred to in *The Hearing Trumpet* as 'a form of planetary hypnosis', which has caused humans to act and think according to what they have been told 'by advertisements, cinemas, policemen and parliaments' (126).

Read against *Down Below*'s chilling depiction of the gaze, the thematisation of listening in *The Hearing Trumpet* emerges as a non-violent resistance to the death-dealing logic of absolute doctrine. Marian's hearing trumpet serves symbolically to undermine such dogma. The object makes Marian think of the horn of the archangel Gabriel, but in reverse, as she hastens to add: 'I believe he is supposed to blow his and not listen through it, that is, according to the bible, on the last day when humanity rises to ultimate catastrophe' (20). She continues to muse:

> Strange how the bible always seems to end up in misery and cataclysm. I often wondered how their angry and vicious God became so popular. Humanity is very strange and I don't pretend to understand anything, however why worship something that only sends you plagues and massacres? and why was Eve blamed for everything? (20)

Marian's analysis here is that communication in society's patriarchal institutions (including Christianity) is one-directional; Gabriel's unmistakably phallus-shaped horn emits sound but is not able to receive any. By inverting the function of the biblical horn, Carrington disturbs not only the binary between active and passive, but also the whole foundation of logocentrism: Gabriel's trumpet symbolises the word of God, presence and absolute meaning. The hearing trumpet – and indeed the whole novel – can be seen as a critique of such a belief in the absolute, which for Carrington is bound up with violence, thoughtlessness and a lack of the ability to listen. Marian's own inverted use of the horn thus subverts the idea of the quest for the self as a discovery of an inner true core that can be articulated. Rather, the novel suggests, it is through the intimate act of listening that the subject is revealed, however imperfectly, to itself.

In *The Way of Love* (2002), Luce Irigaray proposes a philosophy of love that resonates remarkably closely with Carrington's vision of intersubjectivity. Wishing to outline an alternative to the Western philosophical tradition, Irigaray champions a broadened understanding of the term 'philosophy' as not merely the 'love of wisdom', but also the 'wisdom of love'.[33] In such a 'philosophy in the feminine', 'the values of intersubjectivity, of dialogue in difference, of attention to present life, in its concrete and sensible aspects, will be recognized and raised to the level of a wisdom'.[34] Like Irigaray's earlier writings, *The Way of Love* also insists on the need for a new language that allows space for the feminine. As she stated in *Speculum of the Other Woman* (1974), all Western theories of subjectivity have been 'appropriated by the "masculine"', thus allowing no space for feminine specificity and difference.[35] In *The Way of Love*, she continues to insist that in order to speak a philosophy of love and intersubjectivity, originating in the recognition of the 'feminine',

> descriptive and narrative language, those to which we most often resort today, are no longer appropriate. They correspond to something or someone who already exists, and is even already in the past, or put into the past by what is said. The task here is different. It is a question of making something exist, in the present and even more in the future. It is a matter of staging an encounter between the one and the other – which has not yet occurred, and for which we lacked words, gestures, thus the means of welcoming, celebrating, cultivating it in the present and the future.[36]

The hearing trumpet, as the inversion of both phallocentrism and logocentrism, similarly proposes a new language of intimacy rather than of absolute truth (whether such a truth is elaborated in rationalist, Christian or alchemical terms); a language that depends as much on listening as it does on enunciation. More than merely a representation of such a new language of self-narration, we might also consider *The Hearing Trumpet* to be Carrington's own alternative narration of *her* self. The fact that it is a fictional text distinguishes it from the memoir *Down Below*, which purports to give an accurate account of a portion of Carrington's own life. Perhaps the autobiographical genre, which is traditionally concerned with presenting a coherent story of the self, ultimately cannot accommodate Carrington's narration of subjectivity. Instead, it is the fictional, fantastical and surrealist genre that allows Carrington to narrate the construction of subjectivity – of *her* subjectivity – in a way that does not heed a Western, 'masculine' ordering of the world. Like Irigaray's 'philosophy in the feminine', the novel invents a new representational language of the self; it 'mak[es] something exist'.

The novel's eccentric and telepathic character Carmella is seen by Marian as having a 'curious sense of humour' (1); nevertheless, her judgement sometimes seems to be clouded by her overly vivid imagination. She has a distinctive passion, Marian tells us at the beginning of her narrative: she 'writes letters all over the world to people she has never met, and signs them with all kinds of romantic names, never her own. [. . .] No-one ever replies. This is the really incomprehensible side of humanity, people never have time for anything' (4). The novel thus starts with an expressed desire for communication and connection. But Carmella reveals that perhaps her prompting is too presumptuous, as she has already conjured up the personalities of the people she writes to, according to her own desires. 'This letter is addressed to Monsieur Belvedere Oise Noisis, rue de la Rechte Potin, Paris Ile', she tells Marian; 'You could hardly invent anything more sonorous even if you tried. I see him as a rather frail old gentleman, still elegant, with a passion for tropical mushrooms which he grows in an Empire wardrobe. He wears embroidered waistcoats and travels with purple luggage' (6). Marian, however, realises that the key to connection is not just being heard, but to listen: 'You know, Carmella,' she responds, 'I sometimes think that you might get a reply if you didn't impose your imagination on people you have never seen' (6). Suleiman reads this scene as a 'Lewiscarrollesque way to remind us of the power of the imagination and fancy';[37] however, even though the description of Carmella's letter-writing is rendered in a humorous and gentle manner (Varo, on whom the character Carmella is based, was Carrington's closest friend), I believe that it also contains an implicit warning about the dangers of not allowing for the otherness and opacity of the other.

The position of holding back and letting the other exist on their own terms that Marian is suggesting here is at once a critique of Western rationalistic belief systems and of their understanding of the self as coherent and autonomous. Again, we are reminded of Irigaray's philosophy of love, which suggests that subjectivity is essentially relational. Unsettling Hegel's master–slave dialectic, Irigaray advocates an attitude to the other and to difference that emerges from a reciprocal relationship between two subjects, rather than between subject and object. As she proposes in the introduction to her volume of collected essays, *Key Writings* (2004),

> Too often we do not take into consideration clearly enough the difference between approaching another and approaching a thing. Relations with things cannot be reciprocal, and the resistance of a thing to us does not really result from its own mystery.[38]

In order to make space for the other as subject, we must refrain from trying to control them by incorporating them or solving their mystery. This in turn requires what Irigaray elsewhere calls an 'opening of a world of one's own, experienced as familiar, in order to welcome the stranger, while remaining oneself and letting the stranger be other'.[39] Ultimately, 'in a philosophy of intersubjectivity, we have rather to return behind or beyond all our discourses and knowledge, to keep silent and to listen to the speech of the other and enter into a communication with him, or her'.[40]

Even though Marian is nearly deaf, she is, when the novel opens, spiritually ready to transform her relationship with the world into one based on an ethics of listening. In fact, if we consider surrealism's preoccupation with violated or enucleated eyes,[41] which are usually interpreted as an attempt to access the world of the unconscious through blinding oneself to the world of rationality, we might say that in such a surrealist vein Marian's deafness is a necessary condition for her being able to truly hear the other. Held up in humorous contrast to Marian is the character Anna Wertz, one of the old women at Lightsome Hall, whom the novel overtly lampoons for her inability to listen. 'Her talk', Marian ponders, 'was like the wheel of fortune that has certain variations but always gets back to the same point' (27). And Marian worries that the institution and the 'Personality Work' they perform, which is of course the ultimate institutionalised conformism, will make her the same as Anna Wertz: 'Would I also have to work all day and night until I couldn't stop talking?', she wonders (26). Although Anna Wertz's talk prevents listening, the most malicious violence here is enacted by a system that coerces its subjects to behave according to a doctrine, like puppets on a string. Such an attitude, represented in *Down Below* by the institutional gaze, not only fails to admit the other into itself, but renders the other absolutely powerless.

The image of the all-seeing eye, which dominates *Down Below*, is unsettled in *The Hearing Trumpet* not only by its focus on listening, but also by the trope of the wink. In the institutional dining hall, Marian is immediately fascinated by a portrait of a nun, who seems to wink at her 'with a most disconcerting mixture of mockery and malevolence' (29). As Natalya Lusty notes, 'the Abbess's wink, a performative gesture of irony, reinforces Carrington's comic tone throughout the novel'.[42] The winking nun in the portrait is Doña Rosalinda Alvarez, an eighteenth-century abbess, who, we find out, was working undercover as a nun; in actual fact she was a secret agent working to disrupt and undermine the Christian doctrine from within. Soon after Marian has started noticing Doña Rosalinda's winking, she is presented with a book containing the 'true and faithful rendering of the life of Rosalinda Alvarez della Cueva' (73). Her story within the story of the novel provides Marian and her cohabitants with the knowledge they need in order to revolt against the institution and, ultimately, to find the Holy Grail.

Simultaneously, the book about Doña Rosalinda is a narrative *mise-en-abîme* that works to destabilise any belief in original or truthful narratives. In tandem with the dizzying intertextuality of the novel, its overlapping narrative levels suggest that one knowledge system might hide a multitude of others underneath, which can emerge if we adopt a different perspective or construct the world differently. This view of knowledge as a kind of palimpsest resonates with the theory Carrington had encountered in Graves's *The White Goddess*, which similarly suggests that a repressed proto-feminist mythology hides under the surface of Western patriarchal monotheism. Indeed, the narrative of Doña Rosalinda chimes closely with Graves's account of how such a goddess-focused religious practice was eclipsed by Judeo-Christianity. With an overt nod to this alternative theology, Marian's double explains in the cavern scene at the end of the novel: '"This is Hell", she said with a smile. "But Hell is really a form of terminology. Really this is the Womb of the World whence all things come"' (137).

The account of Rosalinda's life, which takes up a substantial portion of *The Hearing Trumpet*, is recorded by a Dominico Eucaristo Deseos, 'ancient confessor of the Convent of Santa Barbara de Tartarus' (100), and presented to us in translation 'from the original Latin by Friar Jeremias Nacob of the Order of the Holy Coffin' (73). Within this narrative there are four letters or documents written by various other characters, which compete with each other for truthfulness, and render the narrative frames even more porous; as Suleiman observes, 'the effect is that of a multiple *mise en abyme*, with the usual unsettling and destabilizing of "reality" characteristic of such mirrorings'.[43] Thus, in a multitude of voices, renditions and translations, Marian and the reader are provided with an alternative version of the Christian Grail legend. Through the account of Doña Rosalinda's life, we learn that the holy cup originally belonged to the Goddess Venus, who dropped it 'in her birth pangs' while giving birth to Cupid, after which it fell into the safe hands of the subterranean, bearded and hermaphroditic Goddess Barbarus (91). We learn that 'later stories sprang up around the Grail, and its magic was erroneously attributed to Christian sources' (92). As Suleiman puts it,

> The story that emerges as Dona Rosalinda's life [...] is a story of antipatriarchal and anti-Christian subversion: the good abbess and her homosexual friend, the bishop of Trève les Frêles, are devotees of 'the Goddess', working to destroy the Christian edifice from the inside – which means, to *rewrite* its story.[44]

Importantly, Carrington does not replace an old myth with a new one; hers is rather a strategy of recovery – of clearing away the 'Dogmaturd' so that we can make space for listening. Such a strategy has implications for our capability to rediscover non-normative forms of knowledge, as well as for a construction of a subjectivity that allows space for the other. Thus, *The Hearing Trumpet* not only subverts the belief in absolute meaning, but also, ultimately, a rationalistic conception of a self that is able fully to know and articulate itself.

Upside Down and Inside Out

When Marian re-emerges from the underworld cavern, she discovers that a new Ice Age has arrived. Mirroring Marian's self-transformation, the earth has overhauled our known civilisation and installed a new order in its place. This happy apocalypse, heralded not by Gabriel's horn but by Marian's hearing trumpet, disturbs the earth's axis so that the equator ends up where the North Pole used to be and ushers in an era that promises empathy among all beings – both human and non-human. Marian's community now consists of five crones (including her friend Carmella), a bard/postman,[45] a driver, an old friend who has serendipitously arrived from Marian's native Britain, his sister who is a werewolf, a pack of wolves, a few cats, and an army of bees that can transform themselves into the body of the Goddess. It transpires that the other elderly women have all, like Marian, already visited the cave and encountered themselves. This motley community of humans, werewolves, wolves and bees manages, in a very swift turn of events in the last few paragraphs of the novel, to recover the Holy Grail from a greedy Archbishop and restore it to its rightful owner in the cavern: the Goddess (of whom Rosalinda Alvarez della Cueva/of the Cave, as her name indicates, was of course a reincarnation).

Noheden convincingly reads the new world order established at the end of *The Hearing Trumpet* as an 'ecological gnosis'; 'an anarchist flash of gnostic light that illuminates possibilities conveniently repressed by a patriarchal civilization predicated upon the doctrine of human exceptionalism'.[46] Indeed, Marian relates to us that the new order, which she hopes will be 'an improvement on humanity', is one marked by harmony between humans, nature and all animals. 'We did not consider hunting [animals]', she says; 'The New Ice Age should not be initiated with the slaughter of our fellow beings' (142). I would add that the novel also imagines, in the New Ice Age, a way of constructing subjecthood that is based on an intimacy with others and achieved through receptive listening. Marian's hearing trumpet, which she still needs and uses up until the end of the novel, again shows that listening openly, and not necessarily in our own familiar language, might transform our relationship with the world and everything in it. 'Although I was still in need of my trumpet', Marian tells us, 'I had recently developed a premonition of sound which I could translate afterwards through the trumpet.' 'Through a slight tingling on my scalp', she confesses, 'I detected a new sound quite near and strangely reminiscent of mince pies' (148). While this synaesthesia is an example of surrealist juxtaposition of incongruous realities, Marian's hearing smells through physical sensation is also evocative, again, of the ethical philosophy of Irigaray, who writes in *To Be Born* (2017):

> the matter is one of learning how to perceive again, including through our sensory perceptions, what we meet. For example, we have to learn again not to reduce a tree to a mere generic term, but to find time to perceive what it is in the present, a presence that is specific to each individual of its species, but also to each moment of the year, not to say of the day.[47]

As the novel draws to a close, the previously hot Latin American setting has transformed into a world covered in snow and ice. The earth has been unsettled in its orbit and the poles of the earth have changed places, so that Marian is now in the region where Lapland used to be. Fortuitously, Lapland happens to be the place Marian has always dreamed of going. Everything thus turned topsy-turvy, the novel ends with a reversal of the old proverb 'If the mountain will not come to Muhammad'.[48] 'If the old Woman can't go to Lapland,' Marian concludes, 'then Lapland must come to the old woman' (158). This new maxim indicates that structures that appear unchangeable – whether they pertain to the way in which we organise reality or how we configure our subjectivity – might be less fixed than we think.

Ultimately, then, *The Hearing Trumpet* replaces the quest for knowledge of the self with a relational intimacy achieved through listening to the other. What will defy the kind of robotic life Carrington fears so much in *Down Below* is ultimately intersubjectivity, in which one is heard without being obliged to inhabit a coherent self; in which one listens without demanding anything from the other. *The Hearing Trumpet* is underpinned by precisely such a poetics of listening.

Notes

I gratefully acknowledge the Swedish Research Council (2018-01419) for supporting my research towards this chapter.

1. See Jonathan P. Eburne, 'Poetic Wisdom: Leonora Carrington and the Esoteric Avant-Garde', in Catriona McAra and Jonathan P. Eburne (eds), *Leonora Carrington and the International Avant-Garde* (Manchester: Manchester University Press, 2017), p. 162n24.
2. Cited in Susan L. Aberth, *Leonora Carrington: Surrealism, Alchemy and Art* (Farnham: Lund Humphries, 2004), p. 79.
3. Eburne, 'Poetic Wisdom', p. 152.
4. Leonora Carrington has so far been best known for her painting, which has been the subject of several books, exhibition catalogues and academic articles. See, for example, Aberth, *Leonora Carrington*; Teresa Arcq, Joanna Moorhead and Stefan van Raaij, *Surreal Friends: Leonora Carrington, Remedios Varo and Kati Horna* (Farnham: Lund Humphries, 2010); and Dawn Ades, Giulia Ingarao and Alyce Mahon, *Leonora Carrington* (Dublin: Irish Museum of Modern Art, 2014). Eburne and McAra's edited volume *Leonora Carrington and the International Avant-Garde*, which focuses equally on Carrington's visual and literary output, provides a crucial complement to these earlier works.
5. See Tessel M. Baudin, *Surrealism and the Occult: Occultism and Western Esotericism in the Work and Movement of André Breton* (Amsterdam: Amsterdam University Press, 2014).
6. Kristoffer Noheden, 'The Grail and the Bees: Leonora Carrington's Quest for Human–Animal Coexistence', in Harri Veivo, Jean-Pierre Montier, Françoise Nicol, David Ayers, Benedikt Hjartarson and Sascha Bru (eds), *Beyond Given Knowledge: Investigation, Quest and Exploration in Modernism and the Avant-Gardes* (Berlin: de Gruyter, 2018), p. 242.
7. See Robert Graves, *The White Goddess: A Historical Grammar of Poetic Myth* (New York: Farrar, Straus and Giroux, 2013).
8. Leonora Carrington, *The Hearing Trumpet* (London: Virago, 2005), p. 1. All further references are to this edition and are given parenthetically in the text.
9. Eburne, 'Poetic Wisdom', p. 142.
10. Leonora Carrington, 'Commentary', in *Leonora Carrington: A Retrospective Exhibition* (New York: Center for Inter-American Relations, 1975), p. 24.
11. Eburne, 'Poetic Wisdom', p. 142.

12. Ibid. p. 160.
13. Perhaps this attitude of openness to otherness was an additional reason why Carrington found Graves's *The White Goddess* so compelling; this work identifies an alternative, matriarchal religious system operative in culture before the emerge of patriarchal, monotheistic frameworks. Graves is able to uncover evidence of this worship through a different sort of listening: a close study of ancient poetry and myth.
14. Leonora Carrington, *Down Below*, in *The House of Fear: Notes from Down Below* (London: Virago, 1988), p. 200. Like *The Hearing Trumpet*, *Down Below* has a labyrinthine publication history. The original text was written in English, after which it was lost. It was subsequently orally narrated by Carrington to Jeanne Mégnen, in French. A portion of this oral account was translated back into English and published as 'Down Below' in the surrealist journal *VVV* in 1944. The entire text was finally published in English in 1972 and in French (*En bas*) in 1973.
15. Susan Rubin Suleiman, *Subversive Intent: Gender, Politics, and the Avant-Garde* (Cambridge, MA: Harvard University Press, 1990), pp. 171–2.
16. See Joanna Moorhead, *The Surreal Life of Leonora Carrington* (London: Virago, 2016), pp. 109–21.
17. Carrington, *Down Below*, pp. 167, 168, 173, 199.
18. Ibid. p. 195.
19. Ibid. p. 195.
20. Ibid. pp. 188, 195.
21. Ibid. pp. 188, 197.
22. Eburne, 'Poetic Wisdom', p. 142.
23. Carrington, *Down Below*, p. 164.
24. Eburne, 'Poetic Wisdom', p. 142.
25. Ibid. p. 143.
26. Ibid. p. 161.
27. Carrington, *Down Below*, p. 191.
28. Ibid. pp. 191–2.
29. Ibid. p. 193.
30. Ibid. p. 173.
31. Ibid. p. 173.
32. Ibid. p. 166.
33. Luce Irigaray, *The Way of Love*, trans. Heidi Bostic and Stephen Pluháček (London: Continuum, 2002), p. 2.
34. Ibid. p. vii.
35. Luce Irigaray, *Speculum of the Other Woman*, trans. Gillian C. Gill (Ithaca: Cornell University Press, 1985), p. 133.

36. Irigaray, *The Way of Love*, p. viii.
37. Suleiman, *Subversive Intent*, p. 171.
38. Luce Irigaray, 'Introduction', in *Luce Irigaray: Key Writings* (London: Continuum, 2004), p. 7.
39. Luce Irigaray, 'Approaching the Other as Other', in *Key Writings*, p. 25.
40. Irigaray, 'Introduction', p. 3.
41. The most well-known example of surrealism's violated eyes is doubtless the opening scene of *Un Chien andalou* (1929), in which a woman's eye is sliced through with a razor.
42. Natalya Lusty, *Surrealism, Feminism, Psychoanalysis* (Aldershot: Ashgate, 2007), p. 75.
43. Suleiman, *Subversive Intent*, p. 174.
44. Ibid. p. 174.
45. This bard goes by the name Taliessin, which is a direct reference to the protagonist in one of the poetic works (*Hanes Taliesin*) through which Graves elaborates his theory in *The White Goddess*.
46. Noheden, 'The Grail and the Bees', p. 252.
47. Luce Irigaray, *To Be Born: Genesis of a New Human Being* (London: Palgrave, 2017), p. 66.
48. The proverb originates from a story about Muhammad retold in Francis Bacon's Essay XII, 'Of Boldness', from 1625. See Francis Bacon, *Complete Essays* (Mineola, NY: Dover Publications, 2008), p. 36.

10
'Je me trouve très sympathique': Dada Intimacies

Marius Hentea

On one level, the story of Dada intimacy is as old as the hills: artists working and sleeping together.[1] The couple Hugo Ball and Emmy Hennings cofounded the Cabaret Voltaire; husband and wife Hans Arp and Sophie Taeuber were among the earliest adherents to the movement and introduced the Laban Dance School and its dancers to the other members, which resulted in close collaborations on stage and off (Tristan Tzara had a serious relationship with Slovak dancer Maya Chrusecz). In Berlin Raoul Hausmann and Hannah Höch pursued an extramarital affair, while in New York the Baroness Elsa von Freytag-Loringhoven engaged in a sexual politics of the body. Céline Arnauld, the editor of the Parisian little review *Projecteur*, was married to Paul Dermée, who sought out the position of Dada publicity manager in France, while Francis Picabia brought into the Dada fold not only his wife, Gabriële Buffet, but also his mistress, Germaine Everling. While *Dada au grand air* (1922) was a close collaboration between Tzara, Arp and Max Ernst, the real *ménage à trois* that rocked the avant-garde world that year was between Ernst and the Parisian couple Paul and Gala Éluard.[2]

The other relatively straightforward way of thinking about Dada intimacy is to think about close friendships and artistic collaboration among its members. As Hans Richter put it of the 'six-piece band' at the Cabaret Voltaire:

> Each played his instrument, i.e. himself, passionately and with all his soul. Each of them, different as he was from all the others, was his own music, his own words, his own rhythm. Each sang his own song with all his might – and, miraculously, they found in the end that they belonged together and needed each other.[3]

In this reading, Dada owed its force to the collaboration between close friends; as these friendships became strained, the movement lost its way. There was some self-awareness of this dynamic: with Zurich Dada activity petering out in the summer of 1919, Arp and Tzara sent the press the (false) notice that they would fight a duel with pistols.[4] While this hoax was meant to expose media gullibility, physical violence and major disagreements between Dadaists were not always off the table. There was 'a real bullfight among Dadaists' over the movement's direction and scope, recalled one of its more cantankerous adherents, Richard Huelsenbeck, who had been implored to join Dada by his old friend Hugo Ball but soon became a divisive figure (he waged a decades-long battle with Tzara and split Berlin Dada over his rejection of Kurt Schwitters).[5] Tzara was introduced to the Cabaret Voltaire by Marcel Janco, with whom he had collaborated on the review *Simbolul* as teenagers in Romania in 1912; but over time the two squabbled over money, and Janco, dismayed by Tzara's nihilism, joined a group of socialist-revolutionary artists in 1919. For his part, Ball had to be constantly brought back into the Dada fold by entreaties from Arp, Janco and Tzara. Dada operations moved to Paris because Picabia offered Tzara room and board, but it was not long before he publicly disavowed his Dada friends as posers and fakes. While André Breton idolised Tzara as a father figure, his animosity towards Tzara grew to such a level that their exchange of insults over the proposed Congress of Paris (1922) led to the dissolution of Paris Dada.

While physical love and deep friendships are undoubtedly important factors in understanding Dada, they encourage an anecdotal history of the movement structured around conflict, scandal and great passions – the very things that Dada itself played on and encouraged with its strident manifestos and over-the-top performances. The temptation to pitch Dada history at the level of the anecdote is also strong because of the raft of Dada memoirs to mine as source material and because the (scandalous) anecdotal Dada story leads to exciting (scholarly) copy. My aim in this chapter is to stake out another area of Dada intimacy, what I call self-intimacy, in order to better illuminate the dynamics of the avant-garde. Before there could be intimacy between individuals, I argue, Dada sought to pave the way for the individual to understand the intimate within him- or herself, the spontaneous nature of one's deeply held being, what is 'most inner' – an intimacy that aligns itself with what the *Oxford English Dictionary* defines as pertaining to 'one's inmost self; closely personal'.[6] As Raoul Hausmann put it, 'anyone who frees his own tendencies in himself is Dada', for 'in Dada you will recognize your real state of mind'.[7] This claim might seem to push Dada close to the reconceptualisation of interiority found within canonical modernist writers like Henry James or Katherine Mansfield. But whereas modernist writers followed in the tradition of Flaubert, convinced that language could unlock those deep recesses if only it were properly ordered (Joyce spending hours working on a sentence in which he has all the words but not the order; Pound taking years to whittle down 'In a Station of the Metro', etc.), Dada was premised on the idea that the 'closely personal' could not be recovered because false social conventions – among them language, the family, the nation and the entire art world – had so warped the individual that nothing uniquely personal remained underneath. A fundamental uprooting of the entirety of social life was necessary so that the individual could have something of his or her own to share with others: 'Let each man proclaim: there is a great negative work of destruction to be accomplished. We must sweep and clean.'[8]

Dada self-intimacy can be thought of as the antecedent to the mutual recognition found within the modern, secularised project of intimacy that Anthony Giddens describes as 'emotional communication, with others and with the self, in a context of interpersonal equality'.[9] Essentially, I am intimate with you, you are intimate with me, and we are equals in this shared moment. This account by Giddens presupposes that what I share as intimate is fundamentally mine, chosen for uniquely personal reasons. Yet if what people believe to be 'closely personal' turns out to be a social convention, a product of a cultural environment, it was the role of the avant-garde to release the primal self from the shackles of inherited values: 'Dada was born of a need for independence,' Tzara wrote, 'of a distrust toward unity.'[10] It was an attempt to move away from transcendent universals into the deep core of selfhood:

> What good have philosophical theories served? Have they helped us make a step forward or backward? Where is 'forward', where is 'backward'? [...] What we have now is spontaneity. Not because it is more beautiful or better than something else, but because it emerges freely out of us without the intervention of speculative ideas, it represents us.[11]

Representation of the self is impossible if one remains within the conventional strictures of inherited thought; the first obligation of the individual is to cast off these conventions so that what is truly the core of one's being can come out. For all the destruction Dada promised to wreak, no hammer was raised to splintering classical beliefs in the primal self or the sanctity of interiority. If anything, this primal self was the utopia that Dada sought – anything that impeded the full flowering and emergence of this internal self had to be destroyed. That not enough which impeded this primal self could be destroyed, since it was the panoply of social relations and inherited customs which were perceived to make individuals unwittingly false to their true selves, only heightened the tantalising prospect of recovering the self-intimacy that society and civilisation had rendered impossible.

This chapter proceeds along three main strands. First, I begin by looking at how Dada challenged conventional views of the transparency of language through sound poetry, the magic of 'Dada' as a word to be intoned, and multilingualism. I then look at how Dada dismantled the intimacies presupposed by the two most basic units of social organisation, the family and the nation, for Dada revolted against both formations in order to recapture the inner core of the self. Finally, I conclude by an assessment of Dada's relationship to the audience, which is nothing less than the moment when the quest for self-intimacy finds expression in a public setting. The cabaret form allowed for closeness to the audience, but it also created moments of opposition and failed intimacy between audience and performer, particularly when Dada attempted to impart a programmatic message of social and cultural reform.

The 'innermost alchemy of the word'

It is hard to know what a boisterous audience of drunk students and local down-and-outs in *anno domini* 1916 in the prosperous city of Zurich would have made of a 'sound poem' performed in the musty backroom of a red-light district steakhouse by a penniless German socialist-anarchist wearing a pointed cone on his head while a robotic shell encased his tall, rail-thin body, constricting any fluid movement but the warbling of the tongue:

> jolifanto bambla   o   falli bambla
> grossiga m'pfa habla horem
> egiga goramen
> higo   bloiko russula   huju
> hollaka   hollala
> anlogo bung
> blago   bung   blago bung
> bosso fataka
> ü   üü   ü.[12]

All interpretive keys seem to be useless for making sense of the particular verbal cacophony that is Hugo Ball's 'Karawane', one of his early 'sound poems' (*Lautgedichte*). Disgusted by the destruction and slaughter of World War I, Ball felt that the world had to be reformed root and branch by renouncing 'the language that journalism has abused and corrupted. We must return to the innermost alchemy of the word.'[13]

The 'innermost alchemy of the word' is a suggestive way of thinking about Dada's attempt to reform language if 'the word is incapable, as a vehicle of logic, of expressing sentiments'.[14] In response to this felt insufficiency of the word as a component in logocentric and orderly linguistic formations such as the sentence, Ball creates a language that is a purely personal materialisation; the primal language of the sound poem has no truck with the social world. Ball's personal disappointment at the failure of revolutionary socialism to stop the outbreak of war no doubt contributed to this turn away from everyday language. Instead, this is poetry as pure *état d'esprit*, with no possibility of representation in the conventional sense since no discernible object is depicted. At the same time, though, the wordscape and linguistic units of the sound poem are more universal than any individual language because they are based on phonemes, and not the particular grammar or linguistic associations of any individual language whose meaning has been shaped by history, politics and cultural exchange. These external factors are removed from the sound poem, which casts language as an intimate bodily phenomenon: as Tzara later put it, 'la pensée se fait dans la bouche' [thought is made in the mouth].[15] The Dada performers' physical bodies carried within themselves a personal language that trumped the legal and political formulations which had led to the mass suicide of civilisation.

The bodily, physical origin of language, the very intimacy of speaking, also found expression in the very word that resounded through the cabaret, soirées and print reviews: 'Dada'. The word held a magical power that adherents intoned like a mantra, from Tzara noting that 'one of these days it will be known that before Dada, after Dada, without Dada, toward Dada, for Dada, against Dada, with Dada, in spite of Dada, it is always Dada'[16] to Ball proclaiming the supremacy of 'Dada psychology, Dada literature, Dada bourgeoisie [. . .] Dada world war and no ending, Dada revolution and no beginning, Dada your friend [. . .] Dada Tzara, Dada Huelsenbeck, Dada m'dada, Dada mhm'dada, Dada Hue, Dada Tza'.[17] Despite the proliferation of manifestos and productions with 'Dada' in the title, there was never anything resembling a cogent definition of the term. This allowed 'Dada' to take on a purely personal meaning for the individual, not only making it easier for the movement to spread (because there was no exclusive set of principles that an adherent would have to sign up to), but also personalising the movement for every adherent. With its thumping sounds, the word 'Dada' had, as Huelsenbeck noted, a 'suggestive power' that turned it into a possession, an object that individuals held within them – their own private Dada.[18] Max Ernst proclaimed that Dada was the only reality he recognised within himself: 'They may call us by any names they please: Surrealists or something else, but they will find that underneath my skin I am always and forever a dyed-in-the-wool Dadaist.'[19] This idea of being Dada to the core – which took up the German Dada distinction proposed by Kurt Schwitters between *Huelsendadaismus* (husk Dada) and *Kerndadaismus* (core Dada) – was a way of interiorising Dada, a mantra that was both meditational and a catchword, within the very self, so that the individual was intimately Dada. No surprise, then, that Tzara painted the word 'Dada' on his forehead, an ersatz tattoo that made Dada and his body one, while Johannes Baader proclaimed himself a resurrected *Oberdada*.

Beyond the invention of sound poetry as private language and the invocation of 'Dada' as a mantra, Dada's other major innovation with language was simultaneous multilingualism. 'All the styles of the last twenty years came together yesterday': that was Hugo Ball's verdict on the performance, in late March 1916, of Tzara's 'L'Amiral cherche une maison à louer' [The Admiral Is Looking for a House to Rent].[20] A simultaneous poem in three languages (French, German and English), it was performed by Huelsenbeck, Janco and the author himself, who read the French lines. As the title indicates, the piece is about searching for a flat after being expelled from one's lodgings. This predicament, made farcical in the figure of an elderly Swiss admiral, was not unfamiliar to the audience: the final line, said in French and in unison by the three performers, 'L'Amiral n'a rien trouvé' [The admiral did not find anything], was a common enough experience for flat-hunters in Zurich.[21] The admiral's homelessness is foregrounded in the ordered, three-columned typography of the written version. Underneath the text Tzara wrote an explanatory 'Note for the Bourgeois'. The ironic title (what bourgeois would have come into possession of the poem?) and the mock-serious tone of Tzara's justification, replete with learned references to predecessors in simultaneism, should be read as a sly acknowledgement of the futility of print as a stable frame for the vocal Dada performance. The reader struggles to find a set of literary codes to decipher the text, which cannot be read in any meaningful way.

The poem thus puts language in competition, showing it to be multiple and various. The printed text also points to something fundamental to Dada's self-understanding, namely written language being defined by a lack because there is no way to capture its physical embodiment in a performance. Tzara's composition of the poem was strongly influenced by the performative possibilities of the original performers. A gifted musician, Janco sang his English lines, creating another layer of opposition beyond language and providing an underlying melody to the piece (after referring to such traditional British tropes as afternoon tea, his song ends in a Molly-Bloomesque orgasm: 'She said the raising her heart oh dwelling oh oh yes yes yes yes yes yes yes yes yes yes oh yes oh yes oh yes yes yes oh yes sir'[22]). Huelsenbeck's aggressive performance style was brought out by the greater number of pure sounds in his lines: 'Ahoi ahoi [...] prrzza chrrza prrrza'.²³ Tzara, whose small frame and young, spectacled face set him apart, had the narrative centre, so that the helpless, gentle little boy who has a simple story to tell struggles against a bombastic Huelsenbeck and melodic Janco.

Finally, Dada's assault on language took the form of questioning the transparency of linguistic meaning by pointing to the commodification of language, a commodification that Dada expanded to the point of naming itself a 'public limited company / For the exploitation of words'.²⁴ While Dada exploited words, it did so haphazardly, without any greater purpose than the immediate pleasure of the moment:

> My words are not mine. My words are everybody else's words: I mix them very nicely into a little bouillabaisse – the outcome of chance [...] My deductions are nothing but the result of fugitive thoughts more or less attuned to desires, the commodities of conversation. They present no absolute interest, they are not applicable [...] they just represent a little need on my part to speak out, to wander about and to complicate things.²⁵

There is no sense of a larger society in which these actions take place, or any responsibility towards others for these actions, but rather the fleeting desires of the moment that have to be followed, the spontaneity of the self which should not be denied.

The Intimacy of Home: Families and Nations

Among the most influential accounts of intimacy in the past few decades, two social institutions have been isolated: the bourgeois family and the nation. In Jürgen Habermas's account of bourgeois intimacy, the 'patriarchal conjugal family' was the traditional zone for the production of intimacy and the wellspring for the development of the 'public sphere' in eighteenth-century Europe.²⁶ For Michael Herzfeld, 'cultural intimacy' took on a national dimension in the nineteenth century, resulting in 'inward acknowledgement' of shared cultural traits.²⁷ The family unit and the nation-state both constitute themselves as a higher authority, discipline bodies and advance an insider/outsider status. More pointedly, both are metonyms for home. As a movement composed of outcasts, the black sheep of families and the deserters of nations, Dada sought out new structures of belonging. And in the context of World War I, the notion that the family and the nation-state had to be defended with arms was considered by the Dadaists as one of the reasons for the world's descent into madness.

Peter Bürger argues that the avant-garde is predicated on being 'an attack on the status of art in bourgeois society'.[28] That Dada was a movement against the bourgeois goes without saying: 'there were artists and bourgeois', Huelsenbeck noted; 'You had to love one and hate the other.'[29] Tzara claimed that 'every product of disgust capable of becoming a negation of the family is *dada*'.[30] Arp stated that Dada was 'devised to show the bourgeois the unreality of his world, the nullity of his endeavors'.[31] For Janco, the Cabaret Voltaire was all about 'shocking the bourgeois, demolishing his idea of art, attacking common sense, public opinion, education, institutions, museums, good taste, in short, the whole prevailing order'.[32] George Grosz noted that German Dada 'simply mocked everything [...] Nothing was holy to us [...] We spat upon everything, including ourselves.'[33] The Dadaists spat on themselves because they themselves were from the bourgeoisie: 'look at me, a kind bourgeois', Tzara proclaimed at the First Dada Soirée in June 1916. Dada was a bourgeois phenomenon, composed of bourgeois youth rebelling against bourgeois forebearers, and the internecine quality of that revolt helps account for its particular bitterness. (It also explains why critics routinely lambasted Dada, for only well-off bourgeois could engage in such frivolity.)

The cultural dominance of the bourgeoisie over European cultural life reached its apogee in the pre-war period, but it is difficult to fully comprehend the grip that it held over cultural life and the emotional compartmentalisation it required of individuals:

> the house of golden nostrils
> is full of correct phrases.[34]

Bourgeois language is empty form, incapable of transmitting genuine thought. In his unfinished novel *Faites vos jeux* (1923), Tzara speaks of the hypocrisy of the bourgeoisie when presenting the otherwise respectable father as a regular visitor to a brothel: 'I should have killed him [...] He didn't see anything wrong, and had the bad taste to tell me that very night how much he loved his wife.'[35] The difficulty of communication in such a stifling atmosphere comes out in one of Tzara's Romanian-language poems:

> Mother, you won't understand but listen
> Suffering can't be versed into a handkerchief [...]
> Mother, you won't understand
> But it's a beautiful thing to be in a poem.[36]

Although a pre-Dada production, Tzara's text points to the inseparable gulf between the demands of the bourgeois family and the temperament of the artist.

The bourgeoisie's preoccupation with material things means that its particular forms of intimacy are stuffed with objects: in this poem, the handkerchief in which emotions are objectified and contained. Dada's well-known fascination with objects (in productions by Duchamp, Man Ray, Schwitters) reveals the desire to upturn the emotional association between the bourgeois home and intimacy.[37] The most telling example is Man Ray's *The Gift* (1921), an iron with spikes. Not only does the work derail the functionality of the object (the iron destroys clothes); it also undermines bourgeois propriety (the self cannot be presented appropriately or correctly in public because no ironing can be done), and while *The Gift* allowed for a closer intimacy between artwork and onlooker, as it was meant to be handled by spectators, it disturbs the safe cocoon of the bourgeois home by introducing a potentially violent (and gendered) weapon into it.

In place of the patriarchal bourgeois family, Dada created intimacy through the 'band of brothers' of its members.[38] This was the collaboration that Richter spoke about, and it was fostered not only through performances at the Cabaret Voltaire or soirées, but also through daily contact where ideas were shared and new collaborations pursued. Unlike other avant-garde groups – most pointedly Futurism or Surrealism (where adherents had to pledge allegiance to Breton) – there was no single Dada leader; as Tzara put it, everyone is a president of Dada because Dada was a family of equals, where individuals worked freely for the common cause of finding spontaneity and the primal self.

The other intimate 'home' that Dada overturned was the nation-state. The most important sociological fact about the Dadaists in Zurich was that they were all foreigners, exiles from a war that they wanted no part in. Ball had entered the country on false papers; Tzara was tenuously listed as a student but had no diplomatic protection to fall back on because he was not a Romanian citizen (native-born Jews were granted the right to Romanian citizenship only after World War I). For Huelsenbeck, it was a matter of pride to remain a foreigner: 'Here in Zurich I was a foreigner, and I wanted to remain one.'[39] It became a point of honour to remain on the margins; Huelsenbeck's statement was very much a reaction to the fact that while Switzerland ideationally considered itself 'a civilizational community above races and languages', the reality of Zurich public life was a growing fear of *Überfremdung* (over-foreignisation) brought on by the arrival of 30,000 *réfugiés militaires* (military refugees) or *Kriegsäuslander* (war foreigners) during the war years.[40]

National marginality translated into cultural freedom for the Dadaists. They had something to react against. Most Europeans in the pre-war period considered culture to be indissolubly bound to the nation. During the war years, just as socialist labour unions refused to back the Internationale, even progressive artists, like those in the German cabaret and café scene, became 'one-sidedly nationalistic'.[41] Guillaume Apollinaire was adamant that Dada had to cut its ties to German artists if it wished to have any presence in France. Censorship in various countries limited the circulation of Dada, even if the decision to print 'international' editions of the review *Dada* was meant to counteract those policies. Multilingualism was not only very much part of Dada's print agenda; it was also a poetic practice. This was most famously on display in Tzara's 'L'Amiral cherche une maison à louer' and the 1919 simultaneous poems between Walter Serner (a German-speaking Swiss living in Geneva), Tzara (whose native language was Romanian) and Arp (who spoke Alsatian, French and German). By connecting languages through chance and uncovering previously hidden associations, multilingual poetry showed the poverty – and perniciousness – of the view that the soul of the nation could be found in a national language. The desire to keep a language 'pure' had an obvious political equivalent in the nationalism of the era; for Dada, both notions had to be combatted through the creation of internationalist intimacies. By directly questioning the politics of nationalism, private artistic form was used to unsettle the boundaries of belonging that had been employed to mobilise citizen-soldiers and inflame war hysteria.

Besides cutting the supposedly essential link between nation and language, the Cabaret Voltaire declared itself open to art from all of the warring nations, without prejudice, hosting soirées devoted to Russian, French and Swiss art. Anti-nationalism was at the heart of Dada's agenda:

> The collaborators of the *Cabaret Voltaire* review belong to the following nations: French (G. Apollinaire, B. Cendrars), Italian (F. Canguillo [sic], F. T. Marinetti, L. Modegliani [sic]), Spanish (P. Picasso), Romanian (M. Janco, Tr. Tzara), German (Hans Arp, J. van Hoddis, R. Huelsenbeck), Dutch (O. van Rees), Austrian (Max Oppenheimer), Polish (M. Slodki), Russian (W. Kandinsky), and stateless – Emmy Hennings.[42]

Zurich Dada was in many ways a calculated response to the marginality forced upon its members as wartime exiles: they embraced cultural and political marginality but did so in ways that undercut the majority's right to define the bases of power. But rather than debilitating Dada, Swiss anti-foreign prejudices made Dada self-conscious of its origins as a movement by and for aliens and outcasts; it would proudly carry the banner of internationalism to set itself apart from the war.

'Intimacies' with the Audience

The vernissage for Max Ernst's 1921 show in Paris had a curious item on the programme: at 11.30 p.m. there would be 'intimacies' with the audience.

While it was unclear what kind of 'intimacies' were shared, Dada prided itself on breaking down the rigid barrier that separated the artist from the audience. This was a consequence of its origins in cabaret, an art form that was traditionally close to the audience.[43] The intimate atmosphere of the small stage and the confined quarters of the Cabaret Voltaire's back room helped to eliminate the traditional hierarchy between performer and spectator. The performances by Emmy Hennings were critical to developing this intimacy, as Huelsenbeck noted: 'The songs created the "intimate" atmosphere of the cabaret. The audience liked listening to them, the distance between us and the enemy grew smaller, and finally everyone joined in.'[44] The audience was also a driver for Dada spontaneity and creativity. Dada had to 'rewrite life every day', as Ball put it:

> Our attempt to entertain the audience with artistic things forces us in an exciting and instructive way to be incessantly lively, new, and naïve. It is a race with the expectations of the audience, and this race calls on all our forces of invention and debate.[45]

The desire for novelty and closeness with the audience was tempered, however, by the need to 'educate' the public:

> Our cabaret is a gesture. Every word that is spoken and sung here says at least this one thing: that this humiliating age has not succeeded in winning our respect. What could be respectable and impressive about it? Its cannons? Our big drum drowns them. Its idealism? That has long been a laughing-stock, in its popular and academic edition. The grandiose slaughters and cannibalistic exploits? Our spontaneous foolishness and our enthusiasm for illusion will destroy them.[46]

'Both buffoonery and a requiem mass', Dada had a conscious desire to make the audience aware of the essential vacuity of European culture.[47] Huelsenbeck admonished the audience: 'The Cabaret Voltaire is not a common music hall. We have not gathered here to offer you *frou-frous* and naked thighs and cheap ditties. The Cabaret Voltaire is a cultural institution!'[48] Ball too grew exasperated: 'The people get terribly agitated, as they expect the Cabaret Voltaire to be a normal night club. One first has to teach these students what a political cabaret is.'[49]

Dada intimacy with the audience, then, straddled two poles. On the one hand, with the audience expected to actively take part in proceedings, performer and spectator came into contact on relatively equal planes, a structural precondition for mutual intimacy.[50] Yet this convergence was mitigated by the fact that Dada had a deeper cultural and political message to impart. While the audience was keen on Dada antics, it was less enamoured of Dada's politics. This created frustration and resentment, as Francis Picabia's 'Manifeste Cannibale Dada' shows:

> It is like your hopes: nothing.
> Like your paradise: nothing.
> Like your idols: nothing.
> Like your politicians: nothing.
> Like your heroes: nothing.
> Like your artists: nothing.
> Like your religions: nothing.
> Keep on booing, keep on screaming, beat me up, and then what? What? I will still tell you that you are all suckers. In three months' time my friends and I will sell our paintings to you for a tidy sum.[51]

Laying bare Dada's assault on traditional values, Picabia's text not only refers to the audience's violent refusal of these positions but also to the hypocrisy of the audience railing against Dada yet hoping to profit from it (by speculating in its art). While the Dadaists, focusing on self-intimacy, had gone through a kind of cleansing of their own selves and had reoriented their understandings of the self accordingly, the audience considered Dada a kind of Bakhtinian carnival, a sanctioned interruption in the norms governing daily life, not a full-on demolition of those norms. The move towards closer mutual intimacy between artist and audience broke down because the process of self-intimacy was one-sided. Tzara experienced this in his first public appearance in Paris when noting that 'anything I might have said really had no importance' because the audience would only be interested in the surface of things, his body, not his interiority or ideas.[52] In the end, Dada proved too personal to spread widely. Without a set of ready-made beliefs that potential adherents could sign up to, Dada signified absolute personal freedom – but it was this very absolute freedom, which required a commensurate absolute honesty and introspection, that the public found frightening.

Conclusion

What did Dada self-intimacy accomplish? Language was not returned to uncorrupted roots, families and nations continued to enforce their stifling worldviews upon individuals, and audiences continued to find greater comfort in banal classics than daring experiments. When judged against its lofty ambitions, Dada was a failure. But perhaps that is the wrong way to evaluate Dada's reorientation of artistic intimacy. Dada's truly revolutionary impact was to throw a question on everything, to cast into doubt every single certainty that the world had provided. No other avant-garde was so comprehensive in its absolute critique of the world. Symbolism, Futurism and all the other *isms* of the time coupled their critique of outworn aesthetic or social principles with another body of directives to be followed. But there was no greater freedom or truth in that replacement doctrine: as a parody of that, Tzara provided his famous recipe for making a poem (cut up the words in a newspaper article, place them all in a hat, shake gently, pull them out one by one, transcribe faithfully). This was not so much a new way of writing poetry (Tzara never 'wrote' a poem this way) but a spoof attempting to show that all external doctrines are false. The other avant-gardes wrote manifestos:

> A manifesto is a communication addressed to the whole world, in which there is no other pretension than the discovery of a means of curing instantly political, astronomical, artistic, parliamentary agronomic and literary syphilis. It can be gentle, good-natured, it is always right, it is strong, vigorous and logical.
>
> A propos logic, I consider myself very charming [je me trouve très sympathique].[53]

Everything comes back to the self and the spontaneity that has to be found within. There is no larger message or mission to this spontaneity but recognition of its internal force, making it a drive not for social communication but rather a reckoning with the intimacy of the self. As Hugo Ball put it, 'we have to lose ourselves if we want to find ourselves'.[54] Dada would always remain a 'purely personal adventure', an attempt to find the deeper springs of one's personality and perhaps to reach out to like-minded individuals.[55]

Notes

1. See Bibiana K. Obler, *Intimate Collaborations: Kandinsky and Münter, Arp and Taeuber* (New Haven, CT: Yale University Press, 2014).
2. On the collaboration between Ernst and Éluard, see M. E. Warlick, *Max Ernst and Alchemy: A Magician in Search of Myth* (Austin: University of Texas Press, 2001), p. 58.
3. Hans Richter, *Dada Art and Anti-Art*, trans. David Britt (London: Thames and Hudson, 1997), p. 27.

4. Although Swiss newspapers faithfully reprinted some of the goings-on, the *St. Galler Tagblatt* reported: 'When the fourth shot grazed Arp's left thigh, the two opponents, not reconciled, left the battleground.' (Quoted in Brigitte Pichon and Karl Riha (eds), *Dada Zurich: A Clown's Game from Nothing* (New York: G. K. Hall, 1996), p. 248.)
5. Richard Huelsenbeck, 'En avant Dada: A History of Dadaism (1920)', in Robert Motherwell (ed.), *The Dada Painters and Poets: An Anthology*, 2nd edn (Cambridge, MA: Harvard University Press, 1989), p. 34.
6. 'intimate, adj. and n.' A. adj. 2, *OED Online*, available at <https://www.oed.com/view/Entry/98506> (accessed 30 September 2020).
7. Raoul Hausmann, 'New Painting and Photomontage', in Lucy R. Lippard (ed.), *Dadas on Art* (Mineola, NY: Dover, 2007), p. 60.
8. Tristan Tzara, 'Dada Manifesto 1918', in Motherwell (ed.), *The Dada Painters and Poets*, p. 81.
9. Anthony Giddens, *The Transformation of Intimacy: Sexuality, Love and Eroticism in Modern Societies* (Stanford: Stanford University Press, 1993), p. 130.
10. Tzara, 'Dada Manifesto 1918', p. 77.
11. Tristan Tzara, 'Conférence sur Dada', in Tzara, *Œuvres Complètes*, ed. Henri Béhar, 6 vols (Paris: Flammarion, 1975–91), vol. 1, p. 421. Hereafter cited as *OC*. All translations mine unless noted.
12. Hugo Ball, 'Karawane', in Karl Riha (ed.), *Dada Zürich: Texte, Manifeste, Dokumente* (Stuttgart: Philipp Reclam, 2010), p. 66.
13. Hugo Ball, *Flight Out of Time: A Dada Diary*, ed. John Elderfield, trans. Ann Raimes (Berkeley: University of California Press, 1974), p. 71.
14. Tzara, 'Essai sur la situation de la poésie', in Tzara, *OC*, vol. 5, p. 11.
15. Tzara, 'Dada manifeste sur l'amour faible et l'amour amer', in Tzara, *OC*, vol. 1, p. 379.
16. Quoted in Michel Sanouillet, *Dada in Paris*, trans. Sharmila Ganguly (Cambridge, MA: MIT Press, 2009), p. 248.
17. Quoted in DADA, V: 7. Kunsthaus Zürich Dada Archive.
18. Huelsenbeck, 'En avant Dada', p. 26.
19. Quoted in Matthew Josephson, *Life among the Surrealists: A Memoir* (New York: Holt, Rinehart and Winston, 1962), p. 183.
20. Ball, *Flight Out of Time*, p. 57.
21. Tristan Tzara, 'L'Amiral cherche une maison à louer', *Cabaret Voltaire* (1916), pp. 6–7.
22. Ibid. pp. 6–7.
23. Ibid. pp. 6–7.
24. *Dadaphone* (March 1920), p. 5.
25. Marguerite Bonnet, *L'Affaire Barrès* (Paris: José Corti, 1987), pp. 44–5.

26. Jürgen Habermas, *The Structural Transformation of the Public Sphere: An Inquiry into a Category of Bourgeois Society* (Cambridge, MA: MIT Press, 1989), pp. 43, 44.
27. Michael Herzfeld, *Cultural Intimacy: Social Poetics in the Nation-State* (New York: Routledge, 1997), p. 6.
28. Peter Bürger, *Theory of the Avant-Garde*, trans. Michael Shaw (Minneapolis: University of Minnesota Press, 1984), p. 49.
29. Huelsenbeck, 'En avant Dada', p. 27.
30. Tzara, 'Manifeste Dada 1918', in Tzara, *OC*, vol. 1, p. 367.
31. Jean Arp, 'Dadaland', in Lippard (ed.), *Dadas on Art*, p. 29.
32. Marcel Janco, 'Dada at Two Speeds', in Lippard (ed.), *Dadas on Art*, p. 36.
33. George Grosz, 'Dadaism', in Lippard (ed.), *Dadas on Art*, p. 86.
34. Tristan Tzara, 'Un Beau Matin aux dents fermées', in Tzara, *OC*, vol. 1, p. 217. On the cultural dominance of the bourgeoisie, see Franco Moretti, *The Bourgeois: Between History and Literature* (London: Verso, 2013).
35. Tristan Tzara, *Faites vos jeux*, in Tzara, *OC*, vol. 1, p. 270.
36. Tristan Tzara, 'Prietenă mamei', in Tzara, *Primele poeme ale lui Tristan Tzara*, ed. Saşa Pană (Bucharest: Editura Cartea Românească, 1971), pp. 70–1.
37. On the tactile intimacy of avant-garde objects, see Janine Mileaf, *Please Touch: Dada and Surrealist Objects after the Readymade* (Hanover, NH: Dartmouth College Press, 2010).
38. I borrow the phrase in the context of the avant-garde from Stephen Voyce, *Poetic Community: Avant-Garde Activism and Cold War Culture* (Toronto: University of Toronto Press, 2013), p. 14.
39. Richard Huelsenbeck, *Memoirs of a Dada Drummer*, ed. Hans J. Kleinschmidt, trans. Joachim Neugroschel (New York: Viking Press, 1974), p. 12.
40. Claire Raymond-Duchosal, *Les Étrangers en Suisse (Étude géographique, démographique et sociologique)* (Paris: Félix Alcan, 1929), p. 34.
41. Peter Jelavich, *Berlin Cabaret* (Cambridge, MA: Harvard University Press, 1993), p. 119.
42. *Cabaret Voltaire* (1916), p. 32.
43. On the cabaret tradition, see Harold B. Segel, *Turn-of-the-Century Cabaret: Paris, Barcelona, Berlin, Munich, Vienna, Cracow, Moscow, St. Petersburg, Zurich* (New York: Columbia University Press, 1987).
44. Huelsenbeck, *Dada Drummer*, p. 10.
45. Ball, *Flight Out of Time*, p. 54.
46. Ibid. p. 61.
47. Ibid. p. 56.
48. Quoted in Günter Berghaus, *Theatre, Performance, and the Historical Avant-Garde* (Basingstoke: Palgrave Macmillan, 2005), p. 144.

49. Quoted in ibid. p. 145.
50. Lynn Jamieson, *Intimacy: Personal Relationships in Modern Societies* (Cambridge: Polity Press, 1998), p. 1.
51. Francis Picabia, 'Manifeste Cannibale Dada', *Dadaphone* (March 1920), p. 3.
52. Tristan Tzara, 'Memoirs of Dadaism', in Edmund Wilson, *Axel's Castle: A Study in the Imaginative Literature of 1870 to 1930* (New York: Charles Scribner, 1931), p. 304.
53. Tristan Tzara, 'Dada manifeste sur l'amour faible et l'amour amer', in Tzara, *OC*, vol. 1, p. 378; translation from Tzara, 'Dada Manifesto 1918', p. 86.
54. Ball, *Flight Out of Time*, p. 15.
55. Tristan Tzara quoted in Sanouillet, *Dada in Paris*, p. 277.

11

Overlapping Intimacies: Russian Fever, Domestic Morale and the BBC Home Service, 1941–5

Claire Davison

> Only in the dark green room beside the fire
> With the curtains drawn against the wind and the waves
> There is a little box with a well-bred voice:
> What a place to talk of war.
>
> – Louis MacNeice, 'Cushendun'[1]

Critical engagements with the modernist valencies of early broadcasting have pulled in two directions over the past years, pointing to the airwaves as the almost ideal medium for staging the labyrinthine depths of memory and desire in the theatre of the mind, or for bearing the powerfully interconnected, politically transformative dynamics of sonic art across the globe. However radically experimental or vibrantly transnational such panoramas of radiophonic arts might be, state-sponsored wartime broadcasting still tends to stand out as a subdued but worthy parenthesis, putting an end to kaleidoscopic polyrhythms, hauntingly expressionist streams of consciousness, and visionary internationalism in the interests of state. The warmly familiar, intimate appeal of 'listening in' from the 'dark green room beside the fire' – as epitomised in the epigraph above – even appears ideally suited to protect and comfort the nation. Radio becomes a Home Guard of sorts: a local guardian of domestic morale, speaking in what Woolf described as the BBC's 'dreary false cheery hero-making strain'.[2] Here was a daily fare of either sing-along favourites and relaxing entertainments, or familiar voices earnestly entreating the nation to stand as one. This perception of wartime radio as, at best, a sober and homely monosphere (seeping from 'the cells of [the listener's] most intimate life', as Adorno puts it), at worst an insidiously invasive voice of state-controlled consensus 'which no longer appears to come from outside',[3] has been bolstered and embellished ever since in the national and international imaginary.[4] To this day, almost every film and television series set in wartime Britain will include its iconic wireless set in a cosy living room, emitting either band music, Vera Lynn ('the nation's songbird'), or topical updates delivered by an archly correct male voice.

Any quick browse through Home Service schedules in late 1939 and early 1940 bears out these entrenched representations, as do the Ministry of Information's wartime propaganda programmes and broadcasting blueprints.[5] Homespun, domestic achievements take pride of place, with newly commissioned series that include: 'Somewhere in England', 'The Showmen of England', 'Forty Years in England', '... Forever England', 'The England I Know' and 'England Expects'. Coverage in the *Radio Times* likewise celebrates insular perkiness and home-grown talents as the finest guarantors of domestic security:

2 December 1940 Peter Warlock – A recital of his songs [...]
If nationality in music counts for anything at all, then Warlock counts for a great deal, for his songs are imbued with the very essence of the spirit of England, both his technique and his highly original idiom being firmly based on the great traditions of the Tudor period. In short, he is one of the most English of English composers.[6]

10 October 1941 Muriel Gale
Muriel Gale has been broadcasting since 1934, and it is her boast that she is truly an 'all British' singer, never having been abroad, even for a holiday.[7]

However, if we 'turn on the wireless and rake down music from the air',[8] it becomes clear that even on the Home Front, private and public psychometers were not so straightforwardly synchronised. The urge to action was very differently interpreted by: BBC programme commissioners and producers; senior politicians and cabinet ministers; domestic and (increasingly far-flung) overseas listenerships; and foreign envoys and cultural diplomats, for instance, all urging better 'sound alliances' and sonic bridges to showcase the nation's undaunted cultural strength and its predisposition to the cultural achievements of its Allies. The result was a gradual but massive redefinition of broadcasting policy in response to these varied, and, on the surface of things, sometimes very mutually hostile interest groups. Close scrutiny of the *Radio Times*, *The Listener*, *The Gramophone* and the BBC Script and Sound Archives even reveals that by the mid-war years, the Home Service was actually broadcasting its most aesthetically and technologically challenging productions to date, and frequently retransmitting them abroad via the Overseas Service and Forces Programme.

This subtle revival of modernist praxis and broader modernist spatialities and geographies on the closely monitored airwaves of wartime radio is multifaceted. It reveals that the intimate scale and familiarity of home listening could prove amenable not only to the transnational dynamics of sonic modernity but also to a number of broadcasting agendas which, on the surface of things, were highly incompatible. The full scale of change being beyond the scope of a single chapter, my focus here is the most ideologically complex of radio's wartime projects: the 'Projection of Russia' campaign, launched in mid-1941. Initially an uncamouflaged home propaganda mission, its evolution soon proved that 'many people's privacies tend to overlap', as Louis MacNeice believed.[9] Conceived before the Nazi invasion of the Soviet Union on 22 June 1941,[10] its mission was to reflect positively on Russia, while avoiding anything too explicitly pro-Communist, and – at least initially – tempering enthusiasms in case the Russian Front collapsed.[11] Given the complex agenda and constant War Office monitoring, broadcasters were urged to demonstrate British appreciation of Russian arts, particularly music – believed to be ideologically safer than science, history or literature.[12] Behind-the-scenes policy advisers point to the first overlapping of interests: they included Cabinet ministers and the Ministry of Information's Policy Committee, the Soviet ambassador Ivan Maisky – a friend and arch-defender of Prokofiev, and staunch music lover – reporting back to Stalin, and Guy Burgess, former Talks producer and now on the Joint Broadcasting Commission, from where he could gently advocate commissions to enhance Anglo-Soviet interests – including in the eyes of the Kremlin.[13]

The campaign began with musico-documentary retrospectives on Tolstoy, Chekhov and Dostoevsky, the mainstays of early twentieth-century Russophilia. The former, often exoticised megaliths of the cultural avant-garde, however, were now revisited for their endearingly local, small-scale appeal. Louis MacNeice's first contribution to the campaign, for instance, was '"Dr. Chekhov", A Study of the Playwright as a Man', a playful, domestic portrait of a homely genius.[14] Another striking novelty was new presenters whose 'microphone manner' could familiarise home audiences with Russia – allied foreign accents could give a better sense of physical proximity and authenticity than those 'well-bred voices' evoked in the epigraph above. Emigré Pavel Shishikoff thus became a new household name, recounting family memories of Chekhov or almost *Boy's Own* perils during the Revolution. Likewise Lydia Lopokova found new popularity as a radio broadcaster recalling her 1910s glory in the Ballets Russes, and presenting panoramic histories of Russian ballet.[15]

As the Ballets Russes retrospectives indicate, initial recommendations that programmes be kept short, accessible and cheerful were dropped, clearing the way for four years of ambitious, often trans-medial broadcasts with a Russian, Soviet or Anglo-Soviet focus, ten at least produced or partially curated by MacNeice.[16] The first major dramatic commission was Louis MacNeice's radio epic *Alexander Nevsky* broadcast on 8 December 1941, based on the 1938 Eisenstein–Prokofiev film.[17] Proposed by Dallas Bower, whose late-1930s training workshops for BBC technicians and producers had drawn extensively on Eisenstein films to illustrate principles of montage,[18] it was an inspired but daring suggestion. Eisenstein's *Nevsky*, its avant-garde cinematography notwithstanding, was explicitly pro-Stalinist as well as anti-Fascist and pro-Soviet, combining anti-Teutonic historical pageant with tenets of high socialist realism.[19] Transposition for the airwaves thus required turning high Soviet agitprop into British morale-boosting home propaganda capable of passing muster with Churchill and the War Office.

Although shamelessly propagandist in parts – MacNeice's Nevsky delivers a hectoring monologue at the end, for example, whereas Eisenstein's Nevsky looks on, silent and contented, as troops return home – the radio version remains true to the impure poetics MacNeice championed.[20] To do so, it garners all the resources of sonic intimacy to 'en-chant' and interiorise, thereby remediating the lost visual immediacy and externality of film.[21] Eisenstein's Shakespearian borrowings, for instance, are greatly played up, bringing Russian epic grandeur closer to home: Nevsky's appeals to the crowds and the army have a St Crispin's ring; the blind man Iuri is a Gloucester figure through whose eyes we see the battle 'feelingly'. Classical resonances also help rescale the more overtly Bolshevik aura for the British home: the opening leitmotif 'If only we had Alexander' combines echoes of Alexander the Great and the British Grenadiers, for instance. Similarly, the added figure of Mikhail, a reluctant bard who can only recite songs of sorrow when summoned to entertain his hosts, recalls both the Shakespearian fool and classical choric commentary. Appeals to the crowds urged to resist the ruthless Teutonic knights interweave echoes of Henry V before Agincourt, the Spartans in the Peloponnesian Straits, and also the British public in 1940–1, thereby reminding listeners that they no longer stood alone. Iuri the blind man is not only a convenient radio dramatist's ploy to compensate for what cannot be seen. The figure functions as one of the play's allegories of listenership, drawing together listeners in the dark, the dark of blackout; the emotive appeal of sonic intimacy with their Russian fellows counters the bewildering darkness of war by foregrounding a common heritage reaching from present suffering back to the feudal upheavals of times past.[22] Prokofiev's more stridently triumphant 'victory music' is meanwhile scaled down, while 'Olga's Song' – 'The Field of the Dead' – is heard far more extensively, putting the emphasis not on feats of arms and heroics, but on shared vulnerability and grief; as *The Listener* later put it, intimate understanding starts from 'what we have in common': 'learning about their background, their views and their traditions, by trying to see things for a few moments as they see them, to think (again temporarily, as an intellectual experience) as they think'.[23]

The broadcast was a spectacular success. Whether deliberately or unconsciously, it laid down two principles common to a large number of productions in the war years which sought to 'bridge individual and collective functions of audition, and to translate intimate hearing into public listening':[24] first, they create a compelling montage of single spoken voices, choric chant and bold modern music – from symphony orchestra to chamber ensemble – which harnesses the intimate energies and inter-subjective directness of music.[25] Second, they favour blank verse over prose for the spoken lines, thereby rhythmicising the drama and reinforcing its appeal not as informative documentary but as recitation harking back to the pre-print age, when listeners and performers were held together by what Woolf calls the 'less visible connection[s]' of intimacy – these are not public events to observe from a distance, but voices 'singing their songs at the back door', restoring 'the world beneath our consciousness'.[26]

A broad variety of commissions, and the burgeoning number of programmes on Russian themes confirm the instant success of 'projecting Russia', which triggered a 'colossal growth of goodwill and compassion towards the USSR', as the Soviet ambassador reported: 'Everything "Russian" is in vogue today: Russian songs, Russian music, Russian films, and books about the USSR: 75,000 copies of a booklet of Stalin's and Molotov's speeches on the war [...] sold out instantly.'[27] The most ambitious undertakings include an eight-hour long dramatisation of Tolstoy's *War and Peace*, for example, broadcast over four weeks as prime-time Sunday-afternoon-and-evening listening, which again featured Lydia Lopokova as one of the two 'homely' narrating voices, alongside a cast of over fifty and extended orchestral interludes to create an epic feel. Tolstoyan, trans-European panorama and sonic intimacy are likewise the key to D. G. Bridson's 'Salute to Life – The Story of the War in the Soviet Union',[28] as the *Radio Times* underlines:

> A year ago today Hitler treacherously attacked the Soviet Union. This programme is an epic of the bloodiest war in history, in which the adventures of three typical Russian infantrymen are traced from mobilisation, through the autumn campaign, the German advance over scorched earth, the winter guerrilla warfare, until the Russian spring offensives began to sweep forward and reconquer territory from the invader. Every phase of the struggle is thus portrayed against the background of the changing seasons, and the lyrically romantic treatment of the theme admits the use of spoken verse and many fine Soviet marching songs. (22 June 1942)[29]

Musico-dramatic documentaries or dramatisations were not the only means to celebrate 'our comradeship-in-arms with the Union of Socialist Soviet Republics' as *The Listener* confidently affirmed.[30] Bridson's inspiring epic was broadcast on the same evening as the British premiere of Shostakovich's Seventh Symphony, for which audiences were prepared by a musical talk earlier in the day and a detailed *Radio Times* article by musicologist Ralph Hill. Nearly eighty minutes long, the symphony's challenging, strident and unfamiliar melodic patterns inspired ambivalent responses from listeners. It nonetheless remains a splendid example of bold sonic modernism[31] made compelling to unversed ears by the topical and emotional appeal of music from 'our great ally' as the *Radio Times* repeatedly insists, inspired by and even composed during the everyday traumas of a pitiless siege. Other press reviewers struck the same chord:

> The critics saw Shostakovich as the heroic fireman who [...] was inspired by ideas that came to him as he was 'waiting for the next moment of action ... in his duties as an air-raid warden, watching for incendiaries on the roof of the Leningrad Conservatoire.' [...] The critics mattered little. To the British, the music was thick with the mood and heroism of their Russian allies, proof of their humanity, and an elegy to the defiant city on the Neva.[32]

Furthermore, by playing up the popular 'Russian' label and setting the broadcast within the frame of British solidarity with their fellow citizens at war, programmers could steer clear of the ongoing and often acrimonious debates about which 'serious' music was suitable for home listening.[33] This homely, mimetic account of the harsh discords and overwhelming epic scale of the symphony's experimental modernism resonated on in the popular imagination for decades.

Even without camouflaging musical modernism as topical programme music, the purely musical component of the 'Projection of Russia' campaign belies the enduring Adorno-inspired myth of wartime radio hypnotising its masses with monolithically conservative, melodically undemanding, and flatly sentimental tunes:

> the preference for Tchaikovsky among radio listeners is as significant a commentary on the inherent nature of the radio voice as on the broader social issues of contemporary listening habits [...] the radio voice does not present the listeners with material adequate to such desiderates. They are forced to passive sensual and emotional acceptance of pre-digested yet disconnected qualities, whereas those qualities at the same time become mummified and magicized.[34]

As the *Radio Times* makes clear, the Home Service was *not* serving up lukewarm Tchaikovsky; in fact, distinctly less Tchaikovsky was broadcast between 1941 and 1945 than Rimsky-Korsakov, Shostakovich and Borodin, for example. Interestingly, there is also considerably less coverage of Stravinsky than the Russian composers he tends to be associated with, Prokofiev and Shostakovich, which suggests that what mattered was the sonic bridge to Soviet Russia rather than to émigré Russians. Such coverage of a foreign country's late nineteenth- and early twentieth-century composers was unprecedented on the airwaves.[35] Broadcasting schedules also indicate that unfamiliar music was no longer restricted to 'serious', evening concerts – Russian themes featured alongside British favourites in morning, afternoon and early evening concerts, as well as in programmes for schools, as a single 'Schools' slot on 6 March 1942 confirms:

For the Schools.
2pm Travel Talks: Russia. 'A Pipe-Line through the Mountains: Oil from the Caucasus', by William Rennet
2.20 Useful Citizens: Series of imaginary interviews, written by Honor Wyatt, between F. H. Grisewood and people who have worked to make the world a better place than they found it. 'Charles Dickens – the man who showed in his novels that the world could be made better'
2.40 Orchestral Concert Series: 'A Great Russian Composer': Illustrated talk on Rimsky-Korsakov, by Herbert Murrill.[36]

Clearly, there had been a huge mutation since the genteel, proudly patriotic prescriptions for radio's musical entertainments and education in 1939–40. Nor can this change be comfortably classified in terms of 'brows': these musical features and documentaries bridged divides by underlining the common Russian theme, whether geographical, topical or historical, and by endlessly varying the register and accessibility of 'contemporary music', as the following brief overview attests:

15 July 1942, 17.00 'The Don Flows to the Sea: Musical impression of Soviet life given by the Russian Balalaika Orchestra and chorus'.[37]

8 January 1943, 18.45 'Russian Opera: Marches, dances, and choruses from *Ruslan and Ludmilla* (Glinka); *Sorochintsy Fair* (Mussorgsky); *Eugene Onegin* (Tchaikovsky); *The Snow Maiden* (Rimsky-Korsakov); *The Golden Cockerel* (Rimsky-Korsakov)'.[38]

24 October 1943, 13.45 '"Songs of the Soviet Peoples". Introduced, with gramophone records, by Alan Bush.'[39]

Wednesday, 12 January 1944, 18.45 '"Winter Will Pass": Life in War-Time Russia illustrated with records of new songs recently brought to Britain'.[40]

Alan Bush's regular involvement as a presenter underlines another change in broadcasting policy on the domestic front. Here was a committed communist with a rich history of pacifist and Popular Front compositions in the 1930s now addressing the country at large.[41] Nor was the twinning of modernist arts and popular appeal solely musical: Russian and Soviet novels, films, poetry and plays were soon high points for the 'Home': Ardov's 'Tanya', subtitled 'The Modern Cinderella', Afinogenev's 'Distant Point', Simonov's *The Russians*, Mayakovsky's 'A Cloud in Trousers' and Blok's 'The Twelve' were all heard on air. The cultural and historical unity is further illustrated by the shift from programmes specifically showcasing Russian cultural achievements to pro-Russian leitmotifs working their way into all the regular slots of the day. Edward Sackville-West's popular late-evening broadcast 'And So to Bed', which initially mixed soothing familiar favourites and contemporary British verse as an ideal nightcap, introduced Russian poetry evenings.[42] Similarly, 'Music While You Work' took up a Russian theme, as did midday concerts for munitions staff linking causes with Soviet workers.[43]

One of the most impressive, symbolically resonant examples of a domestic, modernist *and* trans-European partnership on the BBC was 'In Honour of Russia', on 8 November 1943. This lasted an entire evening, from 7.25 p.m. until 10.30 p.m., was transmitted on the Home Service and (in slightly different format) the Forces programme, and was announced 'as a tribute to Russia's National Day (November 7) and to the prodigious part the Russian people are playing in the war against Nazi Germany':

> But the programmes will also aim at a deeper purpose, namely the realistic presentation of what the Russian people, the Russian civilisation, the Russian character stand for in the light of their history as well as their present, in the hope of creating a wider and deeper understanding of Russia in this country. (10th September 1943)[44]

The evening began and ended with 'God Save the King' and the 'Internationale' played one after the other. This symbolical feat alone had been unthinkable in the early years of war. By 1943, however, the success of the 'Projection of Russia' campaign, championing the victories of the Red Army and the unquenchable spirit of the Russian people at home, was inflecting on British political interests, domestic morale and BBC programming.⁴⁵

The evening's main feature was MacNeice's 'The Spirit of Russia': an hour-long 'panorama of Russian life described by Rimsky-Korsakov's music'.⁴⁶ Although no recording of the evening's broadcasts appears to have survived, the drafts and script alone attest to the creative vision and topical vibrancy of the programme. Composed as an eclogue between three voices, a poetic form which MacNeice favoured in many of his longer compositions, and blending the intimacy of conversation with the epic dimensions of historical drama, it is pageant-like in conception, celebrating the geography, legends and cultural history of popular Russia. Like *Nevsky*, it offers a rousing tribute to the courage of the contemporary ally, both soldiers and civilians, and a vivid musical soundscape interwoven with evocative commentary, prose extracts (notably Gogol's *Dead Souls*), folklore (Baba Yaga, Ivan the Tsarevitch, Gornych and the Dragon) and poetry (Lermontov and Pushkin).⁴⁷ While informative about Russia, it relies on the powerful appeal of age-old legends and storytelling devices, and the acoustic power of reverberation and echo, to bridge divides and create intimate ties between Russia's folklore and Western favourites, and from contemporary Russia to Britain.

The rich musical fresco assures the bold modernism of the production. Conceived in collaboration with the modernist musicologist Gerald Abraham, the dramatic montage gives listeners what was often their first inkling of Rimsky-Korsakov's late compositions, extracts of which had been used by Fokine and Diaghilev for scenes in the ballets, but which only premiered as operas in London between 1926 and 1936. Ranging from *The Golden Cockerel, May Night* and *Christmas Eve* to *The Invisible City of Kitezh*, the Rimsky-Korsakov broadcasts offered vibrant examples of the striking folk tunes, popular dances, radical harmonic play, polyrhythmic orchestration and chromatic sound mosaics that constitute the distinctive modernist sound of Russian early twentieth-century music, as it shifts with apparently blithe ease between folk idiom, anti-autocratic pastiche, staunch nationalism and formal experimentalism. Meanwhile, the voices of three well-known film actors,⁴⁸ the heightened poetry of the prose sequences, and the incantatory effect of fade-ins, cross-over sound sequences, repetition and echo would have reinforced the collective spirit of shared intimacies. In the central section, for example, after evocations of the great plains and forests of Russia and a recitation of Lermontov's lyrically patriotic 'I Love My Country with a Singular Love', comes a rhythmicised chorus of three voices celebrating what Woolf calls 'the obstinate emotion' of national identity, 'dropped into a child's ears by the cawing of rooks in an elm tree, by the splash of waves on a beach, or by

English voices murmuring nursery rhymes'.[49] In the same wistfully utopian, yet radically engaged mode as Woolf, MacNeice thus dramatises Lermontov's verses to be shared and spoken by favourite British voices; in so doing, he reconfigures nations and patriotism as intimately embodied transnational sensations, shared across territorial and ideological divides: 'this drop of pure, if irrational, emotion she will make serve her to give to England first what she desires of peace and freedom for the whole world'.[50]

> [Speaker 1] A country is something more than a place on a map.
> [Speaker 2] (quick) A country is something you breathe and it runs in your veins.
> [Speaker 3] (quick) A country is something you die for but something that lives when you die.
> [Speaker 1] (quick) A country is something you eat and you drink and you sleep with.
> [Speaker 2] (quick) A country is something you laugh with and weep with. So Russia –
> [Speaker 3] (quick) Russia is the cry of quails and the cornflowers in the corn.
> [Speaker 1] (quick) Russia is a wooden hut with a roof of straw and with red shutters,
> [Speaker 2] (slower) Russia is the smell in the fields after thunder – birch trees, mushroom, violet and thyme.
> [Speaker 3] (slower still) Russia is the people who smell that smell, who live in that hut, who hear that cry.
> [Speaker 1] (very slow) Russia is the Russian people ...
> [Music] (Bring in 'May Night' and to background).[51]

Even without a sound archive to reveal the pitch, tone and pace of the speaking voices, the rich harmonic vibrancy of the 'May Night' overture gives an idea of how British listeners at home could be drawn together by the compelling 'spirit of Russia'. The title of the evening's feature highlights this appeal to affective unity, joining everyday people with a common purpose, common hardships and a shared experience of love, longing and loss. The programme may have glorified the clichéd 'Soul of Russia', but this was a soul with a distinctly political, anti-authoritarian edge to it, unlike the more mystical fin-de-siècle soul that had been extolled during the first wave of Russian fever.[52]

The most remarkable evolution of all, in this championing of the Soviet 'People's War' and their leader, is to be found in the annual commemorations on the Home Service and Forces Programme alike not only of the Bolshevik Revolution and the founding of the Red Army, but even of Stalin himself. For four consecutive years on 21 December, the Home Service broadcast a concert in honour of Stalin's birthday, a programme entitled quite simply 'Greetings to Joseph Stalin'.[53] No other foreign leader had comparable honours. The Soviet ambassador, Ivan Maisky, gives a very favourable account of how this popular appeal radiated out from the wireless to the highest echelons of government and to the everyday home:

> Today the British Government ceremoniously celebrated the 25th anniversary of the Red Army. A British Government, that is, headed by Churchill, that same Churchill who led the crusade against the Bolsheviks during the Civil War! How times change! [...] Admiration for the Red Army in England is now unstinting. Everywhere – among the masses and in the army. To fight this wave would have been dangerous. So the Government has decided to stand at its head – that is, to ride the wave.[54]

Nor does Maisky merely speak for Churchill here. In 1944, the prime minister himself in a 'General Directive for Broadcast' cites the outstanding demonstrations of goodwill towards the Russian Allies resonating over the country's airwaves as incontrovertible proof that 'relations with Russia were never more close, intimate and cordial than at present'.[55]

Beneath the surface, however, enthusiasms were tempered. Even in the earliest months of the campaign, Harold Nicolson discreetly warned the Director of Talks that 'audiences I have addressed pay no attention whatsoever to American production or even to the training of vast American armies. All that they can think about is the glory of Russia.'[56] Another confidential letter written a fortnight later, however, suggests that a second outbreak of Russian fever on a national scale, and its concomitant risk of ideological derivation, was, at least for the time being, less harmful than national morale faltering:

> My dear Maconachie,
>   Bracken is not at all in favour of our starting a series on the truth about Russia. He says that if we once started on that Maisky would send a band of dynamiters to blow up Broadcasting House. The more I think of it the more I feel that he is right in this opinion and that we shall have to keep silent and let the false legend prevail.
>   I hate this as much as you do but I think we would find that once we got down to it we would find ourselves edged by tact and discretion into something almost as untruthful as the legend itself.
>   Yours sincerely,
>   H Nicholson[57]

Nicolson's was not the only voice of concern. While pro-Communist producers and transnational-minded artists 'cement[ed] Anglo-Soviet understanding – true, frank, cordial understanding based on something more than emotional response',[58] memoranda and briefs between the Foreign Office, the War Office and the Director-General of the BBC show senior politicians concerned by ideological deviation but hoping to harness popular affect and modernist dynamics for the good of the nation. Louis MacNeice's role curating the 'Spirit of Russia', for example, worried the Foreign Office, who monitored him more closely from then on, but they continued to tolerate his inspirational Russian coverage in the name of its uplifting appeal.[59] This more cynical approach to the airwaves, often at direct odds with mindsets prevailing at Broadcasting House, paradoxically turns Adorno's instinctive suspicion of state-controlled radio intimacy upside down. Here we find senior politicians acknowledging that to suspend state control might end up serving the interests of state; Russian and Soviet modernist rhythms were therefore to be encouraged within the intimacy of home, precisely because there was solace and enchantment to be found in powerfully interconnected sonic bridges and transnational soundings of harmony. Such politics of tolerance came to an end, predictably, once the war ended. The predominance of broadcasts with a marked Russian theme promptly dropped, a trend accentuated by the reorganisation of broadcasting services from 1946. The 'Third Programme' became the more likely site for Russian music and Russian literature, which in turn reinforced their image as 'difficult', 'demanding' and 'highbrow',[60] suitable for smaller, more discerning audiences. Both coincidentally and deliberately, the stage was thus set for the Cold War's cultural front – a barely camouflaged military and ideological assault to be just as insidiously, but far more lastingly, cultivated on the Home.

*

A close study of what deserves to be acknowledged as a second wave of Russian fever, propagated by the BBC, offers unexpected readings of the 'psychometrical pulse' in wartime England. On the domestic front, listeners within the closed space of the home, however theoretically disconnected from the supposed complexity, intellectualism and remoteness of contemporary modernisms, were forging unsuspectingly modernist links with their Soviet allies. From early morning until nightfall, familiar slots on the airwaves which structured everyday British life were transmitting the daily rhythms of their Russian and Soviet counterparts, and these rhythms could be decidedly modernist – powerfully off-beat, irregular, complex, unfamiliar and challenging. Such intimate ties show that even in times of national emergency, state-controlled broadcasting can prove the finest guarantor of sonic modernity; they confirm that national welfare and a yearning love for one's country can fuel and be fuelled by transcultural, transnational sonic bridges to other territories and homelands. They also prove that immense popularity need not condemn cultural production to abandon aesthetically demanding formal experimentation. But they reflect the vulnerability of intimate bonds and sonic bridges too. Radio waves are notoriously ephemeral and when 'the people's collective image constantly in front of the people's eyes'[61] is reliant only on sound, it quickly fades away, whether gradually growing quieter, or becoming harshly overpowered by louder, more strident noises.

Notes

1. Louis MacNeice, 'Cushendun', in *Collected Poems* (London: Faber & Faber, 1979), p. 165.
2. Virginia Woolf, *The Diary of Virginia Woolf*, vol. 5, ed. Anne Olivier Bell (New York: Harcourt, 1984), p. 292.
3. See Theodor W. Adorno's critical definition of radio intimacy in the 1930s: 'the deeper this voice is involved within his own privacy, the more it appears to pour out of the cells of his most intimate life; the more he gets the impression that his own cupboard, his own phonograph, his own bedroom speaks to him in a personal way, devoid of the intermediary stages of the printed word; the more perfectly he is ready to accept wholesale whatever he hears. It is just this privacy which fosters the authority of the radio voice and helps to hide it by making it no longer appear to come from outside' (*Current of Music: Elements of a Radio Theory*, ed. Robert Hullot-Kentor (London: Polity Press, 2009), p. 141.)
4. See Alex Goody's careful reading of how 'the private domestic space of listening can be articulated in particular ways to the homeland threatened by the forces of war' (p. 79), in 'Radio at Home: BBC Drama and the Domestic Listener, 1935–42', *Modernist Cultures*, 10.1 (2015), pp. 62–82.
5. <http://www.bbc.co.uk/archive/hawhaw/8928.shtml> (accessed 27 October 2017).
6. Available at <http://genome.ch.bbc.co.uk/ef51297f0dfc475fb30ef5b2d9056128> (accessed 27 October 2017).
7. Available at <http://genome.ch.bbc.co.uk/f3802c3d736b48d58523d835f2ecc4ad> (accessed 27 October 2017).

8. This is the means recommended by the narrator of Virginia Woolf's *Three Guineas* to assess the more insidious workings of tyranny. See Woolf, *Three Guineas* (London: Hogarth Press, 1938), p. 147.
9. Louis MacNeice, *Varieties of Parable* (Cambridge: Cambridge University Press, 1965), p. 8.
10. Programme Directive no. 19 (2 July 1940) asks producers to 'keep an eye on programme [sic] dealing with Russia. Ironical or derogatory remarks about Stalin and Russia's motives and probable action are thought to be equally undesirable at present.' Internal directives concerning the projection of Russia viewed at <http://www.bbc.co.uk/archive/ussr/6723.shtml> and <http://www.bbc.co.uk/archive/ussr/6711.shtml> (accessed 27 October 2017).
11. A memo from the Director of Talks stated: 'one side is suspicious of our selling sunshine about Russia and the other that we do not pay tribute to Russian qualities. [...] this means we do not want to describe Russia as a paradise or to invite too many unfavourable comparisons with conditions in this country' (<http://www.bbc.co.uk/archive/ussr/6724.shtml> (accessed 27 October 2017)).
12. Asa Briggs, *The History of Broadcasting in the United Kingdom*, vol. 3 (Oxford: Oxford University Press, 1970), p. 392.
13. See Andrew Lownie, *Stalin's Englishman: The Lives of Guy Burgess* (London: Hodder and Stoughton, 2015), pp. 97–113.
14. Available at <http://genome.ch.bbc.co.uk/29ed6159fa9345d5a15ba75202bfa671> (accessed 26 February 2018).
15. Lopokova, described in the *Radio Times* of 7 March 1942 as 'one of the most delightful and famous of all Russian dancers', had been a successful BBC radio presenter and actress since 1934 (available at <http://genome.ch.bbc.co.uk/5ed5f083af5a462a9d73a53cf804754a> (accessed 27 October 2017)).
16. For broader coverage of epic-scale wartime broadcasting, see Claire Davison, 'Performing Communities: Sound Alliances, Modernist Aesthetics and the BBC Home Service, 1940–1945', in Caroline Pollentier and Sarah Wilson (eds), *Modernist Communities across Cultures and Media* (Gainesville: University Press of Florida, 2019), pp. 215–33.
17. Louis MacNeice, 'Alexander Nevsky', Home Service, 8 December 1941. British Library Sound Archive T3618. The script is held at the BBC Written Archives Centre.
18. See Terence Brown and Alec Reid, *Time Was Away: The World of Louis MacNeice* (Dublin: Dolmen Press, 1974), pp. 98–104.

19. In the USSR, extracts from the film (which nearly cost Eisenstein his life during the months of the Nazi–Soviet non-aggression pact) were shown to boost troops' morale. See Paul A. Cohen, *History and Popular Memory: The Power of Story in Moments of Crisis* (New York: Columbia University Press, 2014), pp. 169–70.
20. Louis MacNeice's *Modern Poetry* begins: 'This book is a plea for *impure poetry*, that is, for poetry conditioned by the poet's life and the world around him' (*Modern Poetry: A Personal Essay* (Oxford: Oxford University Press, 1968), p. 8).
21. See Dominic Pettman, *Sonic Intimacy: Voices, Species, Technics* (Stanford: Stanford University Press, 2017), pp. 81–8.
22. For an account of *Nevsky*'s mediations between interior listening practice and public, external concerns, as reflected by broadcast context, audience figures and listeners' responses, see Ian Whittington, 'Archaeologies of Sound: Reconstructing Louis MacNeice's Wartime Radio Publics', *Modernist Cultures*, 10.1 (2015), pp. 47–8.
23. Unsigned editorial, 'Understanding an Ally', *The Listener*, 702 (1942), p. 810.
24. Whittington, 'Archaeologies of Sound', p. 49.
25. See Georgina Born (ed.), *Music, Sound, Space: Transformations of Public and Private Experience* (Cambridge: Cambridge University Press, 2013), pp. 31–40.
26. Virginia Woolf, 'Anon', in *The Essays of Virginia Woolf*, 6 vols, ed. Andrew McNeillie (vols 1–4) and Stuart N. Clarke (vols 5–6) (London: Hogarth Press, 1986–2011), vol. 6, pp. 582–4. Ideas for the never completed essay began in around 1930, but composition dates mostly from 1939 to 1941.
27. Ivan Maisky, *The Maisky Diaries: Red Ambassador to the Court of St James's 1932–1943*, ed. Gabriel Gorodetsky (New Haven, CT and London: Yale University Press, 2015), p. 394. This huge about-turn in public feeling was not achieved by the BBC alone. The Beaverbrook press played a significant and complementary role, as Maisky underlines (ibid. pp. 361–414).
28. Bridson's agitprop-style contributions to the 'Projection of Russia' campaign include 'Arms for Russia – Programme from the campaign of a British factory which makes them' (7 November 1942) and 'Red Star – to celebrate the 27th anniversary of the founding of the Red Army' (23 February 1945).
29. Available at <http://genome.ch.bbc.co.uk/schedules/bbchomeservice/basic/1942-06-22> (accessed 27 October 2017).
30. 'Understanding an Ally', p. 810.
31. Definitions of modernism in music are notoriously slippery, but it is generally agreed that modern music is technically experimental, subverting

conventional tonal and rhythmic patterns, and favouring an essentially self-reflexive aesthetic.
32. Bryan Moynahan, *Leningrad: Siege and Symphony* (London: Hachette, 2013), p. 242.
33. Many listeners reported preferring Britten's music in Sackville-West's *The Rescue* to the drama it accompanied. See Edward Sackville-West, *The Rescue: A Melodrama for Broadcasting* (London: Secker and Warburg, 1945), pp. 15–16. Sackville-West, meanwhile, acknowledges his debt to Berg and Schönberg's *Sprechstimme* compositions (ibid. pp. 7–8).
34. Adorno, *Current of Music*, pp. 266–7.
35. Modern Russian composers heard on the Home Service between 1941 and 1945 include: Arensky, Balakirev, Borodin, Dargomyzhsky, Glazunov, Grechaninov, Ippolitov-Ivanov, Kalinnikov, Khachaturian, Lyadov, Mussorgsky, Myaskovsky, Rimsky-Korsakov, Scriabin and Taneyev.
36. Available at <http://genome.ch.bbc.co.uk/81eccf1ad1dd4913a55abca86ab6757a> (accessed 1 March 2018).
37. Available at <http://genome.ch.bbc.co.uk/e89109587ae24883954e5a-691c1631ea> (accessed 27 October 2017).
38. Available at <http://genome.ch.bbc.co.uk/aa5547b7af174bf4b33f549f-c1a02fa4> (accessed 27 October 2017).
39. Available at <http://genome.ch.bbc.co.uk/38b8cba5d04d4962ba6db01d3cfe6f3c> (accessed 27 October 2017).
40. Available at <http://genome.ch.bbc.co.uk/667305db7bcd46b49787e312d6939556> (accessed 1 October 2017).
41. For the changing fortunes of Alan Bush on the BBC during the war years, see Joanna Bullivant, *Alan Bush, Modern Music, and the Cold War: The Cultural Left in Britain and the Communist Bloc* (Cambridge: Cambridge University Press, 2017), pp. 96–115.
42. 1 December 1943, 23.20: 'And So to Bed: Four poems from the Russian of Pushkin, Lermontov, Tyutchev and Blok', available at <http://genome.ch.bbc.co.uk/d748538c5ed345cb956f34a14ab8a168> (accessed 7 March 2018).
43. Monday, 16 March 1942, 'Music While You Work', available at <http://genome.ch.bbc.co.uk/63699a81dd544727a4025f5d38c365f3> (accessed 27 October 2017); Friday, 31 December 1943, '"Break for Music": ENSA concert for war-workers from a factory canteen', available at <http://genome.ch.bbc.co.uk/12a158e5aadd4f7b8614dc17e62af64e> (accessed 7 March 2018).
44. Features of the evening included MacNeice's 'The Spirit of Russia'; 'Russia at War – I was there' (a programme of eye-witness accounts); 'Russia's National Day' (evocations by those who had seen the celebrations in Red Square the day before); 'A History of the Red Army'; 'War Songs of the Soviet Peoples',

and 'Greetings to the Soviet Union' (in both languages). 'Russia's National Day', commemorating the anniversary of the Bolshevik Revolution, was celebrated on the BBC Home Service every year from 1941 until 1945. I have found no trace of any similar commemoration after November 1946.
45. A BBC directive dated 22 January 1942 stated: 'The Internationale may now be played in programmes. We are asked not to over do [sic] it, and only to play it when the occasion really does call for it' (<http://www.bbc.co.uk/archive/ussr/6725.shtml> (accessed 1 June 2016)).
46. <http://www.bbc.co.uk/archive/ussr/6730.shtml> and <http://www.bbc.co.uk/archive/ussr/6734.shtml> (accessed 27 October 2017).
47. However topical, 'The Spirit of Russia' occupies an interesting place in MacNeice's oeuvre. Echoes of *Nevsky* (49.00–53.34) make their way into 'The Spirit of Russia' (lines 50–66), and both works contain verses from *Kitezh*. The allegorical resonances of both *Nevsky* and 'The Spirit of Russia' clearly pave the way to *The Dark Tower* (1946), generally acknowledged as MacNeice's masterpiece for radio, and the musico-dramatic frame and sequencing of all three are clearly perceptible in *They Met on Good Friday* (1959). Meanwhile the eclogue structure of many of MacNeice's major poetical writings of the mid- to late 1930s is visibly re-enacted in the intercutting voices of his radio features. The mutually enriching impact of MacNeice's verse dramas, features and poetry on his overall creative evolution has yet to be studied in depth.
48. As in Virginia Woolf's *The Waves*, which MacNeice adapted for radio in 1955, the absence of direct dialogue between characters creates a musical unfolding of voice rather than a conversational pattern. The three actors whose voices interweave in this eclogue were Mary O'Farrell, Roy Emerton and Marius Goring.
49. Woolf, *Three Guineas*, p. 198.
50. Ibid. p. 198.
51. MacNeice, 'The Spirit of Russia', p. 8. Typescript held at the BBC Written Archives Centre. BBC copyright content reproduced courtesy of the British Broadcasting Corporation. All rights reserved. I would like to express my warm thanks to staff at the Written Archives Centre for their invaluable help in tracing this material.
52. See Caroline Maclean, *The Vogue for Russia: Modernism and the Unseen in Britain 1900–1930* (Edinburgh: Edinburgh University Press, 2015); and Catherine Brown, 'The Russian Soul Englished', *Journal of Modern Literature*, 36.1 (2012), pp. 132–49 (especially pp. 132–9).
53. Available at <http://genome.ch.bbc.co.uk/78dc34b71bdc454294874d9dadd7245a> (accessed 27 October 2017).

54. Maisky, *The Maisky Diaires*, p. 487.
55. 27 October 1944, viewed at <http://www.bbc.co.uk/archive/ussr/6713.shtml> (accessed 1 March 2018).
56. The matter was considered serious enough to be followed up by internal memos and telephone calls (<http://www.bbc.co.uk/archive/ussr/6737.shtml> (accessed 27 October 2017)).
57. Extracts from the 1942 correspondence between the BBC Director of Talks and Harold Nicolson (then an MP and parliamentary secretary serving on the Board of Governors of the BBC, after a year at the Ministry of Information), concerning the success of the campaign, and its expediency at the present moment, viewed at <http://www.bbc.co.uk/archive/ussr/6726.shtml>, <http://www.bbc.co.uk/archive/ussr/6729.shtml> and <http://www.bbc.co.uk/archive/ussr/6737.shtml> (accessed 27 October 2017).
58. 'Understanding an Ally', p. 810.
59. Scripts were vetted by the Foreign Office, who objected not only to excessive glorification of 'the regime', but also to MacNeice's place in the prime-time slot: 'they are somewhat perturbed by the appearance of MacNeice's name in the 7.35 period – "Spirit of Russia"'. Similarly, his contribution to the Albert Hall meeting met with disapproval; the Foreign Secretary considered it 'much overdone' (<http://www.bbc.co.uk/archive/ussr/6738.shtml> (accessed 27 October 2017)).
60. Similar terms recur during BBC negotiations before the launch of the Third Programme in 1946, and were unquestioningly repeated, usually appreciatively, by early historians of radio. See Humphrey Carpenter, *The Envy of the World: Fifty Years of the BBC Third Programme and Radio 3* (London: Weidenfeld & Nicolson, 1996); and Briggs, *The History of Broadcasting*.
61. Hermione Lee (ed.), *The Mulberry Tree: Writings of Elizabeth Bowen*, London: Vintage, [1986] 2009, p. 181.

12

The Modernist Nonmodern: Provincialism and the Intimacy of Space

Saikat Majumdar

Great art is provincial. Let us not temper that with the softer, politically neutered word 'regional'. 'Cosmopolitan', much like the glossy magazine that carries its name, and the shiny airport lounges it adorns, has dominated well-meaning conversations about culture for as long as we can remember, donning ambassadorial goodwill and gaining academic momentum. It has become to culture what multiculturalism has become to affairs of state (and college admissions). It is so much nicer to be cosmopolitan, no? To be provincial is not only to be narrow and mean-spirited, but also almost certainly to be reactionary into the bargain, a religious nut perhaps, backward and excluded from the intergalactic flight of modernity.

What a curious transfer of values this is. In terms of rhetoric, a pathetic fallacy. Where the weeping night ends up containing the tears of the suffering lover – the weeping human being who trades her identity with that of the night incapable of shedding human tears. Cosmopolitanism is what we expect of the sensibility that engages with the art-object, the reader/viewer/listener. It is the magical, sylph-like spirit that can contain multiple aliennesses at the same time, that can step beyond mere markers of alienness such as headgear or vegetarianism and genuinely engage with the alien values that uphold them, indeed, that which has no visible markers at all. There exists no particular burden on the work of art that it be cosmopolitan; human perhaps, but not cosmopolitan in any sense of the term. Its artistic power hangs on its ability to embed itself as deeply as it can within its cultural milieu, not leave it behind in gay abandon and show how easily it can travel across the globe. Asking a work of art to be cosmopolitan is similar to asking it to be moral; for cosmopolitanism is the goodwill of the nations, the moral impulse of its embassies. In a world where embassies often sponsor the dissemination, indeed, the creation of artwork speedily inserted into the free market, culture that can lay the curious claim to cosmopolitanism has, behind it, the fatally effective combination of national goodwill and global marketability joined together.

How did it happen, this great historic pathetic fallacy? The version of cosmopolitanism that circulates in the realm of culture today is essentially a creation of Western modernity. Arguably, there are other forms of cosmopolitanism, but that is a discussion for another day. If the European Enlightenment of the eighteenth century gave us the modern notion of aesthetics, with its sense of interiority and artistic originality, it was the intense flowering of this modernity in the artistic modernism of the late nineteenth and early twentieth centuries that turned cosmopolitanism into the most desired whorl of not only the art-object, but of the life of the artist as well. Urban bohemiana, cafes and art galleries, the hip art district, artistic and intellectual migrancy – in most cases, living in and soaking in the atmosphere of the Left Bank, Bloomsbury or Greenwich Village – owe their birth to the emerging cityscape of nineteenth-century Europe, especially Paris. Much of what we take for granted about artistic life goes back to modernism – that to create art you must leave the dull backwater where you were born, move to the hip art district in the hip happening city where 'on or about December 1910 human character changed'[1] (or a couple of other cities like it, across the Channel and the Pond). And once you are there, you must lead an angst-ridden, hard-drinking, chain-smoking life and trade sexual partners as often as you shed your goth-hipster outfit. And this is where the world gathers, the world that matters anyway, and fine art emerges, winged by the blithe spirit of the cosmopolitan. James Joyce and Katharine Mansfield trekked this path of artistic migration from their provincial hometowns, as did T. S. Eliot and Ezra Pound; Gertrude Stein not only did it herself but became a sponsor of all who aspired to do so; Virginia Woolf, of course, was already there and deepened the definition of the cosmopolitan through the fantastic assemblage of minds at Bloomsbury.

But once they reached the heart of the cosmopolis – London–Paris–Trieste–Zurich – what did they write about? The contrast between 'home-grown' American modernists like Wallace Stevens and William Carlos Williams and the expats like Pound and Eliot are easily obvious, and there are the celebrated international locales of Joseph Conrad and E. M. Forster, but is not some of the best modernist literature set in the same provincial locations its exponents supposedly fled from? Joyce's Dublin, D. H. Lawrence's Nottinghamshire mining country, William Faulkner's rural American South – their celebration in literary modernism seems to mock the very cosmopolitan aspirations with which the movement is overwhelmingly identified. The dull idyll of the New Zealand countryside vies with

London society and Paris cafes in Katherine Mansfield's fiction, and while the quotidian rhythms of Stevens's Hartford may not have the paralysing deadness of colonial Dublin or the illiterate savagery of the Lawrentian mining country, all of these locations can safely be called provincial, a long way from the artistic, political and economic centres of the Western world, if not always in terms of physical distance, certainly in the yardstick of culture.

Modernism's seductive import of provincialism to the metropolis has deepened the delusion. The organic and visceral power of the provincial has fallen farther and farther out of artistic and intellectual memory. John Marx has reminded us that the relationship between provincialism and cosmopolitanism in literary modernism is more dialectical than simply oppositional. He quotes Robert Crawford, who made the apparently counter-intuitive, but eventually convincing argument that 'Modernism's cosmopolitanism can be seen as partly the result of "provincial" concerns.'[2] Marx goes on to delineate the hidden and seductive ways in which 'modernism brought provincialism to the metropole – in the form of dialect and regional idiom punctuating modernist prose and poetry – and reciprocated by bringing the city to the country – via the cosmopolitanism that frames modernist literature as a whole'.[3] The nonmodern forms of intimacy embedded in the provincial formulations have continued to thrive in literary modernism but lost critical attention with the eventual canonisation of literary modernism as the pre-eminent movement of cultural cosmopolitanism in the twentieth century.

Modernity can be understood not only in temporal terms, but in spatial terms as well. If metropolitan centres of culture embody modernity, the provincial backwater always embodies the lack of it. The provincial, in that sense, is the spatialisation of the nonmodern. Franco Moretti has argued that the *Bildungsroman* tends to involve a spatial as well as a temporal trek; the provincial youth's aspiration for growth also symbolises a national aspiration for modernity, which necessarily involves a journey from the provincial backwater to the big city.[4] Modernism has staged a relentless trajectory of aspiration for modernity, hiding its deep roots in the provincial and the nonmodern in a deceptive manner. Perhaps it is time that we try to recuperate the affective power of the nonmodern and the provincial. Such a recovery, carried out in the realm of the aesthetic, might help the return of the provincial in wider spheres of popular and political life. At a time when many of the premises of modernity, such as secularism and cosmopolitanism, seem to be failing miserably before the rise of authoritarian governments backed by jingoistic populism, the aesthetic recovery of the provincial might offer some answers and open up new possibilities.

*

It should be easy to celebrate the provincial in modern India, no? After all, the miracle of national statehood in India is upheld by a plethora of provincialisms – linguistic, religious, those driven by caste and clan and class, wealth and poverty, a literal maelstrom of sartorial and gastronomic cultures. But *celebrate* the provincial? In a country where progress and modernity have, for the most part, been synonymous with the colonial and the Western for the last two hundred and fifty-odd years? Those who have seen Satyajit Ray's film *Aparajito*, based on the Bengali novelist Bibhutibhushan Bandopadhyay's great modernist *Bildungsroman* of that name, might recall the poignant hierarchy between the provincial and the cosmopolitan enacted when Apu, the teenage protagonist, holds a globe in his hands and shows it to his poor, widowed mother in the yellow lamplight of their dilapidated mud hut, tracking places to which they have never been.[5] For Apu, who will soon make the long and arduous trek from the province to the nearest metropolis, Calcutta – then the capital of British India – this moment embodies the provincial's dream of leaving his impoverished home behind and travelling far and wide, especially to the places that promise modernity and cosmopolitanism. In India, in the provinces, more often than not, provincialism is a miasma to claw through, a monster to fight. The long legacy of colonial modernity has ensured that there is very little, if anything at all, to celebrate about being a provincial in modern India.

Independence could not rid the provinces of the long shadow of neo-colonialism and global capitalism. More importantly, it introduced a new anxiety in provincial cultures: the independent state and the subsequent importance of a national imagination, heavy in its ethical burden. Here again, celebrate the *provincial*? Amit Chaudhuri has repeatedly pointed out how the national narrative, allegorical or otherwise, gripped the novelistic imagination of English India in the decades of its high global visibility following the publication of the pioneering national allegory, *Midnight's Children*.[6] This obligation to the pan-Indian imagination was rarely felt by vernacular-language writers, most of whom remained, if not provincial, certainly regional. Chaudhuri gives the examples of Bibhutibhushan Bandopadhyay's Nischindipur (the birthplace of Apu), the Lucknow or Sylhet of Qurratulain Hyder's short stories, and even spaces that, he argues, are situated outside the physical boundaries of India but not 'outside the consciousness of what it means to be Indian': Hyder's London, Nirmal Verma's Czechoslovakia, the Africa of Bandopadhyay's *The Moon Mountain*, a place the author had never visited.[7]

Post-millennially, the grip of the national seems to have, happily, loosened, or at least reinvented itself radically enough that it is unrecognisable from its previous, Nehruvian avatar. So has the definition of the cosmopolitan, suddenly far more diffuse and decentralised than the term's previous fixation on colonial and postcolonial modernity would allow. The new economic energy of India and its global diaspora has much to do with it, doubtless, as has the re-emergence of English as an Indian vernacular, liberated, as it were, from its entrapment in Western modernity.

What are the aesthetic and political limitations of this modernity? Bibhutibhushan's *Bildungsroman* gives us clear hints that within India's bhasha or vernacular-language modernism, questions of modernity and cosmopolitanism occupy a richly problematic space. I would like to push this position farther. The most excited, if perhaps submerged, impulses in key works of Indian modernist literature in the vernacular-language tradition disown the trappings of modernity and the cosmopolitan bourgeois sensibility that has been quickened into life by the nation-building aspirations of its anglophone counterparts. They do it through irrational kinds of intimacy and self-construction.

*

'The Weed', by the Punjabi writer Amrita Pritam, is the most mind-blowing short story that I have ever read.[8] The three-page story is told by an educated urban woman, an adult of unknown age, and consists almost entirely of a series of conversations between her and her maid, Angoori, a young, illiterate, rural woman, over a couple of days. The narrator describes Angoori in seductive language that says much about the young woman's appeal, and perhaps also something about the narrator's own immersion in it:

> They say a woman's body is like a lump of dough, some women have the looseness of under-kneaded dough while others have the clinging plasticity of leavened dough. Rarely does a woman have a body that can be equated to rightly-kneaded dough, a baker's pride. Angoori's body belonged to this category, her rippling muscles impregnated with the metallic resilience of a coiled spring. I felt her face, arms, breasts, legs with my eyes and experienced a profound languor.[9]

Angoori is married off to an elderly widower, Prabhati, 'old, short, loose-jawed, a man whose stature and angularity would be the death of Euclid'.[10] Thinking of him, a funny idea strikes the narrator: 'Angoori was the dough covered by Prabhati. He was her napkin, not her taster.'[11] It is an ominous thought in a narrative universe where little girls are promised to older men at the age of six. In Angoori's village, it is widely believed that that girls who fall in love do so because they are fed a wild weed that their lovers smuggle from a faraway land, usually in sweets or paan. Why else would they go against their family's wish, flee their community with their lover? It is madness. The women who are fed the weed go crazy, refuse to comb their hair, sit awake all night, singing.

Angoori also comes from a world where it is believed that it is a sin for women to read and write. 'I read', says the narrator. 'I must be sinning.' Angoori has the answers ready. 'For city women, it's no sin. It is for village women', she says, even as they both laugh at the remark. The narrator does not try to 'reform' or 'educate' the young, illiterate woman. She tells herself, 'If she found peace in her convictions, who was I to question them?'[12]

The story ends with Angoori falling sick, after a fashion. Suddenly, she is silent and desolate, quiet in one place. Suddenly, she says, 'Teach me reading, *bibi*.' 'Teach me to write my name.' 'Why do you want to write?' asks the narrator. 'To write letters? To whom?' Angoori falls silent again. 'Won't you be sinning?' the narrator asks again. Angoori does not answer.[13]

That afternoon, the narrator finds Angoori sitting in desolation, singing, and singing the same song her friend used to sing after she was 'fed the weed'. The narrator's attempts at conversation reveal that Angoori has not cooked or eaten for three days, nor has even had tea. Why not even tea? 'Ram Tara', says Angoori, and the narrator realises that Ram Tara, the night watchman, fetches the milk for her, with which she makes tea. In a flash, the narrator remembers Ram Tara: 'good-looking, quick-limbed, full of jokes. He had a way of talking with smiles trembling faintly at the corner of his lips.'[14]

'Angoori', asks the narrator. 'Could it be the weed?' Angoori's voice trembled and her words were quickly drowned in a stream of tears.[15] The story ends there.

*

This magical story puts the refusal of private agency at the heart of one's sense of the self. Angoori often reminds me of the Santal in the historical accounts of the subaltern historians, especially when the Santal declares that his fight against the British will not really be fought by him but by his god, Thakur. If modernity means the belief that one is capable of real action, the Santal's subjectivity is a radical denial of that modernity. Angoori's is much the same. The very possibility of falling in love with someone — of owning the agency to do that — lies far outside the pale of her belief. One can 'fall in love' only under the toxic influence of the wild weed. To her, it is just an absurd idea. Suddenly, it becomes an experience when she feels her own desire for Ram Tara, the night watchman. It is a desire that makes no sense to her. Except through the only possible explanation that Ram Tara, whom she misses achingly, must have fed her the weed. And yet it is all bewildering to her – since she took nothing from him but tea. No sweets or paan.

For Angoori, then, falling in love is both an impossibility and a violation, one made possible only by a force outside her.

There is also another thing that is a violation for a woman like her: reading and writing. Or at any rate, for her as a village woman. Her educated mistress spends most of her day reading and writing – to Angoori that is fine for a city woman.

But not for herself. That is, not till she has committed the other violation – that of falling in love. Is it or is it not the weed? Does she really believe it is? It is a moment like the end of Mahasweta Devi's story 'Arjun', which leaves us confused as to whether Ketu Shabar, the tribal protagonist, really was visited by his god in his dream and forbidden by him to cut down the Arjun tree, against the will of the corrupt politician who holds power over him. Or whether or not Ketu believes in that visitation, or if he is simply pulling a fast one.

I suspect that Angoori knows that she has fallen in love – that is, she knows that she is responsible for her emotion. The awareness of this responsibility inserts the modern in her consciousness, which has lived stubbornly outside its pale so far. She becomes modern, one might say, the moment she realises her own agency in the emotion over that of the weed. There is, however, no acknowledgement of this realisation in the story. Angoori's tears, in the end, simply embody a great confusion – but one, I would say, that is also tarnished by guilt. Without a sense of agency, there is no guilt.

The main reason I ascribe this awareness to her is because when she is swallowed up by this emotion, she wants to learn to read and write. To learn to write her own name. To commit the other great sin. And to etch her own self, its very name. For the first time in her life, she is eager to assume personhood. She is ready to commit sin, because, in her heart of hearts, she knows that she already has.

*

If 'The Weed' ends with this aspiration for modernity in the form of private agency, the story's wild appeal, I feel, lies in its depiction of the nonmodern. The weed, as well as the community that believes in it, is a savage force of the nonmodern that is, in this story, no mere metaphor but a reality. But at the very core of this nonmodernity is Angoori's refusal of agency. Her fear of it. Her refusal to be responsible for the emotion for which the modern subject assumes personhood most passionately – romantic love.

Some of the most compelling modernist works of Indian vernacular-language writing call for literature to reassess its relation with modernity, often through irrational and transgressive forms of intimacy. If Bibhutibhushan's modernist *Bildungsroman* reveals a more conventional yearning for cosmopolitanism, Amrita Pritam, who was part of the Progressive Writers' Movement in Urdu and Hindi, shows, in this story, a clear hesitation with that aspiration as experienced in the rural and vernacular lives of women.

The material reality of literature, as a written and printed art form expressed through language, we all know, did not exist, at least in Western culture, before the wide spread of print media and the rise of a large middle class with the means, leisure and literacy to sit and read in private. Even more important is the fact that the very spirit of literature as we know it today, with its preoccupation with authorial subjectivity, artistic interiority and creative originality, was impossible to imagine before the European Enlightenment of the eighteenth century. This, we now know, is true of European culture as well as the non-Western cultures that came under the purview of its modernity through the global spread of colonialism.

The most direct impact of this modernity in literature, as we know, is to be found in the rise and development of the novel, and specifically, of the narrative mode of realism. Realism is in tune with the secular rationality unveiled by the Enlightenment, and becomes the natural worldview of the emergent middle class – the bourgeois reality principle, as Franco Moretti has called it.[16]

Writing such as Pritam's and Devi's articulates a restlessness with this modernity, the modernity within which both the idea and practice of literature, especially anglophone postcolonial literature, are still embedded for the most part. This is not a restlessness with narrative realism. 'The Weed' is rooted in an everyday realism throughout. Realism, as Amit Chaudhuri has argued, can be read as a hegemonic worldview *only within* the context of the European Enlightenment.[17] It simply does not have the same uneasy location within Indian culture, where the classical epics as well as other genres of music and performance have had deep, organic relations with the real. I read this as a restlessness not with realism per se, but with the larger worldview that gave rise to realism in modern Western culture.

I have written a book celebrating literature's rootedness in what I felt was the most distinctive aesthetic legacy of Western modernity. This was modern literature's preoccupation with the banal – in stories about marks on the wall and entire novels about men and women walking along city streets. The prose of the world, as in the title of the book, might have been disdained by Hegel as the trivial stories of daily life, but it was, I argued, the most defining characteristic of literature since the Enlightenment and Romanticism, and in a more radical way, of the broken interiority of modernism in the late nineteenth and early twentieth centuries.[18]

It is not that this vernacular modernism calls for a breaking away from the ordinary and the quotidian. The Pritam story is nothing if not quotidian. Nothing happens there except in the course of routine domestic life; action there is nothing but a series of conversations between two women.

But the power of a story such as this makes one increasingly sceptical of the worldview of realism as the bourgeois reality principle, as for instance Franco Moretti has defined it. One feels restless with the stolid culture of modernity that was the cradle of literature as we understand it today. The nonmodern elements that got lost or subdued in the transition to modernity – the religious, the ritualistic, the communal and the performative – these were fascinating things, morally and politically no less than aesthetically, and their depletion comes across as a profound loss. The very emergence of literature as an epistemological category is inseparable from this loss.

The modernist celebration of nonmodernity, as for instance canonised by Irish nationalist drama and poetry during the period of the Celtic Twilight, provides rich examples of such elements of ritual, community and performance. The pre-ordained laws of life and death, reminiscent of the world of Greek tragedy that, for instance, defines the universe of J. M. Synge's *Riders to the Sea* sit in quiet and profound contrast to the modernity that is traditionally understood to constitute the spirit of modernism. This is part of Stephen Dedalus's unique struggle – to choose between community and the individual, the province and the cosmopolis, the religious and the liberal. Stephen's choice of the latter in each case is traditionally highlighted and celebrated, and his – and modernism's – commitment to the former elements is all too easily forgotten. Abandoning provincial intimacy – Joyce's scepticism of the Celtic Twilight is well known – Stephen moves towards a more cosmopolitan model of intimacy where the Irish nation includes the immigrant Jew Leopold Bloom as much as any of its Irish Catholic citizens.

It is admirable how English-language modernism battles this erosion. Joycean celebration of the secular ordinary is contrasted with the celebration of the ritualistic, the performative and the nonmodern in the Irish Revival, from the plays of Lady Gregory and J. M. Synge to the poetry of W. B. Yeats. D. H. Lawrence, the quintessential writer on modern love, is perpetually on the quest of primitive instincts and the energy of primal forms of life. Even within Joyce, the archetypal modernist, the aesthetic celebration of cultural provincialism is inseparable from his deeply intense love–hate relationship with the Catholic Church, whose language and discourse made him as an artist as it made Stephen Dedalus. But at the end of the day, English-language modernism remains predominantly identified with its aspiration to a certain global cosmopolitanism — no doubt partly due to its celebrated theorists such as Ezra Pound and T. S. Eliot — that places it along the sharp trajectory of modernity.

This is why, I feel, Pritam's story stands out in its location of South Asian modernism. The power of 'The Weed' lies in the modern, bourgeois subject's searing encounter with the nonmodern. This encounter does not translate into form, which stays true to the real depiction of everyday life that is the worldview of bourgeois modernity. But here is a disruptive appearance of the religious, the ritualistic and the communal — of all that is irrational and regressive to the progressive value system of the urban, educated narrator. That she does not try to reform the nonmodern is her great beauty — and that of the story.

A story such as 'The Weed' tells us that one of the most vital things literature can do today is to disrupt its embeddedness in the modern. That it should seek to find its closest connections with the nonmodern — whatever and wherever such connections may lie. The possibilities are endless. The celebration of the provincial over the cosmopolitan. The disruption of bourgeois reason. The betrayal of the individual, the private and the original. Most of all, the celebration of transgressive intimacies that violate both the liberal notion of the individual as well as the traditional conception of community. The relations etched in fiction such as Pritam's and Devi's illustrate such intimacies beautifully — and dangerously — but such intimacies also define the texture of the fiction of Katherine Mansfield and Virginia Woolf, sometimes in more latent and muted form. In 'The Weed', the narrator's refusal to question Angoori's notions and to 'enlighten' her about liberal notions of individual desire and romantic companionship is a striking, if implicit, critique of that liberal modernity. Such an artistic disavowal of liberal modernity is a crucial gesture to understand a present that seems to have reached its last frontier.

What is perhaps the most radical about this disruption of modernity is that it leads to the very displacement of the notion of literature itself.

The betrayal of reason as a legacy of the modern is a tricky thing. And yet, as Pritam's story shows, such a betrayal is a powerful aesthetic and political event. It is tricky because reason, like realism, has had its own troubled history within the metropolitan West, that bared by poststructuralist philosophers like Michel Foucault and Jacques Derrida, and by thinkers of the Frankfurt School. It is only too easy to export this internal unease outside the limits of the metropolitan West and name non-Western cultures and narrative traditions as naturally irrational. That has been a new rebranding of Orientalism. It becomes hard to tell whether magic-realist, fabulist and mythical worldviews are part of the natural fabric of a culture, or merely the import of the very portable philosophies of poststructuralism to newer soil.

But the crisis of reason has also been a rich predicament for historians of the subaltern school, most memorably in their encounter with tribal or indigenous narratives. The tribal who refuses agency and claims that his god will fight the British for him is not unlike Pritam's Angoori, who is terrified at the thought of assuming agency in love. History cannot ascribe agency to the supernatural. And hence it stops right there. That is not a problem with literature at all. The explosive appeal of 'The Weed', or a story like Mahasweta Devi's 'Arjun', comes from the very rational indeterminacy of the situation – in effect, of its frustration of modernity. The celebration of poetic language over history writing by Ranajit Guha, the founding father of the subaltern school, is clearly rooted in poetry's freedom from the strictures of modernity. The disruption of the modern is one of the places where a political utopia finds articulation only in the poetic.

*

The *Bildungsroman*, it is sometimes said, is not only the individual's trek towards adulthood, but also an allegory of the nation's aspiration for modernity. This may very well be the case. It has always reminded me of a fateful conversation I once had with the American novelist Fae Myenne Ng, in which she had told me: 'The first five years is all you need.' The first five years, she had argued, is the material for a lifetime of fiction writing.

In spite of having spent seventeen years in North America, I have repeatedly returned to the city, and especially the neighbourhoods of my childhood – Calcutta, where most of my fiction, barring maybe a couple of stories, has been set. I have never been accused of the romantic nostalgia of the diasporic writer, not only because there is nothing diasporic in my writing, but also because the Calcutta I have written about can hardly be called the subject of either romance or nostalgia. If both my novels have drawn on the stalled modernity of Calcutta as their backdrop, it is because this stalling has created an intense, atmospheric kind of decay, with sensual contours that are painful, indelible and utterly unforgettable.

Why the first five? Or ten, perhaps fifteen at the most? Before adulthood, at any rate?

Because, I now realise, that is the period when one forms a relation with place that is non-cerebral, or at least primarily so, raw and visceral, full of primitive joys and terrors, sensual memories, absurd connections made on the basis of daily habits and bodily experience.

Before *Bildung* socialises one into modernity. The bourgeois modernity of the abstract intellect. Of cosmopolitan aspirations.

But the escape from personal modernity does not easily translate into the same in the fiction one writes. The universe of my first novel, *Silverfish*, was the universe of modernity – quotidian life, the deadening impact of bureaucracy, the pulsating banality of modern cities – the realities theoretically foregrounded in *Prose of the World*. Even the longings of the past were contained within the aspiration for the modern – the memoirs of a nineteenth-century widow whose *Bildung* paralleled the Bengal Renaissance, that great force of colonial modernity.

But it is in my second novel, *The Firebird*, that I found my voice as a novelist. I have been deeply moved by people's response to it, and perhaps there is much that can explain that response, but one thing has been particularly gratifying for me. As the responses came, I realised that *The Firebird* sought to capture the wilderness of the nonmodern in the composure of prose fiction. The milieu, as before, was the stalled modernity of late twentieth-century Calcutta, and the aesthetically intoxicating decay set in motion by that stalling. But the real force in the novel, I now feel, is that of the nonmodern. It came through the primal terrors of childhood, the obsession with blood kinship and its violation, and a persisting engagement with the spectacle of death. Most importantly, the novel sought to capture the ritual and energy of performance, which long predate the modern category of literature.

It is a novel about a young boy's destructive obsession with his mother's life as a theatre actress. It explores some fundamental questions: what does it mean to see a loved one on stage? A loved one dying, romancing a stranger, leading an everyday life where the person in the audience has no role to play? What impact might this experience have on personal and social relationships, and on the social image of the actor? Consumed by a hatred of the stage, the boy-protagonist is drawn into a pattern of behaviour that can only have catastrophic consequences.

The failure to distinguish between art and life that unleashes deadly consequences in the novel also stalls the *Bildung* of the protagonist – his growth into modernity, as it were. If the *Bildungsroman* is the exemplary genre of modernity, *The Firebird* is, as some have called it, an anti-*Bildungsroman*.

*

The project of Western modernity that had a robust, confident run since the Enlightenment had a catastrophic crisis in the Holocaust. It led to a profound questioning of modernity, most notably by the philosophers of the Frankfurt School. Suddenly, progress and reason, and its corporeal body, technology, did not feel like such a good thing. Was the Holocaust the logical conclusion of the Enlightenment? Such were the questions being asked.

Historical comparisons are always risky, and often unfruitful. And yet one cannot but think of 2016 as a watershed year. After Brexit and the election of Donald Trump, and most recently, the way he exercised – and tried to exercise – his executive powers, one cannot help but feel gloom for the future of neoliberalism, the post-World War II embodiment of modernity, progress and globalism.

Over the subsequent years, it has become clear to all that what we have here is a profound crisis of liberal, globalist modernity that has for many been reminiscent of the early twentieth century. Almost none of the various totalitarian governments that rule a number of nations around the world today have captured power by force or a coup – most are democratically elected, which only drives home the power of populist totalitarianism, redolent of early twentieth-century Europe.

It is not coincidental that state leaders who use Twitter as their bully pulpits hate much of mainstream media with their gut and are no friends to celebrated outlets of print journalism, including iconic ones such as *The New York Times*, which was shut out of the tragicomic farce of President's Trump's press conference in 2017. The pattern of relationship between the current state government in India and the English-language media is eerily similar. The feeling is mutual, all around.

I think it is okay to admit that here was a US president who did not read, willed into power mostly by people who did not. Much has been made of President Obama's deep and wide reading habits, especially of literary fiction. It is all part of the devastating nostalgia for a better world. As with all nostalgia, it is misplaced, but that is a different story.

*

For the crisis of literature in the public sphere is essentially the crisis of literary modernity. A ranting, tweeting president at the helm of the so-called free world feels like a fitting climax to a longer trajectory of erosion of the liberal, progressive, modern values held dear by the global bourgeoisie. More immediately, it also marks a longer arc of erosion of the social, psychological, aesthetic and material conditions within which literature came to form an essential experience and institution of modernity.

It was from a very different viewpoint that I read Pritam's story as a call for a reassessment of literature's rootedness in modernity. It charted what is perhaps an inevitable restlessness with the worldview of bourgeois modernity. It is a huge aesthetic loss to have the religious, the irrational, the communal and the performative subdued or domesticated to shape the modern space in which the literary begins to emerge. The secrets of this subversion are latent in the transgressive intimacies and irrationalities of local and vernacular modernisms. It is this spirit that has become overshadowed by the bourgeois spirit of modernity, and it is this very spirit that has the secret of aesthetic and political redemption today.

We need to recognise that the great period of print modernity that encased the existing idea of literature is facing a profound crisis. A crisis not necessarily in a negative sense but at least in a profound, transformative one. Our reassessment of the categorical modernity of literature must take place in this light. At a time like this, the invocation of the nonmodern, as articulated in the celebration of the provincial and the irrational in works of Indian-language modernism such as 'The Weed', is at once essential and the best possible gesture of literary activism.

The best way in which literature can enact this activism is by embodying the rhythms and patterns of art forms that predate the modern – those that appear far less affected by its current crisis than the culture of writing and reading has been. Modernism's war cry, 'Make it new', is also at the same time one that says: make it really, really old, so old that it is new again. I am imagining literature that is more musical, more rhythmic, more visual, more theatrical, more performative. Poetry, for several decades the neglected stepchild to the mainstream publisher, has renewed its vibrant micro-lives across Indian cities through a culture of performance, be it in cafes and galleries or in informal social collectives, and now on YouTube channels. Long before modernity, poetry has been communal, religious, ritualistic and performative before it became a new art form in print and the culture of private reading. Even as we continue to delight in the modern genre of written poetry, it is heartening to see poetry reclaim its old premodern life, which is also its new postmodern one. And it is the delight of inevitability to see William Shakespeare inaugurate a hearty new career as the most masala of Bollywood film producers, as the Shakespearean scholar Jonathan Gil Harris argues provocatively in his book *Masala Shakespeare*.[19]

It is prose, and especially prose fiction, for which the challenge to disrupt or transcend modernity is the greatest. Prose fiction, particularly that which hinges on the invented story to be read in private, is the special child of Enlightenment modernity. The material body of this genre faces a crisis today, in that neither print nor the culture of reading is what it used to be. But its inventive soul is also in crisis as aesthetic value gets increasingly overpowered by the sociological – people reading novels because of the socio-historical importance of their themes and not because of how such themes are treated. At the same time, the expanding appetite for the creative reworking of mythical stories indicates an affinity with premodern audiences, who had no expectation of an original story but looked for retellings of stories shared by the collective memory of the community.

Prose fiction's disruption of modernity is, in many ways, a disruption of its own origin. It has been achieved before, by the fictions of literary modernism, a movement that is as much a continuation as a crisis of Enlightenment modernity. This disruption is evident in the forbidden intimacies of D. H. Lawrence and the provincialisms of William Faulkner and James Joyce. Personally, I am keenest on prose fiction that pushes to the limit its own literariness – its containment in the abstract artifice of language, its capacity to be anthropological, its rootedness in secular reason. I imagine fiction that is variously performative, musical, rhythmic, visual. Fiction that confronts the bourgeois subject with profound alienness. This is the natural spirit of the modernist nonmodern that is so deeply worthy of celebration.

Notes

1. Virginia Woolf, 'Character in Fiction', in *The Essays of Virginia Woolf*, vol. 3, ed. Andrew McNeillie (San Diego: Harcourt Brace Jovanovich, 1988), p. 421.
2. See John Marx, *The Modernist Novel and the Decline of Empire* (Cambridge: Cambridge University Press, 2005), p. 169.
3. Ibid. p. 169.
4. Franco Moretti, *The Way of the World: The Bildungsroman in European Culture*, trans. Albert Sbragia (London: Verso, 2000).
5. *Aparajito*, film, directed by Satyajit Ray. India: Epic Films, 1956. DVD, Sony, 2003.
6. Amit Chaudhuri, 'The Construction of the Indian Novel in English', in Chaudhuri (ed.), *The Picador Book of Modern Indian Literature* (London: Picador, 2001), pp. xxv–xxvi.
7. Ibid. pp. xxiv–xxv.
8. Amrita Pritam, 'The Weed', trans. from Punjabi by Raj Gill, in Stephen Alter and Wimal Dissanayake (eds), *The Penguin Book of Modern Indian Short Stories* (New Delhi: Penguin Books India, 2001), pp. 22–7.
9. Ibid. pp. 23–4.

10. Ibid. p. 24.
11. Ibid. p. 24.
12. Ibid. p. 23.
13. Ibid. p. 25.
14. Ibid. p. 26.
15. Ibid. p. 27.
16. Franco Moretti, 'Serious Century', in Moretti (ed.), *The Novel*, vol. 1 (Princeton: Princeton University Press, 2006), pp. 364–400.
17. Chaudhuri, 'The Construction of the Indian Novel in English'. See also Chaudhuri, *Clearing a Space: Reflections on India, Literature and Culture* (London: Peter Lang, 2008).
18. Saikat Majumdar, *Prose of the World: Modernism and the Banality of Empire* (New York: Columbia University Press, 2013).
19. Jonathan Gil Harris, *Masala Shakespeare: How a Firangi Writer Became Indian* (Delhi: Aleph, 2019).

Index

Abel, Elizabeth, 66
Abraham, Gerald, 205
Accent: A Quarterly of New Literature, 140
Adorno, Theodor, 140, 197, 202, 208, 209n3
advance-guard art, 93, 103
affect, 4–5
    in Loy, 130–42
    in Richardson, 79–80
    unity of (radio broadcasts), 206, 208
    in West, 109–25
Afinogenev, Aleksandr, 'Distant Point', 204
Allan, Maud, 34
Allendy, René, 155
Andersen, Hans Christian, 'The Snow Queen', 165
Anderson, Nels, 130
Apollinaire, Guillaume, 190
Ardov, Viktor, 'Tanya', 204
Arnauld, Céline, 181
Arp, Hans, 181, 182, 188, 190, 194n4
art *see* visual art
Artaud, Antonin, 157

Baader, Johannes, 186
Bagguley, Paul, 2
Ball, Hugo, 181–93
    'Karawane', 184
ballet, 199, 205

Bandopadhyay, Bibhutibhushan
    Aparajito, 218, 219, 222
    The Moon Mountain, 218
Barbellion (Bruce Frederick Cummings)
    The Journal of a Disappointed Man, 153–4
    A Last Diary, 154
Barnard, Rita, 110, 119, 121
Barthes, Roland, 141
Bashkirtseff, Marie, *Journal*, 154, 155
BBC wartime radio, 12, 197–209
    'Projection of Russia' campaign, 12, 199–209
    documentaries, 199–200
    drama, 200–1, 204
    music, 199–208
    tributes to Russia, 204–8
    PROGRAMMES
    Alexander Nevsky, 200–1
    'In Honour of Russia', 204–6
    War and Peace, 201
Bell, Angelica, 94
Bell, Clive, 77, 89n17
Bell, George, Bishop of Chichester, 94, 95
Bell, Quentin, 94
Bell, Vanessa, 31, 92, 93, 94
    Annunciation (church mural), 95
Bennett, Jane, 77–8, 87

Berlant, Lauren, 2, 74, 83, 110–11, 116, 120; *see also* cruel optimism
Berman, Jessica, 3, 7, 57
Bernini, Gian Lorenzo, 32
Bersani, Leo, 2
Berwick Church murals, 94–6
Bibesco, Princess Elizabeth, 54
Bildungsromane, 217, 225–6
   Bandopadhyay, *Aparajito*, 218, 219
   Majumdar, *Silverfish* and *The Firebird*, 225
   Roche, *Vessel of Dishonor*, 96–100, 104
birth control, 37, 57–8, 63
Bjørnson, Bjørnstjerne, 16–17, 23, 24, 26
Blanchot, Maurice, 156
Blok, Aleksandr, 'The Twelve', 204
Bloomsbury Group, 92–6; *see also* individual members
Bonaparte, Marie, 36
Booster (journal), 150
Borodin, Alexander, 203
Bower, Dallas, 200
Bowler, Rebecca, 89n27
Bracken, Brendan, 207
Bradshaw, David, 64
Brennan, Teresa, 4
Breton, André, 31–2, 182, 189
Bridson, D. G., 211n28
   'Salute to Life – The Story of the War in the Soviet Union', 201–2
broadcasting *see* BBC wartime radio
Bromley, Amy, 4
Brown, Bill, 77–83
Bryher (Annie Winifred Ellerman), 86
Buffet, Gabriële, 181
Bürger, Peter, 188
Burgess, Guy, 199
Bush, Alan, 204, 212n41
Butler, Josephine, 55

Cabaret Voltaire, 181, 182, 188, 190, 191
Café Royal, 99–100, 105n28
Cailleux, Roland, 158
Cangiullo, Francesco, 190
Carrington, Dora, 92
Carrington, Leonora, 10–11, 164–78
   quest for self-knowledge, 164, 168–70
   spirituality and beliefs, 164, 166–7
   visual art, 164, 178n4
   wartime trauma/psychotic breakdown, 166–7, 168–9, 170–1
   WORKS
   Down Below, 168–71, 173, 174, 177–8, 179n14
   The Hearing Trumpet, 10–11, 164–78
Carroll, Dennis, 151, 160n24
Cendrars, Blaise, 190
Charleston farmhouse, 92–3, 94, 95, 100, 101
Chaudhuri, Amit, 218, 222
Chekhov, Anton, 153, 154, 199
Childs, Donald, 66
Chitty, Susan, 160n20
Christianity, intimacy and, 93–104, 111–12
Chrusecz, Maya, 181
church murals, 8–9, 93–6, 100–4
Churchill, Winston, 207
Clarke, Darren, 100
Clarke, Stuart, 64
cold intimacy, 110–25
Cold War, 116–17, 127n52, 167, 208
Cole, Sarah, 3
Colebrook, Claire, 60
compassion, 108–25, 128n86
Conover, Roger, 142–3n10
Conrad, Joseph, 216
contraception *see* birth control
cosmopolitanism, 215–29
Crane, Hart, 153
Crawford, Robert, 217
cruel optimism, 110–11, 115–21
cultural intimacy, 187–90

INDEX

Dada, 11–12, 181–93
   intimacies between members, 181–2, 189
   and intimacies of family and nation-state, 183–4, 187–90
   intimacies with audience, 190–2
   and language, 184–7, 190
   and self-intimacy, 182–4, 192–3
   WORKS
   Congress of Paris, 182
   Dada au grand air, 181
   Faites vos jeux (Tzara), 188
   'Karawane' (Ball), 184
   'L'Amiral cherche une maison à louer' (Tzara), 186–7, 190
   'Manifeste Cannibale Dada' (Picabia), 192
   'Prietenă mamei' (Tzara), 188–9
   simultaneous poems, 190
   'Un Beau Matin aux dents fermées' (Tzara), 188
Das, Santanu, 3
Davies, Margaret Llewelyn, 53
Dedalus, Stephen *see* Joyce, James
Dermée, Paul, 181
Derrida, Jacques, 59–60, 224
Devi, Mahasweta, 'Arjun', 221, 222, 224, 225
Diaghilev, Sergei, 205
diaries
   intimacy of, 10, 146–59
   journaux intimes, 146–7, 153–4, 156, 159n9
   lost and rediscovered, 147–8, 150
   and psychoanalysis, 147, 151–2, 155, 156, 157, 160n24
   terminology, 159n1
Dodson, Betty, 47
domesticity, intimacy of
   Bloomsbury Group, 92–3
   in Richardson, 80–1, 87, 92–3, 97
Dostoevsky, Fyodor, 199
Doty, Mark, 104

du Coudray, Hélène, *Another Country*, 66
Duchamp, Marcel, 189
DuPlessis, Rachel Blau, 133
Durrell, Lawrence, 148–9, 159n8
   The Black Book: An Agon, 148, 159n8
   'Paris Journal: For David Gascoyne (1939)', 148–9, 151–2, 153, 160n12

Eburne, Jonathan P., 164, 166, 167, 169, 170
Eco, Umberto, 141
Edelman, Lee, 112, 123
Eilert, Heide, 29n11
Eisenstein, Sergei, *Alexander Nevsky*, 200, 211n19
Eliot, T. S., 216, 224
   The Waste Land, 18
Ellis, Havelock, 122
Éluard, Paul and Gala, 181
Emerton, Roy, 213n48
emotional capitalism, 5, 113
Ernst, Max, 168, 181, 185–6, 190–1
erotic intimacy
   as liquid music, 16–28
   in Loy, 129–30, 132–4, 136
   see also orgasm
ethnographers, writers as, 129–42
eugenics, 62–5, 67–9
Evans, Karl, 37–8, 40
Everling, Germaine, 181
'extimacy', 156

family planning, 37, 57–8, 63
fascism, 56–7, 62–9, 109, 166–7, 170–1
Faulkner, William, 216, 229
feminism, 41–2, 46–7, 52–6, 58, 59, 63–9
First World War
   Dada response to, 184–5, 187, 189–90
   feminism and, 53, 56

Fish, Stanley, 141
Flaubert, Gustave, 183
fluid eroticism, 16–28, 33
Fokine, Michel, 205
Fondane, Benjamin, 161n32
Fontane, Theodor, 18, 22, 23
    L'Adultera, 5–6, 17, 18–23, 27–8, 29n11
Forster, E. M., 97, 216
Freud, Sigmund, 5, 34, 35–6, 47, 152–3; *see also* psychoanalysis
Freytag-Loringhoven, Baroness Elsa von, 181
Fromm, Gloria, 75–6
Frost, Laura, 3, 143n16
Frost, Robert, 130
Fry, Roger, 92

Gale, Muriel, 198
Garber, Marjorie, 112
Gascoyne, David
    connection with Durrell, 148–9, 151–2, 153, 160n12
    connection with Nin, 149–50
    diaries/journals, 147–50, 151–2, 153–5, 158–9, 161n38
    psychoanalysis, 152, 153
    relationship with White, 150, 158
    and surrealism, 152, 158, 161n32
    WORKS
    'The Fabulous Glass', 153
    A Short Survey of Surrealism, 152, 158
Gee, Emily, 74
Giddens, Anthony, 37, 183
Gide, André, 24, 154
Glinka, Mikhail, 203
Gogol, Nikolai, 205
Gold, Mike, 117
Goodman, Paul, 93, 103
Goody, Alex, 134, 209n4
Goring, Marius, 213n48
Grant, Duncan, 8–9, 92–104
    friendship with Roche, 96, 102–4
    portrayal by Roche, 96–100
    relationship with religion, 95–6, 104
    representations of intimacy, 92–6, 100–4
    WORKS
    Berwick Church murals, 93–6
    Lincoln Cathedral murals, 94, 100–4
    'The Story of Narcissus', 102, 106n43
Graves, Robert, *The White Goddess*, 164, 165, 170, 175, 179n13, 180n45
Green, Julien, 147
Greenberg, Jonathan, 116–17
Gregory, Lady Augusta, 223
Grieg, Edvard, 16
Grisewood, F. H., 203
Grosz, George, 188
Guha, Ranajit, 225
Guiler, Hugh Parker (Hugo), 157
Gurdjieff, George, 166

Habermas, Jürgen, 187
Hall, Radclyffe, *The Well of Loneliness*, 34, 59, 66
Hamer, Mary, 157
Harris, Frank, 105n28
Harris, Jonathan Gil, *Masala Shakespeare*, 228
Hausmann, Raoul, 181, 182
Heller, Agnes, 80–1
Hennings, Emmy, 181, 190, 191
Herzfeld, Michael, 187
Hill, Ralph, 202
Hite, Shere, 35, 46–7
Hitler, Adolf, 23–4, 66, 171, 201
Höch, Hannah, 181
Holland, Norman, 141
home
    Bloomsbury Group, 92–3, 100, 101
    as family and nation state, 187–90
    in Richardson, 80–1, 87, 92–3, 97
homelessness, 136–40, 144nn34–5, 145n48, 186

Huelsenbeck, Richard, 182, 185–91
Hussey, Mark, 89n17
Huxley, Aldous, 24
Huysmans, Joris-Karl, 20
Hyder, Qurratulain, 218

Illouz, Eva, 2, 4–5, 110, 113–14, 121, 127n40; *see also* cold intimacy
incest, 157
India, 218–19, 222, 225–6
indispensables, 86–7
intimacy and 'intimate'
  context, 1–5
  definitions, 1, 3, 56, 82, 115, 127n40, 182
Irigaray, Luce, 165, 172, 173–4
  To Be Born, 177
  Key Writings, 174
  Speculum of the Other Woman, 172
  The Way of Love, 172
Iser, Wolfgang, 141

Jagose, Annamarie, 32
James, Henry, 182
  The Ambassadors, 86
Janco, Marcel, 182, 186, 188, 190
Jauss, Hans Robert, 141
Jelliffe, Smith Ely, 39–40
Johnson, Virginia, 35, 46
Jong, Erica, *Fear of Flying*, 46
jouissance, 123
journals (diaries) *see* diaries
journals (periodicals) *see individual titles*
Jouve, Blanche *see* Reverchon-Jouve, Blanche
Jouve, Pierre Jean, 152–3
  Hecate, 152–3
  Vagadu, 152–3
Joyce, James, 24, 34, 183, 216, 216–17, 223, 229
  Ulysses, 18, 33, 142–3n10, 186, 223
Joynson-Hicks, Sir William, 59

Kandinsky, Wassily, 190
Kenney, Annie, 56
Kierkegaard, Søren, 159
Kingsmill, Dorothy, 160n24
Kinsey, Alfred, 46
Klein, Melanie, 157
Koedt, Anne, 47
Krafft-Ebing, Richard von, 122
Kreymborg, Alfred, 131–2
Kristeva, Julia, 139, 144n34, 156

Lacan, Jacques, 32, 156
Laqueur, Thomas, 35
Lasch, Christopher, 34
Lawrence, D. H., 34, 40–1, 42–6, 216–17, 223, 229
  Aaron's Rod, 40
  'The Bad Girl in the Pansy Bed', 42, *43*
  Lady Chatterley's Lover, 40, 44–6, 67
  Pansies, 42
  The Plumed Serpent, 40, 42–4
  'Tickets, Please', 40
  'The Woman Who Rode Away', 40, 42
Lawrence, Frieda, 41
le Bas, Edward, 95
Lejeune, Philippe, 146
Lennard, John, 134
Leppert, Richard, 17
Lermontov, Mikhail, 205–6
lesbian desire, 33–4, 36, 58–9, 65–6, 67–8
Levinson, Marjorie, 3
Lincoln Cathedral murals, 94, 100–4
liquid intimacy, 16–28
The Listener, 200–1, 202
listening, intimacy of, 164–78; *see also* radio intimacy
The Little Review, 142–3n10
Lopokova, Lydia, 199, 201, 210n15

Loy, Mina, 9–10, 129–42
  economy of intimacy, 131, 136
  on genocide, 139–40
  on homelessness, 136–40, 144nn34–5, 145n48
  and interiority, 134, 143n19
  sexual imagery, 129–30, 132–4, 136
  typography, 134–5, 143n22
  WORKS
  'Chiffon Velours', 140, 145n48
  'Crowd Soul', 138
  'A Hard Luck Story', 138
  'Hot Cross Bum', 131, 137–9
  'An Idiot Child at a Fire-Escape', 137
  'International Psycho-Democracy', 135–6, 144n28
  Lunar Baedeker, 142–3n10
  'Mass Production on 14th Street', 136
  'Photo after Pogrom', 131, 139–40, 145n48
  'Songs to Joannes' ('Love Songs'), 129, 131–6, 142–3n10, 142n5
Luhan, Mabel Dodge, 34, 37–42, 46
  'The Ballad of a Bad Girl', 40–1, 42, *43*
  Intimate Memories, 37–8, 40, 41
Luhan, Tony, 40
Lusty, Natalya, 175
Lydon, Susan, 47
Lynn, Vera, 198
Lysistrata (magazine), 54

McCabe, Susan, 133
McCarthy, Molly, 53
MacNeice, Louis, 199–200, 211n20, 213n47–48, 214n59
  Alexander Nevsky, 200–1, 211n22
  'Cushendun', 197
  The Dark Tower, 213n47
  'The Spirit of Russia', 205–6, 208, 213n47, 213n51, 214n59
  They Met on Good Friday, 213n47
Maconachie, Richard, 207, 210n11
Madge, Charles, 158
Maines, Rachel, 35
Maisky, Ivan, 199, 201, 207
Majumdar, Saikat
  The Firebird, 225
  Prose of the World, 225
  Silverfish, 225
Malinowski, Bronislaw, 130
Man Ray, 189
  The Gift, 189
Mann, Thomas, 18, 23–4
  Buddenbrooks, 5–6, 17, 23–8, 30n23
  Doktor Faustus, 18, 23
  Tristan, 29n18
  Zauberberg, 23
Mansfield, Katherine, 147, 153, 154, 182, 216–17
Marcus, Jane, 67
Marinetti, F. T., 134, 190
marriage, 31, 43–4, 57–8, 75–6, 78, 87
Martin, Jay, 111, 115
Marx, John, 217
Marx, Karl, 110
Masters, William H., 35, 46
masturbation, 26–7, 35, 36, 148–9
Mayakovsky, Vladimir, 'A Cloud in Trousers', 204
Mayor, Edward, 101
Mégnen, Jeanne, 179n14
Mendelssohn, Felix, 20
Millay, Edna St. Vincent, 133
Miller, Henry, 148, 155, 156, 157, 159n8
  Mon Journal, 150
Millett, Kate, 47
Modigliani, Amadeo, 190
Moglen, Seth, 109–10, 124, 127n52
Montagu, Edward Douglas-Scott-Montagu, 3rd Baron, 103
Moran, Patricia, 160–1n27
Morel, Edmund, 72n68
Moretti, Franco, 217, 222, 223
Mörike, Eduard, 19
motherhood, 38–40, 57, 64, 69, 97

Mulholland, Terri, 85, 88n8
Müllen, Bent von, 152
Murrill, Herbert, 203
music
   at Cabaret Voltaire, 181
   as fluid eroticism, 16–28, 33
   and modernism, defined, 211n31
   on wartime radio, 197–208
Mussorgsky, Modest, 203

nationalism, 187, 189–90, 198, 205–6
   see also fascism
The New York Times, 227
Ng, Fae Myenne, 225
Ngai, Sianne, 112, 115, 118–25, 127n58
Nicolson, Harold, 207, 214n57
Nieland, Justus, 3, 4, 116–17, 118, 120
Nietzsche, Friedrich, 16, 18, 23
Nin, Anaïs, 33, 34, 149–50, 151, 155–8, 159n8
Nin, Joaquim, 157
Noheden, Kristoffer, 164, 176
nonmodern intimacy, 215–29
Nordau, Max, 16

Obama, Barack, 227
'objects', intimacy with, 77–8, 189, 195n37; *see also* 'things', intimacy with
occultism, 164
oceanic sexuality, 17, 23–5, 28, 33
O'Farrell, Mary, 213n48
opera, 16–28, 203, 205
Oppenheimer, Max, 190
orgasm
   female, 6–7, 31–47
      as agency and autonomy, 33–4, 37–8, 46–7
      and gender conformity, 35–6, 37–46
      and lesbian desire, 33–4, 36
      as reproduction imperative, 39–40
   male, 32–3
   pianistic, 25–7

Orwell, Sonia Brownell, 147
Others: A Magazine of the New Verse, 132

Pankhurst, Emmeline and Christabel, 56
Penrose, Valentine, 158
Peppis, Paul, 133
Péret, Benjamin, 32
Picabia, Francis, 181, 182
   'Manifeste Cannibale Dada', 192
Picasso, Pablo, 190
Pitt-Rivers, Michael, 103
Ployé, Philip, 160n24
Podnieks, Elizabeth, 147, 160–1n27
poetics
   of intimate sensation, 45
   and liquid music, 16–28
   of listening, 164–78
   radio poetics, 200–1, 205–6, 213n47
poetry, 19, 20–1, 41–2, 58, 110, 183
   Dada, 184–90, 193
   Durrell, 148–9, 151–2, 153, 160n12
   Gascoyne, 152, 153
   in India, 225, 228
   Loy *see* main entry
   MacNeice, 197, 211n20, 213n47
   on wartime radio, 204, 205
   and Woolf, 52–3, 58, 61–5
Potter, Rachel, 135
Pound, Ezra, 134, 216, 224
   'In a Station of the Metro', 183
precarity, 108–25
Pritam, Amrita, 'The Weed', 219–25, 228
Prokofiev, Sergei, 199, 200, 203
provincialism, 215–29
psychoanalysis, 39–40, 147, 151–3, 155, 156, 157, 160n24
Pushkin, Alexander, 205

queer intimacy
   and Grant, 94, 96, 100, 101–4
   in Stopes, 68
   in West, 123
   in Woolf, 33–4, 58–60, 65–6, 67

Queneau, Raymond, 32
Quennell, Peter, 72n78

Rabaté, Jean-Michel, 3
radio intimacy, 197–209, 209n3; *see also*
　listening, intimacy of
Radio Times, 198, 201, 202, 203
Raleigh, Sir Walter, 63
Rank, Otto, 155, 156, 157
　The Double, 162n64
Ray, Satyajit, *Aparajito*, 218
Reed, Christopher, 92
Rees-Jones, Deryn, 66–7
Reid, Colbey Emmerson, 140
relational intimacy, 164–78
Rennet, William, 203
Reverchon-Jouve, Blanche, 152, 153, 161n38
Rhondda, Margaret Haig Mackworth, Viscountess, 53
Richardson, Alan, 86
Richardson, Dorothy, 8, 74–88
　and 'indispensables', 86–7
　intimacy of style, 81–3
　on shared living and intimacy with 'things', 8, 74–81, 83–8
　and 'significant form', 77, 89n17
　WORKS
　Pilgrimage, 74, 82–3, 88n8
　The Trap, 8, 74–88, 89n31
Richardson, Mary, 56
Richter, Hans, 181, 189
Rimsky-Korsakov, Nikolai, 203, 205
Roche, Paul, 8–9, 96–104
　friendship with Grant, 96, 102–4
　influence of Grant and Bloomsbury, 96–100, 104
　as model for Grant, 101–4
　WORKS
　O Pale Galilean, 104
　'Reminiscences', 101, 106n36
　Vessel of Dishonor, 96–100, 104

Roudinesco, Elizabeth, 152, 153
Rudnick, Lois Palken, 39, 41, 42
Rushdie, Salman, *Midnight's Children*, 218
Russia on BBC wartime radio, 199–209

Sackville-West, Edward, 204, 212n33
Sackville-West, Vita, 56, 60
　Passenger to Teheran, 60
Sanger, Margaret, 37
Sanger, Tam, 2
Schumann, Robert, 19, 20, 21
Schwitters, Kurt, 182, 186, 189
Second World War
　Berwick Church murals, 94–5
　Leonora Carrington's breakdown during, 166–7, 168–9, 170–1
　diaries during, 157–8, 159
　Holocaust and modernity, 227
　Loy works on, 136, 139–41
　radio broadcasting *see* BBC wartime radio
Serner, Walter, 190
sexual intimacy
　as liquid music, 16–28
　in Loy, 129–30, 132–4, 136
　see also orgasm
Seymour, Julie, 2
Shakespeare, William, 200, 228
shared living, intimacy of, 74–81, 83–8
Shishikof, Pavel, 199
Shostakovich, Dmitri, 203
　Seventh Symphony, 202
'significant form', 77, 89n17
Simonov, Konstantin, *The Russians*, 204
Sinclair, May, 82
Slodki, Marcel, 190
sonic intimacy, 197–209
sound poems, 184–5
space, intimacy of, 215–29
Spark, Muriel, 66
Spivak, Gayatri Chakravorty, 59, 60, 68
Stalin, Joseph, 199, 201, 206–7, 210n10

Stein, Gertrude, 37, 133, 134, 216
Stevens, Wallace, 216–17
Stopes, Marie, 7, 56, 57–8, 62–9
   Love Songs for Young Lovers, 66
   Love's Creation, 57, 58, 66–9
   Man, Other Poems and a Preface, 58
   Married Love, 31, 36, 58, 60, 62, 68
Strachey, Lytton, 102, 103–4
Stravinsky, Igor, 203
Stutfield, Hugh, 155
suffragettes, 55–6
Suleiman, Susan Rubin, 168, 170, 173, 175, 176
superrealism, 108, 117, 118, 121, 125n1
surrealism, 152, 158, 164–78, 180n41, 189; *see also* Dada
Swinburne, Algernon Charles, 104
Synge, J. M., *Riders to the Sea*, 223

Taeuber, Sophie, 181
Tanguy, Yves, 32
Taos, art colony, 40, 41
   Laughing Horse (journal), 42, *43*
Taylor, Julie, 3
Taylor, Yvette, 2
Tchaikovsky, Pyotr Ilyich, 202–3
teleopoiesis, 59–60, 66, 67
textual intimacy, 7, 56–7, 59–61
'things', intimacy with, 76–81, 83–8; *see also* 'objects', intimacy with
Thomson, George, 74
Tolstoy, Leo, 199
   War and Peace, 201
Trump, Donald, 227
Turing, Alan, 103
Tzara, Tristan, 181–93, 194n4
   Faites vos jeux, 188
   'L'Amiral cherche une maison à louer', 186–7, 190
   'Prietenă mamei', 188–9
   'Un Beau Matin aux dents fermées', 188

ugly feelings, 112, 115, 118–19, 122, 123, 125
Utell, Janine, 3

Vaget, Hans Rudolf, 23–4, 30n20
van Hoddis, Jakob, 190
van Rees, Otto, 190
Van Vechten, Carl, 42
Varo, Remedios, 166
Veitch, Jonathan, 115
Verma, Nirmal, 218
violence, 109–12, 118–24
visual art, 93–6, 100–4, 136, 164, 178n4
von Reinhold, Shola, *Lote*, 60

Wagner, Richard, 16–28
   extramarital sentiments, 20
   perceived as lewd and libidinous, 16, 22–3
   performed in private sphere, 17–18
   references and imagery in
      Fontane, 5–6, 17, 18–23, 27–8
      Mann, 5–6, 17, 18, 23–8
   translated into reality, 18
   WORKS
      'Im Treibhaus', 20–1
      Tannhäuser, 19
      Tristan und Isolde, 16–17, 18, 20–1, 24, 25–7
      Die Walküre, 18
      Wesendonck-Lieder, 20
war *see* Cold War; First World War; Second World War
Warlock, Peter, 198
Watney, Simon, 95, 100
Wesendonck, Mathilde, 20
   'Im Treibhaus', 20–1
West, Nathanael, 9, 108–25, 127n52
   'Burn the Cities', 110
   The Day of the Locust, 116
   Miss Lonelyhearts, 9, 108–25

West, Rebecca, 53
Whistler, James Abbott McNeill, 99–100
White, Antonia, 150–1, 158, 160nn20/24/27
   The Lost Traveller, 151
   The Sugar House, 150
Wilde, Oscar, 99–100, 105n28
Wildeblood, Peter, 103
Williams, Linda, 32
Williams, William Carlos, 216
Wilson, Kabe, '*Of One Woman or So* by Olivia N'Gowfri', 60
Wolfe, Jesse, 3, 75, 92
Woolf, Leonard, 31
Woolf, Virginia, 7, 52–69
   and birth control, 57–8, 63
   chastity as fetish, 61–2
   on consciousness, 160n13
   and cosmopolitanism, 216
   diaries, 147
   on eugenics, 62–5, 67
   and fascism, 55–6, 57, 62–9
   on feminism, 52–6, 58, 59, 63–9
   influence on Roche, 97–8, 99
   on lesbian desire, 33–4, 58–60, 65–6, 67
   musical models of time, 24
   on national identity, 205–6
   on orgasm, 31, 33–4, 46
   and textual intimacy, 56–7, 59–61
   and wartime BBC, 197, 201
   WORKS
   'Anon', 201, 211n26
   Jacob's Room, 53
   A Letter to a Young Poet, 143n19
   Mrs Dalloway, 33–4, 46, 99
   Night and Day, 53
   Orlando: A Biography, 4, 66
   A Room of One's Own, 38, 46, 53, 56, 57–69
   Three Guineas, 54, 56, 59, 63, 64, 65, 198(n8), 205–6
   The Waves, 213n48
   'Why?', 54
Wyatt, Honor, 203

Yeats, W. B., 130, 223

Zola, Émile, 20
Zöllner, Karl, 22

EU representative:
Easy Access System Europe
Mustamäe tee 50, 10621 Tallinn, Estonia
Gpsr.requests@easproject.com

www.ingramcontent.com/pod-product-compliance
Lightning Source LLC
Chambersburg PA
CBHW070343240426
43671CB00013BA/2389